Natural Learning

for a

Connected World

Natural Learning for a Connected World

Education, Technology,
and the Human Brain

Renate N. Caine
Geoffrey Caine

Foreword by Joseph Chilton Pearce

Teachers College, Columbia University
New York and London

Published by Teachers College Press, 1234 Amsterdam Avenue, New York, NY 10027

Library of Congress Cataloging-in-Publication Data

Caine, Renate Nummela.
  Natural learning for a connected world : education, technology, and the human brain / Renate N. Caine, Geoffrey Caine.
    p. cm.
  Includes bibliographical references and index.
    ISBN 978-0-8077-5189-3 (pbk.) — ISBN 978-0-8077-5190-9 (hardcover) 1. Learning, Psychology of. 2. Cognition in children. 3. Educational technology—Psychological aspects. 4. Education—Effect of technological innovations on. 5. Education—Aims and objectives. I. Caine, Geoffrey. II. Title.
  LB1060.C334 2011
  370.15'23—dc22

                                                                    2010046705

ISBN 978-0-8077-5189-3 (paper)
ISBN 978-0-8077-5190-9 (hardcover)

Printed on acid-free paper
Manufactured in the United States of America

18 17 16 15 14 13 12 11   8 7 6 5 4 3 2 1

We dedicate this book to Arthur W. Combs and all our teachers.

Contents

Foreword

OF THE MANUSCRIPTS sent me in recent years, the majority have concerned educational reform. And right here I stick my neck out and state unequivocally that *Natural Learning for a Connected World* towers over all and is easily the most remarkable, intelligent, and challenging work I have read on the subject of learning, schooling, social crises and the like, and weighs heavily into the whole issue of development. Were I younger and more vigorous, I would go on the road again just to promote this book.

The challenge at the heart of *Natural Learning for a Connected World* is serious, for it recognizes the bottom-line issue largely missed today, an issue the Caines face here in all its raw, destructive power. It exposes the organizational thinking and practices that fail to address emergent technology and the phenomenon they call *videotech*. They document its sudden sweep of our whole social scene, its near-complete capturing of the mind-set of our time, particularly our young, and the strange unthinking, easy acquiescence of this monumental, unprecedented, and near-worldwide takeover.

But even as they point out what is wrong, the book turns things upside down and shows how education can make use of technology on behalf of the child. But to do so the system itself must change and adopt a more complex view of learning.

In essence, the book presents an entirely new idea of how children learn naturally and how videotech can serve and be used for a new approach to education. The book does this by exposing a physiological process that is totally natural and based in biology. Everyone is familiar with this process, as it operates in our lives and we can recognize it, but we have never thought of it as a way of learning in schools as they exist now. It turns the old system upside down even as it invites the flexible inclusion of technology on multiple levels. The process the Caines describe is simultaneously compatible with project-based learning of all kinds, and encourages creativity and thinking, an essential gift that schools need to provide for a generation born into this time.

Without a new view of learning and schools that understand this underlying message, technology by itself can easily fail to teach children to think but instead to become quintessential consumers who serve the processes and those producing those consumables. This compulsion may be one of those underlying memes to which the Caines refer, or, perhaps one of those underlying if unspoken and unrecognized fields of influence that physicist David Bohn pondered. These fields, or-memes, create large-scale social-cultural acceptances that drive us unbeknownst from behind the scenes of our own minds. They are seldom recognized as the less-than-conscious motivations they actually are.

Children are taught to think by allowing, encouraging, and training their imagination. That requires the formulation of genuine questions, making decisions, and applying new understanding or creating something for feedback. Without genuine guidance and a new vision of what it means to learn, the love affair with videotech sweeping our very planet could result in nothing more than cultural counterfeits of the real that supplant, take the place of, or even eliminate the very grounds of imagination.

The ultimate message, however, is that children learn from everything and everyone and therefore education is never limited to school or technology. The culture, including parents and community, teach. This is also why America cannot compare itself to other cultures such as India or China on the basis of test scores. The challenges are much bigger. America has always excelled in creativity and to lose that gift may be far more devastating than testing poorly. The journey calls for the creative inclusion of technology, and this book shows how to get there.

—*Joseph Chilton Pearce*

Acknowledgments

THIS BOOK WAS CREATED on the shoulders of giants. It integrates an enormous amount of research and we owe much to all those who have dedicated their lives to the various disciplines, fields, and questions from which we draw. We mention many in the text itself, but many more influenced our thinking and understanding. Thank you to all.

We owe much to the work of Dr. Joaquin Fuster at UCLA, who helped with our many questions and puzzles. The bridge from neuroscience to education is indeed a complex one. From our point of view, he provided a crucial foundation for the bridge.

On a more personal note, there are people we must thank. First and foremost is our dear friend and colleague Carol McClintic. Her belief in us and in our work, along with countless hours of dedicated effort, places her at the top of our list.

Our editor, Jean Ward, encouraged us throughout the years and never gave up. She just believed that we could write this book. It probably would not have been finished without her faith in us.

Margaret Arnold came to us on a scholarship from Germany and helped to focus our reading and thinking, and Anne Richards helped with the editing of the manuscript.

Next come our associates, and in particular those whom we call the IdyllAssociates. These are educators who have worked with us over the years, both in our summer institutes and in meetings in Idyllwild during the year. They include Andrea Bond, Lance Fogle, Karl Gustafson, Adam Gratt, Michael Voell, and JoAnne Lawrence. They are superb educators. Others associated with this group are Noel Tan, Bette Moore and Sharon Delgado. Each is someone who not only knows content, but understands that children learn from everything around them. They understand what isn't happening in schools and families, what is needed for students at this time, and what the future demands.

Our heartfelt thank you goes out to Margo Foster, the manager of Learning to Learn in South Australia, and to all the schools and educators who participated in that program. Thanks also to the principal, Rosslyn Shepherd, her teachers, students, and the parents of Bridgewater Primary School in Adelaide Australia, and Larry Rosenstock and many others at High Tech High in San Diego, California. They most closely approximate what we mean by the Guided Experience Approach.

We also thank friends and colleagues who listened to our ideas and entered into difficult dialogues with us. And finally, we thank the teachers at Rose Warren Empowerment School in Las Vegas, Nevada, especially Rosanna Galagher, the principal, along with her entire staff, parents, and students. They represent the kind of educators who will be needed in the future.

Introduction

I T IS NOW KNOWN that the brain can generate new neurons and create new connections until the day we die. And if the latest research is any indication, human beings are capable of intentionally altering their own brain, sometimes by way of changed behavior, through meditation, and by use of devices that literally retrain the brain.

It is also clear that the role of technology is growing exponentially. No longer do teachers and students and content need to be in the same place at the same time. Sophisticated video games are showing the way of the future, where three-dimensional learning, alternate realities and universes, and an expanding cornucopia of fact and expert knowledge will be available for anyone wanting to find them.

So how do we deal with learning in this age of almost limitless potential? And how can today's education, frozen in a model created for another time, transform into something that is relevant?

This book is not about the latest in technology nor does it focus on the latest brain research, although it includes both. Instead, it sets out to show that if we look at learning in a new way, it may just be possible to reconcile what is occurring all around us and find a way through to a radically different and expanded type of education.

This book provides evidence for the fact that public education is at the center of an immense number of competing forces and that the center cannot hold. And we have few illusions about the daunting shift that is needed. We have worked with countless schools and programs and have tested these ideas in programs we have conducted in our own center in Idyllwild, California. Our work with schools and districts in the United States became increasingly difficult with the U.S. effort to standardize teaching. While our workshops and courses, as well as our work in Australia, often reaped rich rewards and true transformation, the current U.S. emphasis on making test scores the primary and often only criterion for learning, all too often left great education further and further behind. Again and again we have witnessed the ways in which mandated procedures, enforced by sometimes draconian regimes of rewards and punishments, and implemented by top-down management policies and practices, have led to compliance driven by fear and helplessness.

Happily, for those who can master the way human beings naturally learn and also manage to transform the systems in which learning takes place, "teaching" can morph into a process that is much more exciting, meaningful, and coherent. The answers are waiting to be understood, but they are very challenging. However, armed with the amazing contributions from technology, psychology, and neuroscience, we have remained optimistic about the future.

The shift can be excruciating for anyone involved in education at this time. The reason is that educators have to let go of much of the control that comes with being the content expert in a classroom and being responsible for everything that happens. What is needed is the very opposite of what is happening. Teachers need to be empowered with new skills and knowledge about how human beings learn—knowledge that is now available. The information age requires educators who can lead learners into *their* unique interests, talents, understandings, and expertise, while simultaneously embedding and dealing with the academic, social, and emotional capacities that students have and will need for the future they will face.

Fortunately, there are solutions. At the core lies an instructional approach grounded in a capacity to learn that is biologically built into every human being from birth. The challenge we therefore face, individually and collectively, is to implement what is known to be possible. Our goal in writing this book is to contribute to that possible future.

A BRIEF SUMMARY OF THE BOOK

We have had to literally create new vocabulary in order to make clear what is initially immensely complex, is documented across multiple disciplines, and is grounded in physiology. At times we have shortened or abbreviated these terms.

The book is divided into four major parts. Part I looks at what is happening to students in and out of school. Chapter 1 describes the ubiquitous use of electronic media by today's youth and demonstrates the great divide that exists between traditional education and what we call *videotech*. As the average student in the United States spends more than 50 hours per week being engaged and entertained by electronic media of one type or another, schools are rapidly being left behind. Chapter 2 takes a closer look at the degree to which technology is actually impacting education and how educators are attempting to protect themselves from what is certainly here to stay, using firewalls, banning cell phones, and employing other means for keeping technology out. Chapter 3 takes a hard look at the beliefs that are at the heart of current education. It suggests that these beliefs constitute what is known as a *meme*—an idea that keeps replicating itself. We call it the *transmission/direct instruction meme*. Chapter 4 summarizes the skills and capacities required of students working and living in a technologically connected world or what is sometimes called the "knowledge age." It relates those skills and capacities to what psychologists call *higher order functioning* and what neuroscientists call the *executive functions* of the human brain.

Part II introduces a new approach to learning and teaching—one that emerges out of biology and is supported by psychology and neuroscience. Chapter 5 introduces a more organic and natural approach to learning grounded in biology, and framed in terms of the dance between perception and action. We suggest that understanding the perception/action dynamic (which is always operating) and the perception/action cycle (which is the foundation of natural learning) is essential to shifting the current and prevailing view of learning and teaching in order to accommodate knowledge age education. Chapter 6 introduces the science that explains how perception/action is fundamental to learning from life. It also introduces an approach to the organization of the brain, based on the parallel functions of perception and action, and highlights the critical nature of learner- or actor-centered adaptive questions in natural learning. It also shows how video games and much of technology take advantage of this process already. Chapter 7 introduces what we call *Perception/Action Learning*, and shows how video games and much of technology take advantage of this process. It unpacks the critical phases of Perception/Action Learning and lays the foundation for how to teach to how the brain/mind learns naturally. Chapter 8 looks at outcomes in a new way. It describes how the brain organizes experience and knowledge in terms of *knowledge networks*, and shows that creating rich knowledge networks needs to be the goal of education. It spells out the differences between rich knowledge networks and the relatively impoverished knowledge networks created during traditional education. Chapter 9 contrasts two approaches to teaching using the topic of digestion. One approach is a traditional lesson; the other approach models Perception/Action Learning. The two examples are followed by an introduction to the various phases that are needed for effective instruction, drawn from the phases of the Perception/Action Learning Cycle introduced previously.

Part III explores the body-mind connections that influence learning. Chapter 10 introduces the notion of motivation and the distinction between *intrinsic* and *extrinsic motivation.* It shows intrinsic motivation to be the primary force that keeps the *perception/action cycle* functioning, and identifies some powerful aspects of intrinsic motivation. The interaction between learning and motivation is explored in some depth, with a look back to how behaviorism "sideswiped" education and is still having an impact. Chapter 11 deals with mind states and introduces *Relaxed Alertness* as the optimal state of mind for learning. It does so by drawing on the distinction between the *high road* and *low road* of the brain, and explains how the high road supports deep learning and the low road suppresses it. The chapter also introduces research from a wide variety of fields to support the distinction between the two roads. Chapter 12 shows how many of the features of education today, ranging from standardized instruction to an obsession with standardized test results, work together to induce the low road, and so suppress and undermine deep learning and great teaching. Chapter 13 introduces what we call *biological predispositions* that explain natural behaviors that are largely reflexive and outside of the field of awareness. It shows how they are always operating in schools and explains that they must be acknowledged and worked with rather than suppressed. It then suggests ways to elevate these more basic behaviors into awareness where they can be managed via higher order thinking. Chapter 14 focuses on the intrinsically social nature of learning. It introduces recent research on what are called *mirror neurons.* This research suggests that children, students, and adults alike learn much from watching others and from the social context in which they find themselves. It discusses some of the relevant factors and describes the importance of imitation and modeling in great education. This makes sense of the adage "action speaks louder than words."

Part IV presents what we call the Guided Experience Approach to learning and teaching, and demonstrates how two schools implement the approach. Chapter 15 introduces three elements that are essential to mastering the Guided Experience Approach—*Relaxed Alertness, Immersion in Complex Experience,* and *Active Processing of Experience.* Chapter 16 provides a closer look at how two schools (one in the United States and the other in Australia) have created a climate of Relaxed Alertness. Chapter 17 takes a closer look at many of the procedures and processes that both schools use to insure that learners are immersed in complex experience and that all the phases of Perception/Action Learning are implemented. Chapter 18 describes the process that is essential to consolidating learning by way of continued challenge and questioning. Chapter 19 provides a brief but critical look into the future of learning, and into the immense importance of implementing Perception/Action Learning and the Guided Experience Approach.

Part I

TWO FUNDAMENTALLY DIFFERENT VIEWS OF LEARNING

CHAPTER 1

Who and What
Are Educating Our Children?

When you lose your mobile, you lose part of your brain.
—A Japanese student (Prensky, 2006, p. 128)

The future has arrived. We are the beneficiaries of a revolution in the under-standing of the brain and of human potential.
—Sharon Begley (2007, p. 243)

IMAGINE THAT SOMEONE told you we could have an outstanding kind of education, one compatible with a world deeply steeped in technology, innovation, academic excellence, global communication, and cultural diversity—what would you think? And suppose that we could finally educate almost all citizens to live successfully in a society infused with healthy relationships as well as instant messaging and instantaneous access to information—what would you do?

Ultimately, this vision could become reality provided that cultural forces permit it. One way to begin is with what science is revealing about how people learn naturally. When we take the brain research seriously, for example, and synthesize it with developments in cognitive psychology and other fields, we find that children learn from just about everything around them. The division between learning in school and learning from life outside of school was always artificial, but this new understanding helps us to recognize learning as something that consumes kids all the time. We can acknowledge what most gifted educators have always known, that learning in school, as most of us recollect from our own school experience, is artificially limited by a lens fabricated for another time. When we replace and update that lens and honor research and technology now available, we have the opportunity to recognize and take advantage of a miracle in action.

In the following pages and throughout the book we will be adding our voice to all those who are calling for a new and different kind of education. One chapter at a time we will lay out the critical shift that educators and policy makers need to embrace if public education is to survive as an essential platform for the ways in which we prepare our children for the future.

TWO COMPETING WORLDS

The journey begins with the fact that most of our children are being educated by at least two competing worlds.

One of those worlds, the world of television, technology, and video gaming—which we call *videotech*—is not generally perceived as a system of education. It is digital, media driven, exciting, challenging, inviting, and "fun," and is largely disconnected from what many educators would call school. The other, the world recognized as school, *is* perceived to be a system of education, but it largely suppresses the dynamic, interactive, creative, exciting, and social aspects that videotech engages.

The time has come to grasp the essence of each world—to see what each does, to test the assumptions upon which each is built, and to come to terms with how education needs to function if it is going to meet the goal of preparing our children adequately for the knowledge age into which they are being born.

How Does the Videotech World Educate Our Children?

Let's look at two students, typical of those found in most elementary and middle schools today. Jake and Dan are 9 and 11 years old respectively. Their parents have come to us because both boys are worried about their grades. Each one is failing at least one subject. These are good kids who are popular and are well liked by other students and their teachers. In many ways they are like their classmates, articulate and frank. Their main problem is that they cannot grasp some of their subjects. They literally feel that they can't learn, and they both tell us that they don't listen well and fail to pay attention.

And yet, like so many kids their age, they seem to have no trouble mastering the world of digital technology. They have grown up with computers, video games, cell phones, and all the most recent "toys" that represent the information age. Jake in particular tells us that his favorite thing to do is to play video games, and Dan has a gadget that he holds in his hands and "plays with" continuously all through our interview. Both boys have a TV and video game setup in their respective bedrooms. They represent thousands of middle-class kids in this country. They are immersed in a digital, media-driven world, which presents some revealing data.

How Are Students Engaged with Media and Technology Outside of School?

Media now reach into almost every corner of the lives of children of all ages. Here we take a look into their bedrooms, in particular, and their homes, in general.

Media in the Bedroom. In 2009 alone, Americans spent $10.5 billion on almost 230 million computer and video games according to the Entertainment Software Association (2010). This means that sales revenues have roughly tripled over the past 10 years.

A large number of these purchases by adults find their way into the bedrooms of children. According to the Kaiser Family Foundation (Rideout, Foehr, & Roberts, 2010), children's bedrooms have increasingly become multimedia centers, with 71% of all 8- to 18-year-olds having a TV in their bedroom and 50% having a video game player as well. And those with a TV in their room spend almost 90 minutes more in a typical day watching TV than those without a set in their room.

Here are some more statistics on the use of media by children in their bedrooms:

- 8- to 18-year-olds devote an average of 7 hours and 38 minutes to using entertainment media across a typical day (more than 53 hours a week). And because they spend so much of that time "media multitasking" (using more than one medium at a time), they actually manage to pack a total of 10 hours and 45 minutes worth of media content into those 7½ hours (Rideout et al., 2010);
- Over the past five years (2004–2009), there has been a huge increase in ownership among 8- to 18-year-olds, from 39% to 66% for cell phones, and from 18% to 76% for iPods and other MP3 players. During this period cell phones and iPods have become true multimedia devices; in fact, young people now spend more time listening to music, playing games, and watching TV on their cell phones—a total of 49 minutes daily—than they spend talking on them—33 minutes (Rideout et al., 2010).

Although Jake and Dan do not have access to cable television they each have a TV in their room as well as video game players. Their TV is largely used for watching movies on DVDs.

Media in the Home. Vicky Rideout, a Kaiser Family Foundation Vice President who directed the study cited here, additionally reports that the TV is constantly on in most homes, according to the young people in the study (Rideout et al., 2010):

- Nearly two thirds (64%) say the TV is "usually" on during meals.
- Just under a half (45%) say they live in homes where the TV is left on "most" or "all" of the time, whether anyone is watching it or not.

These kids are spending the equivalent of even more then a full-time work-week using media.

When casually asked how much time he spends playing video games, Dan thinks for a moment and tells us that after school and homework, he spends about 3 hours a night playing video games. He estimates the time he spends gaming on weekends to be around 10 hours. He is also an avid DVD consumer and prefers the "scary" kinds of movies. Asked about violence, he shakes this off as not important and says that "the scarier stories are great" because they keep him interested.

Media as Teacher. To repeat, our children are immersed in a digital, media-driven world from which they learn. It reaches into every nook and cranny of their lives, pulls at their heartstrings, and engages them in cocreating a world run by it. And it does so all too frequently in the absence of adult supervision and guidance and without an eye to their moral, emotional, physical, or intellectual well-being.

> Based on the data, there is no doubt that children are learning something from their media-driven world. The critical question that emerges has to focus on what exactly they are learning. If experience changes the brain and body, as some neuroscientists suggest (Christakis, Zimmerman, DiGiuseppe, & McCarty, 2004; Healy,1998), then learner immersion and involvement in videotech and technology in general is shaping what learners prefer to do and believe to be important.

As they connect to other game players and TV watchers and use text messaging and cell phones, Twitter, Facebook, and other forms of social networking to share what they are doing, they come away with new skills and information. They are acquiring a new language. They are becoming adept at functioning in a world of images and icons and instant interactions. They are absorbing the culture of games and social networking online. They are adapting and changing in response to their world because their capacities for learning, which are natural and automatic, are being activated and are determining what they value and choose to do.

Some of what is being acquired is valuable, even in terms of the goals of traditional education. In part, media of all kinds are providing learners of all ages with access to enormous amounts of information, often presented in very dynamic ways. In addition, many video games can help learners hone skills in a similar (though more limited) way as flight simulators train future pilots. In the course of playing their games students can develop some capacity to stay with a problem to the end, remain focused even under pressure, pay attention to details, and apply analytical reasoning and logic to some problems.

In fact, a study published in the *British Journal of Educational Technology* concluded that computer games may actually be helpful for children with ADHD because the games motivate students to sit still and concentrate (Farrace-Di Zinno et al., 2001; see also Lawrence et al., 2004; Cloud, 2009; Houghton, Milner, West, Douglas, Lawrence, Whiting et al., 2004).

The well-known game designer Will Wright recently suggested in *Wired* magazine (Wright, 2006) that video games teach the essence of the scientific method because players have to create a hypothesis and through trial and error test and experiment in order to establish a successful result. This process has much in common with the final research phase required for a PhD degree.

Why Could Unsupervised Television and Video Games Be Harmful?

In many ways, however, videotech hurts rather than helps. Here is a small sampling of research into the impact of information technology on children:

- The age of children who play video games is becoming lower: most of the "heavy gamers" are 6–17 years old (Jenkins, 2006).
- Not surprisingly, children who spend more time playing, especially in the bedroom, tend to be more overweight or obese (Vandewater, Shim, & Caplovitz, 2004; Walsh, Gentile, Walsh, & Bennett, 2006).
- There are significant differences in grades between heavy media users (more than 16 hours of media a day) and light users (less than 3 hours of media a day). About half (47%) of heavy media users say they usually get only fair or poor grades (mostly Cs or lower), compared to about a quarter (23%) of light users (Rideout et al., 2010).
- There is growing evidence that children who play violent video games are more aggressive. They also appear to become more and more immune to being able to recognize and fight violence in their

environment (Carnagey, Anderson, & Bushman, 2007; Iacoboni, 2008; Anderson, Gentile, & Buckley 2006).

Susan Greenfield (2008), a leading neuroscientist and former director of the Royal Institution of Great Britain, warns that what we are already seeing will only get worse. She suggests that eventually schools are likely to be filled with students with the following characteristics:

- Think more episodically than analytically (are reactive rather than reflective)
- Have shorter attention spans
- Communicate through pictures rather than words
- Have more learning difficulties
- Are less able to control their impulses and emotions

A study led by Dimitri Christakis at the Children's Hospital and Regional Medical Center in Seattle links violent video games to developing Attention Deficit Disorder (ADD) and Attention Deficit Hyperactivity Disorder (ADHD), and concludes that high amounts of television viewing overstimulate a child's nervous system and permanently alter the child's developing brain. Indeed, the evidence strongly suggests that an overuse of technology-driven media and video, including instant messaging and instant access to any information, at the very least can bypass students' ability to think and make good decisions (Christakis et al., 2004; Small & Vorgan, 2009).

The last claim, however, shows that the picture is a complex one. On the one hand is the contention that violent video games increase ADD and ADHD. Yet a few paragraphs above we referred to the claim that some computer games may reduce ADHD because they may help to improve concentration. In our view, one of the critical differences is the degree of violence in the games, but there is a range of other factors associated with gaming, some of which we address in later pages.

The Problem Expanded: The Absence of Mature Adult Guidance

Many educators would see the research results and statistics as proof that technology in and of itself is the problem. While we understand that point of view, we believe that conclusion is simplistic.

We suggest that neither television nor computers nor video games are intrinsically good or bad. One critical issue is the environment within which they function. The main problem is that kids are primarily on their own or with peers when they engage technology. Most of their exposure to the media and video games is unsupervised and largely unprocessed with mature adults.

Where Are the Parents? To a significant extent technology is replacing parents. By the time an American child is 18, he or she has spent more time in front of the TV than in school, talking with teachers, interacting with peers, or talking and interacting with parents.

While prior studies indicate that parents have strong concerns, the study led by Rideout found that "only about three in ten young people say they have rules about how much time they can spend watching TV (28%) or playing video games (30%), and 36% say the same about using the computer." The study also indicates that "when parents do set limits, children spend less time with media: those with any media rules consume nearly 3 hours less media per day (2:52) than those with no rules" (Rideout et al., 2010).

The unsupervised time spent on television and video games becomes truly frightening when it comes to the amount of violence children encounter. One estimate suggests that the average number of attempted murders that a child will witness by the age of 18 if the home has premium cable channels or a VCR/DVD player is 72,000 ("Youth crime," 1992). Another researcher states, "By the time the average U.S. child starts elementary school he or she will have seen 8,000 murders and 100,000 acts of violence on T.V." (Phillips, 2007). Still another estimate holds that the number of murders seen on TV by the end of elementary school amounts to 8,000 and the number of violent acts seen on TV by age 18 is equivalent to 200,000 and murders 40,000 (Herr, 2007).

Obviously these are daunting statistics. Neuroplasticity refers to the fact that the brain changes as a result of its experience. Can anyone still doubt that this amount of involvement with violence affects how our children think and what they imagine to be "real" or acceptable? Computer games, e-mail, the Internet, cell phones, and instant messaging are integral parts of kids' lives and will not go away.

Where Are the Educators? Most teachers and administrators are woefully out of date when it comes to using computers and technology in the classroom at the level their students consider normal. Use of networking tools such as Facebook and LinkedIn, the use of webinars, Skype, and other video conferencing tools are still not integrated into most teachers' professional lives. But perhaps more problematic is that the videotech world and other uses of technology continue to evolve at an exponential pace while most educators remain frozen into a model of teaching that ignores, rather than engages, what their students see as essential to their lives. And sophisticated video games (Gee, 2007; Jukes & Walker, 2009; Shaffer, 2006) are continually evolving and demonstrating just how amazing and rich teaching can be when a different model of learning is applied.

Today's generation is the first to have grown up in the digital world. According to Marc Prensky (2001a, 2001b), today's college students will spend less than 5,000 hours of their lives reading, but over 10,000 hours playing video games and 20,000 hours watching TV. They have literally grown up with computers, gaming, networking, digital music, YouTube videos, downloading, digital video and still cameras, cell phones and text messaging, to name a few.

Prensky describes this disconnect between today's digital savvy students, whom he calls "Digital Natives," and their adult instructors, whom he calls "Digital Immigrants." The latter try to speak the native language but come at it through a socialization process that is alien and therefore can never equal the language of the natives. "The single problem facing education today is that our Digital Immigrant instructors, who speak an outdated language (that of the pre-digital age), are struggling to teach a population that speaks an entirely new language" (Prensky, 2001a, p. 2).

Of course it would be wrong to categorize everyone in this way. Many students are not digitally savvy, while many adults are. And as we will point out, there are many schools exploring the cutting edge of technology with savvy teachers. However, the general point remains accurate.

And the essential shift is not only about simply gaining expertise with technology. It requires a new way of thinking. Technology gives students choices in what and how they want to explore a topic or subject. Using the Web and multiple search engines, students have access to virtually unlimited information. This means that teachers have to give up their role as the primary providers of information, something that has up to this point defined their profession.

So one readily discernable problem can be identified in terms of how students and teachers relate or don't relate to technology. But this is only the tip of the proverbial iceberg because what is called for is a far more student centered, dynamic, and natural flow to learning. For example:

The teacher we are observing has given her students the afternoon to pursue any project they wish. Some are working with gravity, one is building a birdhouse, but many are putting together electronic gadgets while enthusiastically skipping through the manual. Walking around this combination second- and third-grade class, an observer is struck by the sophistication and ease with which these kids are studying manuals that the teacher would be hard pressed to translate.

INTRODUCTION TO HOW PEOPLE LEARN NATURALLY

Popular technology engages children and adults using challenging scenarios, exciting and relevant social issues, collaboration, ownership, control, relevant engagement, competition, and action that often occurs in real time and at lightning speed.

If we look at some of the emerging research, we will see that much of what is now known about learning is right at the heart of the deep involvement of our kids with video games (and, as we will show, is largely discounted or actively suppressed by most of formal education). Here are some examples:

- The search for meaning occurs through patterning (Caine, Caine, McClintic, & Klimek, 2009; Gee, 2007). Every human being is born with a drive to make sense of experience. Gopnik, Meltsoff, and Kuhl (1999) call it "the explanatory drive." Simply put, in the real world all human beings (and every living organism) have to engage with their environment as a matter of survival. And so videotech activities organized in the context of scenarios with identifiable characters in identifiable settings provides an instantaneously meaningful frame of reference for all that is to follow.

- Cognition is emotional. Among the many factors that influence meaning making is the fact that cognition is affected by emotions. It was once thought that the rational mind functions independently of emotions, but that view has changed. Neuroscientist Candace Pert (1997) suggests that every thought—without exception—is accompanied by the secretion of some "molecules of emotion." And neuroscientist Antonio Damasio (2003) developed what he called a "somatic marker theory" to explain the fact that all decisions and all thought have emotional underpinnings. Others concur (Panksepp, 1998; Roald, 2007). This suggests that people are much more willing and able to master material about which they are passionate or in which they have a genuine personal interest. This is elegantly captured in the *Los Angeles Times* story (Cole, 1999) about Nobel Prize–winning scientist Ahmed H. Zewail, which described him as "the man who loved molecules." Similarly, almost all videotech material triggers the emotional engagement of users in ways ranging from appealing or unappealing characters to situations that activate a range of feelings that potentially engage and motivate.

- The brain/mind is social (Meltzoff, et. al. 2009). No one is an island, not biologically. Even for people who love to spend most time alone, some aspects of learning are intrinsically social. The social nature of people is behind what Wheatley (1999) calls "the longing to belong." In fact, it is not possible to master a language or grasp the meaning of any concept without these being embedded in social relationships. Cognitive scientists call this "situated cognition" (Gee, 2007; Lave & Wenger, 1991), and it refers to how the social environment and relationships impact what someone learns and comes to know. The underlying biological basis for the social nature of human beings has recently been confirmed by neuroscience in the form of mirror neurons (Rizzolatti & Sinigaglia, 2008; Winerman, 2005). We deal with this in depth in Chapter 14. A great deal of the impact of videotech is derived from multiple ways of networking by players of video games and the power of the collective to solve problems in a way that no one can accomplish alone. Much of the learning in the world of videotech comes from players sharing insights, ideas, and strategies with other players in their individual pursuit of mastery.

The world of consumer-driven videotech is thus grounded in a (not always articulated) theory of learning. Those who design, develop, and maintain systems of gaming largely believe that users are motivated by interest. So they develop compelling story lines that incorporate and generate feelings of excitement and other emotions, personal meaning, and social relationships, and that are (in some ways) developmentally appropriate (Shaffer, Squire, & Gee, 2004). Most important of all, participation is a matter of choice. Most game players want to belong to groups of peers who share their interests. This is the context that leads them to pay attention, focus, and concentrate. In this way, gamers and networkers—our children—acquire values and develop an approach to survival, the nature of relationships, the role of loyalty, and what it means to be human (Anderson, 2003; Gee, 2007; Haines, 2005; Shaffer, 2006).

As research in many different domains accelerates, it is revealing that a human being is a learning system in which every aspect of the system—the body, brain, and mind of the person—participates (Damasio, 1994, 1997). As we noted above, the businesses that create video games and operate gaming Web sites are open to, and are making use of, much of this research (Shaffer, 2006). They are intentionally making games more inviting and compelling in both individual and social ways.

And they are competing with formal education (Gee, 2007; King, 2003; Stansbury, 2009).

CHAPTER 2

How Is Technology Impacting the World of Traditional Education?

For the first time in the history of education, the teacher, student, and content do not need to be in the same place or even be together at the same time. If time and distance are dead and if complete integrative technology allows us to have a 2-dimensional and 3-dimensional experience, what will be left of our current education system?

—Ted McCain and Ian Jukes (2001, p. 68)

THE WORLDS OF VIDEOTECH and formal education have different approaches to learning and teaching. In general (and we elaborate in more detail in Chapter 3), the basic form of traditional education is a transmission/direct instruction model (TDI) of teaching characterized by the following features:

- Most teachers use a syllabus, scripted lesson plans, and unit plans that spell out specific assignments and deadlines that leave little or no room for student inquiry, personally relevant engagement, or adjustments to the world that changes around them.
- The concern about cheating (a legitimate concern) and the belief that learning is an individual and sedentary pursuit lead to the suppression of the social and physiological engagement that is both natural and powerful.
- The emphasis on cognitive content, explained by teachers in ways organized to suit them and the educational system, effectively neutralizes the passion and emotional connections that make learning joyful and are essential to deep understanding.

This approach to teaching is based on some core beliefs about learning.

- One belief is that *learning* means memorization and replication of skills and known information, while leaving out how things work or are applied in real-world contexts. Examples include memorizing the names of all the presidents, the procedures for solving equations, the causes of World War II, the structure of a letter seeking an employment interview, and so on. A case can be made that even though this kind of information may be necessary, much of this "learning" is independent of student-generated interest and purpose, something videotech and technology in general supplies in abundance.

- A second belief is that the way to get students to understand complex ideas is by teacher and textbook-based explanations. These can be accompanied by stories, examples, and demonstrations. In essence, however, the formal system believes that understanding can, and all too often must, be transmitted from experts (in the form of textbook or teacher) to learners.

- This largely top-down control model of teaching permeates the educational system and is integrated with a bureaucracy that fragments learning into subjects, time segments, and a belief that time spent or "on task" equals success.

There are many more complex views of teaching and learning than the one we summarize here. For example, a very good introduction to sophisticated direct instruction can be found in an online series funded by Annenberg Media on *The Learning Classroom* (http://www.learner.org/resources/series172.html). We have discussed in detail the continuum of approaches to instruction, ranging from transmission to the guided experience approach dealt with in this book, in our other writings (see Caine & Caine, in press; Caine et al., 2009).

The cry for an alternative has been heard for over a century, and we elaborate upon it later in this book. Indeed, the notion that changing times require changes in education is itself an old notion; that is the theme that drove the commission that produced in 1983 *A Nation at Risk: The Imperative for Education Reform* (now found online at http://www2.ed.gov/pubs/NatAtRisk/index.html). Yet not much has changed. The bottom line is that the transmission model dominates the current thinking of educators and society in general. And it is simply missing the boat.

WHICH SYSTEM OF EDUCATION IS WINNING?

We have no doubt that videotech is winning the battle for the hearts and minds of the vast majority of young people. However, as we note above, the sort of education that children are receiving from the world of videotech leaves a huge void that videotech is not fulfilling, and, to some extent, is helping to enlarge.

Actually, most educators and the public at large seem not to regard the world of videotech as "educating." For many, it is relegated to play outside of school.

It is almost as if education is operating under the illusion that television and technology are not teaching students, just entertaining them.

Meanwhile, some of the developers of the videotech world treat formal education with disdain. Consider, for instance, this strong condemnation of most schools:

> Schools tend to care only about what is inside students' heads as their heads and bodies are isolated from others, from tools and technologies, and from rich environments that help make them powerful nodes in networks. . . . Good workplaces in our science—and technology-driven "new capitalism" don't play this game. Schools that do are, in my view, DOA [Dead On Arrival] in our current world—and kids who play video games know it. (Gee, 2007, p. 202)

Without disrespect to the many exceptional teachers and efforts of innovative school leaders, one could argue that much of the worlds of media, science, and business use a far more sophisticated approach to learning than do most schools. And much of this knowledge remains untapped by teachers and school leaders, even though there are frequent calls for the introduction of more sophisticated technologies into education (see e.g., Federation of American Scientists, 2006).

TENSIONS GENERATED BY INTRODUCING TECHNOLOGY INTO FORMAL EDUCATION

The world of videotech and the transmission/direct instruction (TDI) meme have met each other, and the system of formal education is feeling the tension.

On the one hand, we can observe the new and exciting approaches to education that are being introduced all over the United States. Apple's "Challenge Based Learning" (http://ali.apple.com/cbl/) is one example, and the creative and critical work being supported by the George Lucas Foundation (Edutopia: http://www.globalschoolnet.org/gsnprojects/GLEF/) is another. Organizations like this and the Creative Learning Plaza (http://www.creative-learningsystems.com/prod/clp.asp), the Square One Network (http://www.cef-trek.org/Home.html), and the work being done on sophisticated teaching video games (Shaffer et al., 2004) are a few more examples.

These approaches to education not only make use of more technology, but they also have an approach to learning and teaching that is fundamentally different from the transmission approach. And they are demonstrating that the use of technology often plays havoc with the transmission model. Above all they engross students through learning that empowers them because it includes student decision making, applying creative solutions to complex real-life problems, and negotiating with peers and experts. Of course it includes extensive use of the Web and other sources of technology in multiple, interactive ways. And a small number of schools handle the situation very well.

The bulk of the public education system, however, has immense difficulty with technology. We do not wish to slight the many successful attempts by public schools to implement more sophisticated technology, but most of the time when this is done it has played havoc with traditional schedules, spaces, teacher-designed lesson plans, top-down administrative management, and student discipline programs (Collins & Halverson, 2009). All too frequently teachers are caught between district practices and mandates that do not allow for the sorts of learning that embed complex curriculum in projects like filmmaking, media literacy, video design, creative diagramming, and documentation of research that emerges out of student interests. Yet genuine and effective use of technology is highly dependent on creativity, innovation, and play, as well as collaboration.

Even more tension arises because teachers cannot deal adequately with the world of information open to students. The availability of Wikipedia alone (the free, Web-based, digital encyclopedia) can drastically subvert a teacher's plans and force a reevaluation of what it means to "cheat." In addition, the widespread availability of home computers makes the use of firewalls by schools and districts, even though intended to protect students by limiting access to the World Wide Web, just about irrelevant.

Two recent encounters made it abundantly clear to us that firewalls are relatively ineffective. In one instance, we were in a highly technologically adept high school in Michigan. Students had been creating films using one book they had chosen from literary works assigned by the district. In the course of making a point concerning his character's dialog, the student showing his films mentioned that he had some additional dialog on My Space which was restricted by the district firewall. In a very relaxed and casual voice he promised to copy it from his home computer and bring it in the next day. The teacher, who trusted the student as a responsible young designer, made no objections.

The second incident took place in California in a special education class. A student came up to the teacher to tell him that it was easy to get past the district firewalls. The teacher asked the student to show him how it was done, and sure enough, after entering the instructions, they were out freely surfing the Web. The student had simply Googled the information (when we Googled "bypassing school firewalls," we found 563,000 results). And teacher-stipulated assignments that used to require a great deal of student work, as in the case of preparing a report on some subject, are now easily accessed on the Web and can be downloaded in seconds.

> The point we are making is not that educators need to know all the latest in technology or design better firewalls, but rather that teaching with technology is an entirely different art. And with software and hardware applications changing daily and expected to keep changing for the foreseeable future, the entire question is about how to teach in this new world and how to access a model for teaching that can incorporate the necessary degree of student interest and freedom.

At the very least, this requires a much more dynamic and much less prescriptive approach to learning and teaching that includes the following attributes:

1. Hierarchy between students and teachers is flattened as everyone respectfully exchanges ideas and information, with teachers becoming the facilitators of excellence.
2. Students become more creative and ready to explore and experiment with their own ideas, with teachers preserving some boundaries as they integrate high standards into student-generated products.
3. Learning becomes more complex, with a focus on questions that require uniquely organized research and demonstration of higher level thinking skills rather than the mere gathering of facts and information for written or verbal summaries or reports.

RESCUING THE FUTURE

There is much more to the future of education than finding a way to use technology more effectively. The larger purpose of education itself needs to be revisited. In broad terms, a core purpose of education in any given society is to prepare its youth to survive and thrive in the real world. That calls for more than success on standardized tests, although tests and assessment in general clearly play a role.

A place to begin is with the role of education in preparing students for the world of work—a very complex endeavor. Graduates will need a variety of skills and characteristics:

> Strong skills in English, mathematics, technology, and science, as well as literature, history, and the arts will be essential for many; beyond this, candidates will have to be comfortable with ideas and abstractions, good at analysis and synthesis, creative and innovative, self-disciplined and well organized, able to learn very quickly and work well as a member of a team and have the flexibility to adapt quickly to frequent changes in the labor market as the shifts in the economy become ever faster and more dramatic. (National Center on Education and the Economy, 2007, pp. XVIII–XIX)

And there is more to education than even the goals just listed. There has long been a call for a higher purpose for education and it is time for that purpose to be resurrected. One thread can be found in the writings of John Dewey (1916/2010) and others who thought that, among other things, education should nurture social responsibility and democracy. Many people, ranging from Thomas Jefferson to Eleanor Roosevelt, have argued that a critical purpose of education is to prepare people for citizenship. Here is a comment by Martin Luther King Jr. (1947):

> The function of education, therefore, is to teach one to think intensively and to think critically. But education which stops with efficiency may prove the greatest menace to society. The most dangerous criminal may be the man gifted with reason, but with no morals. (Morehouse College Student Paper, *The Maroon Tiger*)

In a similar vein, Governor Hunt of North Carolina made the following comments in an address to the American Association of Higher Education in 1998:

> Education generally, and higher education in particular, has several purposes—and one of the most important is to promote citizenship. As I

look at the political scene today, having good citizens who care, who understand, who can ferret out truth seems to me to be more and more important. And we ought to say it first when we talk about our purposes.

A second purpose is preparing people to be good human beings, to be good members of families, to be the kind of parents and spouses we ought to be in our families and communities. (p. 3)

This general view, which we ardently support, continues to be reexpressed. Here, for instance, is a position taken by Stoddard and Dalman-Jones (2010) and endorsed by the Educating for Human Greatness group (http://definegreat.ning.com). They argue for a crystal-clear purpose for education: Develop great human beings to be contributors (not burdens) to society. They give seven dimensions of human greatness with accompanying goals:

1. *Identity*—Help students learn who they are as individuals with un-limited potential, develop their unique talents and gifts to realize self-worth, and develop a strong desire to be contributors to family, school, and community.
2. *Inquiry*—Stimulate curiosity; awaken a sense of wonder and appreciation for nature and humankind. Help students develop the power to ask important questions.
3. *Interaction*—Promote courtesy, caring, communication, and cooperation.
4. *Initiative*—Foster self-directed learning, willpower, and self-evaluation.
5. *Imagination*—Nurture creativity in all of its many forms.
6. *Intuition*—Help students learn how to feel and recognize truth with their hearts as well as with their minds; develop spirituality and humility.
7. *Integrity*—Develop honesty, character, morality, and responsibility for self.

RESOLVING THE PROBLEM OF TECHNOLOGY CAN GIVE LIFE TO THE OTHER PURPOSES OF EDUCATION

The exciting and revolutionary possibility is that, in successfully bridging the gap between videotech and formal education, the process is in place for achieving the higher purposes of education at the same time as children are prepared for the basics of work and the future. Even though there is a great deal of room for debate about the purposes of education, we will attempt to demonstrate throughout this book that all those higher purposes can be achieved while at the same time incorporating the highest academic standards.

Irrespective of the specific purposes upon which society settles is the fact that education and educators must come to terms with the emerging research about how people learn and be able to apply it. (This point has been made by others for many years. See, e.g., Strommen and Lincoln, 1992). At the very least they need to understand what exactly attracts students so powerfully to the new technologies. When they do, they will see that the key to integrating technology into education calls for tapping into the power of meaning and motivation that all too often is left untapped in classrooms and that does not engage students sufficiently. It calls for the need to deal with the social and networked way of learning that is found throughout the real world as well as in the world of games. It calls for mature decision making, self-regulation, reflection in action (an aspect of metacognition), creativity, the capacity to think about and work with others, and a host of additional matters.

In short, education needs to find a way to access the inherent capacities of students, and that includes taking advantage of and embracing the worlds of videotech, so that students can be adequately prepared for the massively changing world into which they are being thrust. And as this happens, students have the experiences that help them to mature as human beings.

Unfortunately, traditional beliefs about learning and teaching are held captive by the current culture and its beliefs and practices, and its commitment to what we call the transmission/direct instruction (TDI) model. Cultural forces, then, remain the largest obstacle to change.

CHAPTER 3

What Are the Powerful Beliefs About Learning and Teaching That Keep Education Frozen in Place?

Games provide increasingly complex, customizable learning-by-doing environments. Just as schools are moving toward increasingly standardizing the learning experience, games offer the prospect of user-defined worlds in which players try out (and get feedback on) their own assumptions, strategies, and identities. Thus games have come to typify the essentially subversive nature of computing in relation to schools.

—Allan Collins and Richard Halverson (2009, p. 85)

IN THE PREVIOUS CHAPTER we introduced the transmission/direct instruction (TDI) model of teaching. It is a view of teaching that is so deeply held throughout the education system and in the larger community that it is largely taken for granted as "the" way to teach. And any ostensibly new way to improve education tends to be seen in terms of how it relates to that traditional view.

Even when educators attempt to move toward student-centered teaching or more naturally engaging or constructivist approaches that suggest that the learners should be more directly in charge of their own learning, it rarely takes long before the entire teaching enterprise reverts back to the adult, largely telling students what they need to know (providing answers), verbally explaining, and calling on them to practice until they get it right.

The idea and image of traditional teaching, in fact, is a meme. And it needs to change.

MEMES: IDEAS THAT GOVERN THEMSELVES

A *meme* (Blackmore, 2000; Brodie, 1996; Dawkins, 1976) is an idea that has a life of its own. It refers to a unit of cultural information transferable from one mind to another. It thus acts as an underlying belief that drives how people interpret what is going on around them and organizes what they do. Here is one to test. Tell someone that you are going to Las Vegas next weekend and watch what happens. What assumptions will automatically surface? You will rarely if ever be asked if you are visiting family or going on business. What is done in Las Vegas is taken for granted.

> Memes drive collective action and this is what makes them so powerful. Everyone simply takes for granted that this is how things are done and dismisses alternative interpretations or even evidence to the contrary.

Here are some possible examples of memes or self-replicating ideas that shape interpretations and drive behavior:

- A scientific paradigm according to which only measurable outcomes matter and which discounts, as useful evidence, expert interpretations of phenomena and behaviors that influence outcomes that cannot necessarily be quantified
- A narrow medical model that defines health or illness exclusively in terms of physical symptoms and ignores the effects of stress, state of mind, beliefs, or impact of relationships on health
- An approach to business according to which profit is all that matters, other reasons for being in business like service are ignored, and the value of relationship between employees and customers is discounted.

Traditional education is driven by a powerful meme that keeps replicating itself. One simply has to imagine several people gathering to talk about education to recognize how powerfully the meme is embedded. Individuals will visualize desks and books and a teacher in the front of the classroom. Grades, tests, discipline, and hard work will bind together the beliefs that everyone automatically subscribes to. These beliefs linger as foundational ideas that are rarely, if ever, questioned.

Over the past 20 years we have watched this meme along with its self-replicating assumptions and its hold on education. Despite mountains of research, technological advances, and innovative teaching revolutions, one theme persists: the idea that academic learning is fundamentally about teachers transmitting information, understanding, and skills to learners who in turn replicate essential "work," regardless of personal meaning, motivation, and purpose. And most recently, the heavy emphasis on testing, has largely been used to solidify this view of learning and teaching.

Let us assume (though not all agree) that the transmission/direct instruction (TDI) approach to learning and teaching has served us relatively well historically. Most of the adults living now grew up with it and society has prospered. (Remember, however, that this "success" occurred in a relatively slow-paced and slow-changing world, and those characteristics of the world are gone forever).

There has always been a tension, however, between the direct instruction model and an alternative. The alternative model, associated with Dewey and others (Dewey, 1916/1980, 1938/1997, 1916/2010; Piaget, 1976; Vygotsky, 1993), is that the best way to teach requires students to have experiences within which they can be guided to subject matter mastery while they make personal sense of, and directly engage in, those experiences.

There is much to be said for good direct instruction. There is a great deal, however, that only experience, properly guided, can teach. Most important, direct instruction or the more traditional direct instruction approach is not a good fit with current technology. The approach is simply too limited. So a more learner-centered, experiential model should *include* direct instruction, but transcend it and go much further. We call this more sophisticated mode of instruction the Guided Experience Approach. It embraces a much more open and complex view of learning. We will discuss this more in depth in Chapters 15–18 and establish its foundation throughout this book.

The Transmission/Direct Instruction Meme Is Present Everywhere

The existing meme is so powerful that, on many occasions, teachers who are exposed to, and come to understand, alternative approaches (through such processes as goal-based scenarios, action learning, project-based learning, problem-based learning, and self-directed learning that engages students in technology), find that it is not possible to implement those new approaches in their schools. Sometimes the challenge is psychological because the new approaches are not supported by the teaching context and community (Hirst & Peters, 1970). And sometimes the structure and functioning of the system through time and resource and other constraints make it impossible (Christenson, Horn, & Johnson, 2008; Hirst & Peters, 1970; Masullo & Ruiz, 2000).

The transmission meme infuses every aspect of the system. Its power lies in the fact that it colors everything that people do and operates both directly and indirectly.

One reason why it is so difficult to include sophisticated technology in teaching is not just because of lack of hardware or technical instruction for teachers (although these play a significant role), but because almost every change is almost automatically pulled into the orbit of the TDI meme and ends up serving an old master, even while it purports to be something new.

One example often quoted by more technology-savvy individuals refers to how teachers now use smart boards just the way they used to use the old blackboards and overheads. The same thinking and actions remain, but teachers feel more technologically competent because they can operate this new tool. This false sense of competence can keep them from recognizing that their deeply held beliefs about learning and teaching need to be challenged.

Education Pays a Price for the TDI Meme

Educators are quick to tell anyone what is "in" and what is "out" in education. For many in the profession, whole language is currently "out" as is constructivism, while direct instruction is "in." For instance, this is how the status of whole language is characterized in Wikipedia: "Whole language has thus during the 2000s receded from being the dominant reading model in the education field to marginal status, and it continues to fade" (http://en.wikipedia.org/wiki/Whole_language). Yet from our perspective, the thorough and intense research supporting good whole language was far more sophisticated than the governing meme could accept.

It seems to us that what drives these evaluations is the governing meme, which leads people to interpret and eliminate ideas and research that fall outside standard "truths" or do not directly connect to practices sanctioned by the meme. Because educators themselves are taught in fragments and by way of direct instruction, there are rarely opportunities provided for questioning or processing the deeper issues involved. The meme that drives direct instruction and student compliance also affects educators who all too often do not see themselves as decision makers or powerful professionals whose judgments are based on respectfully analyzed and debated constructs and research. And this entire scenario has been exacerbated by the current emphasis on testing by external authorities as the primary goal and means of assessment.

If the goal is to develop knowledgeable learners who are technologically adept, guided by educators dedicated to tapping human potential and serving humanity, then collective assumptions and the prevailing meme need to be exposed and challenged. If those assumptions don't shift or change, education will continue to erode and crumble, and it will have no way of meeting these deeper needs of students of today who emerge as the adults of tomorrow.

The Perspectives of Key Stakeholders

As we have already pointed out, the transmission meme is built on an edifice that is extraordinarily difficult to shift, in part because it meets the expectations of almost all the stakeholders in the system of education. That calls for us to begin a painful process of looking at the ways in which the TDI meme serves those interests, and in the ways in which many taken-for-granted aspects of education naturally reinforce the meme. We will proceed by looking at groups of stakeholders:

- The meme suits most parents. Most parents want and expect their children to have assignments and homework that can be graded and checked off. They hunger for some simple, clear objective indicators that tell them how well their children are doing. They like the clarity of different subjects and teachers who seem to be preparing their children in familiar ways. And, even though it is often left unsaid, many parents need schools to function as a safe and predictable place so that they can have peace of mind while they are at work.
- The meme suits most administrators. The management concept is understandable. Administrators can check to make certain that state and district curriculum goals are met systematically, relying on teaching as a relatively linear process. And although the highly structured system, which is organized by age, grade, subject, and individual classrooms, can be painfully difficult to control, the familiar management concept is similar to that of any other institution, be it a factory or (dare we say it) a prison.
- The meme suits most teachers. Teachers largely direct and control the learning. They can make up lesson plans for days when they are absent and students can be monitored through assignments checked off as work to be completed or made up in case of absence.
- The meme suits unions in many ways. In the current system, salaries and benefits are defined and determined in accordance with specific numbers of hours in front of students, as dictated by union negotiations. The old meme lends itself to this approach. But when student purposes, projects, and interests drive what they do, time for learning cannot be organized, and benefits assessed, in terms of prespecified hours spent on prespecified goals and products.

- The meme suits most school board members. They can focus on costs, protection of finances, union issues that relate to "work" tied to hours spent in front of well-managed classrooms, and on the physical infrastructure, while largely remaining unaware of how the physical structure and all the other issues with which they deal actually link to learning needed for this century.

- The meme suits many business interests. One enormous source of profit to corporations comes from the sale of textbooks and administration of standardized tests (Garan, 2004; Kohn, 2002). The TDI model is a perfect fit for this type of business, and billions of dollars are at stake for corporations as they market and present books and materials for teachers that produce enormous profits for a relatively low expenditure.

- The meme suits those who thrive on sound bites. These include politicians at every level who want to be seen as doing something to improve schools in quick, readily understandable, and measureable ways. There is nothing easier than calling for money to be spent in ways that look as though they will provide tangible results such as higher test scores. And this category includes those in the media who relish issues that can be addressed in simplistic, black or white terms. It is interesting to note that in the past 10 years the reading level of newspapers has gone from 12th grade to 9th grade ("What's with the Newspapers," 2005; Porter, 2005).

- The meme suits much of academia. Much teacher training and credentialing is framed in terms of the old meme. A structured course sequence assumes that all future teachers must engage in a similar course of separate subjects. Teacher expertise and power is confirmed by the TDI model, as professors use lecture and teacher-centered practices. This includes faculty research and writing that explores improvements in, but does not challenge, the current meme.

In fact, the meme is so powerful that many of the wonderful findings of modern brain research have been interpreted from the perspective of the current meme. For instance, although they have contributed a great deal to informing educators about brain research, and offer a large array of new teaching strategies, many of those who advocate versions of brain-based learning are essentially expanding and enriching the TDI model rather than transcending it.

We need to repeat here that there is a long tradition of attempts to transcend traditional teaching (Annenberg Media, http://www.learner.org; National Board for Professional Teaching Standards, http://www.nbpts.org). Many universities also offer extraordinarily sophisticated programs. An example is the master's program on Holistic and Integrative Education at California State University–San Bernardino, jointly created by our colleagues Sam Crowell and Bob London. The program is one of only three in the country and has been recognized as an exemplar by the Fetzer Institute (http://www.fetzer.org). Six students from the program from only nine cohorts (groups of students that go through a program together) have been awarded Teacher of the Year honors by their school or district.

Yet such programs are still few and far between, and the educators who graduate from these programs can face difficulties in implementing their new understandings and skills in a system riddled with the TDI approach. And although these are more compatible with the teachings we advocate, they are all too often still poorly integrated with sophisticated technology.

Even the Development and Implementation of Standards Supports the TDI Meme

Over the last 15 years there has been an immense effort in the United States to spell out academic standards at the state and national level. One example is the Common Core States Standards Initiative or CCSSI (http://www.corestandards.org). The development of core standards has been seen as essential for a number of reasons. For one thing, the standards have been different in different districts and states, and so students and communities have been treated differently. There have also been many disparities in the education of minority students, much of which has been attributed to the absence of uniform standards (Ready, Edley, & Snow, 2002). Moreover, it seems unarguable to us that some core goals for education need to be set, whether or not they are called "standards." For instance, in a world driven by text and the media, we believe that a fundamental goal of education should be both text and media literacy. Beyond that are other specific needs for changing times, as we discuss in more depth below.

The problem is that the TDI meme permeates and therefore confuses the entire standards debate. Here are two examples, both of which point toward a deeply held belief that education is about the transmission of fixed information and skills.

1. The forced implementation of standards undermines the positive process in which they were developed. The process of development is highly revealing because the standards are actually established using a more natural approach (see Chapters 5 and 9), but are implemented by way of a top-down process tied to the TDI meme.

Developing the standards calls for the asking of critical questions, discussion, gathering evidence, and problem solving based on expert knowledge and research. The experts and volunteers who were recruited to write the CCSSI standards gathered in separate places, usually in a moderately relaxed atmosphere, and discussed their ideas, sought common ground, and spelled out and summarized for publication the standards they believed to be essential for students to achieve. This entire process has aspects of the kind of natural learning we will advocate in the following chapters. The process they used was moderately open, creative, and collaborative and resulted in a product open to continuous feedback from a range of colleagues (we appreciate that the process can be much more limited and contentious than described here).

Now let's look at what happens to those standards. They are transmitted "down" the ladder to others who have to implement them. It will happen now as it has happened in the past. Those who "know" tell those who "don't know" what has to be done. Thus the open process by which the standards were developed is ignored, and implementation follows the TDI meme (Ravich, 2010). Educators in the trenches did not (and do not) have the opportunity to discuss the implementation of the standards and analyze them critically and openly and in collaboration with fellow teachers. There is no time provided for discussion, modification, collaboration, or input from the very people directly responsible for implementing the specified standards. Instead, like their students, they have to comply and do what they are told rather than what makes sense to them. So the very means by which the standards are implemented (enforced by a top-down bureaucracy) reinforce the transmission meme. Notwithstanding an average of 5 to 6 years of college, teachers are largely reduced to technicians, not expected to act like professionals.

2. The obsession with results on standardized tests has forced a massive move toward standardized instruction. Many state and district materials are being produced that call for all teachers of a particular subject in a particular grade level to be on the same page of the same text on the same day—in the name of efficiency. Other materials spell out precisely how and where a teacher should stand in a classroom at a particular moment in a lesson and even what to say (Saxon, 2004). And many are the school principals who march down school corridors and peer into classrooms to police the process.

For example, an outstanding teacher in our community, who was one of the exceptional teachers we reported on in our first book (Caine & Caine, 1991), decided to retire early after her principal insisted that she teach from the prescriptive text the district had adopted. Her own judgment, exceptional record, and teaching were entirely ignored in favor of the approved text protocol. She was repeatedly checked on by the principal, who insisted that she pace her instructions one page at a time.

By analogy, imagine every coach of little league baseball being obliged to teach kids of the same age precisely how to throw a particular pitch at precisely the same time each week. The practice is inherently absurd and makes it literally impossible for teachers to work with individuals and individual groups in anything like the sort of way that high-level performance calls for.

There is, of course, no logical link between standardized tests and standardized teaching. The problem is the meme. As already pointed out, the meme is both culturally and psychologically embedded. The pressure to base success primarily on producing students who can achieve high test scores reveals a gross lack of understanding of how people learn and what great teaching looks like.

The two of us have often observed the mechanical implementation of standards. We recall one math teacher standing in front of her class and listing the standards that would be "worked on" this day. One by one she called out a math problem tied to each standard. As she stated the problem, students were given the opportunity to answer by raising their hand. Once someone had the answer she would declare that that particular standard had been met. Sitting at the back we observed students asking each other if they knew what was going on. The teacher, however, forged ahead, convinced that she was implementing the math standards.

The TDI Meme Is Structured in Our Buildings and Culture

To gain a better idea of how the meme operates, look at the photographs on the following page. Which ones are photographs of schools and which are of prisons?[1]

This is a critical question and one that may seem elusive because we tend *not* to think of a building as housing a meme. Yet we have traveled all over this country and schools inevitably look like factories or prisons. What is it that leads to schools being organized like this? (See Figure 3.1.)

The buildings are sending a message. It is that learning and the education process require obedience and specific product outcomes determined by an authority or authorities. Rooms are organized separately, each governed and

controlled by a teacher. The building is easily organized to manage specific timelines and outcomes determined by mandated goals and parameters all resulting in restricting rather than facilitating natural learning and student interactions. Physical movement and the expression of emotional issues that need to be processed in a respectful way are inevitably suppressed because they do not comply with prestipulated rules. And the dynamic participation of learners in a more natural and lifelike context tends to be treated as an interference with the important work of "learning."

What should concern all of us, in addition, is the use of professional guards in schools, drug searches by outside authorities, and students having to go through metal detectors. All of these mimic the social world of prison far better than the modern workplace calling for creativity, initiative, and social and technological expertise on a national and international level. Given the research on mirror neurons in particular (see Chapter 14), we have to ask ourselves, just what is being modeled?

The TDI meme is rampant. We must find a better way.

FIGURE 3.1. Clip art representations of a factory and a school.

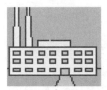 

WHERE DO WE GO FROM HERE?

Times have changed so much that the TDI model has reached its limits.

- There is no conceivable way in which standards of any sort can cover more than a fragment of the ideas, procedures, information, and technologies that are flowing into the world that our students will inhabit. There is now so much information available and change is so quick that it is just not possible to cover more than a fragment of what is known. The key, therefore, is to use an educational process that develops the best foundations for everyone to genuinely be able to adopt learning as a way of life.
- The technologies that are available for transmitting information, collaborating for increased understanding, and experiencing the stuff of any curriculum has more power and possibility than the TDI meme can handle. While sophisticated direct instruction is a very useful tool for educators, it simply cannot adequately incorporate the other tools and processes that are available.

The fact is that the time has come for a more learner-focused approach to prevail (McCombs & Miller, 2008). The reason is that a genuinely learner-centered approach releases additional learning capacities of students in a way that makes it possible to teach for the knowledge age. But change is immensely difficult.

NOTE

1. The answers to this question are as follows: The top two photos are prisons. The bottom two photos are schools.

CHAPTER 4

What Do Students Need in Order to Successfully Prepare for the Future?

I don't want my son to be limited to learning only what his teacher already knows!
—John Couch, Vice President of Education at Apple, Inc.

AS THE DRUMBEAT increases for an education system that works for the knowledge age, and that blends both academic competence and knowledge age capacities and skills, we need to deal with a basic fact: *Education cannot get there from here.*

WHAT DOES EDUCATION NEED TO ACCOMPLISH? AN EMERGING CONSENSUS

Education is in danger of fragmenting everything, from framing outcomes based on last century's standards, to separating totally natural human variations and capacities into an almost endless list of dysfunctions. At the same time, technology is entirely capable of drowning human capacities for depth of understanding, reflection, and the application of unique abilities in a continuous and escalating sea of entertainment and overstimulation.

We as a society face an almost impossible tension. On the one hand, children are immersed in a world of technology from which they learn a great deal with very little adult supervision. But much of what they learn may not serve them. On the other hand, they spend hours in school every day for up to 12 years where they are very tightly controlled and where learning is totally directed, and yet many end up learning very little of value, and much of what happens to them does not serve them in the world they will live in. (How many individuals have attended school for 12 years and can neither read nor spell nor write for public consumption?)

The challenge we all face, and the problem we have to solve, is to find and integrate the best of both worlds. Education and society must come to terms with technology, with the ways that children are beginning to communicate with what engages and interests them, and with the fact that the role of technology is still very much on the rise. Quantum computers and "meat machines" (DNA-based computers) will advance technology in unknown ways. How do we prepare students to deal with such an information tsunami? Higher order thinking, personal decision making, and depth of knowledge will be absolutely essential.

At the same time, education and society have to find out how best to include academic knowledge and mastery, including personal and interpersonal skills. And we have to do this with adults who were immersed in, and largely still believe in, the type of teaching and schools that will no longer serve.

> The solution, it seems to us, must be to think differently. Rather than establish standards in terms of a catalog of facts, concepts, and skills (Resnick, 2010), the goal must be to help students acquire a way of thinking and perceiving and acting that provides an ongoing platform for being able to adapt to a changing world.

In addition to a solid academic foundation, a vision of what else education needs to focus on is coming from multiple sources and disciplines, and that vision is becoming more coherent. In effect, what is emerging is driven by a more interconnected, dynamic, and holistic view of learning and what it means to function successfully in the knowledge age and a new economic reality.

Skills Students Need in Order to Succeed in the New Economy

I have come to understand that there is a core set of survival skills for today's workplace, as well as for lifelong learning and active citizenship—skills that are neither taught nor tested even in our best school systems.
—Tony Wagner (2008, p. 14)

Even if we aim no higher than the preparation of students for the working world, one way of viewing the competencies needed for the economy is represented in Figure 4.1.

Notice that successful students will need to master skills and capacities represented by the top of the pyramid. They will need to know how to research,

FIGURE 4.1. Projections of typical jobs and skills needed in the future. From *Tough Choices or Tough Times: The Report of the New Commission on the Skills of the American Workforce,* by the National Center on Education and the Economy, 2007, San Francisco: Wiley.

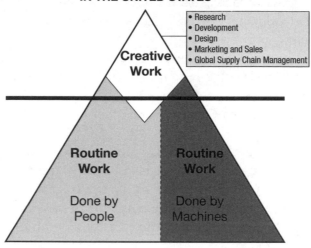

design, and develop new products and services, as well as how to market and sell these while competing in a global market. From the perspective of the United States, note also that many "less developed countries" are moving in a similar direction, and have talented individuals with complex skills, including the capacities to research and develop new products (Iiyoshi & Kumar, 2008).

This is much more a question of education than it is of membership in a more or less developed country. The underlying capacities for doing creative work can be expanded in several ways. For instance, in *The Global Achievement Gap* (2008), Tony Wagner summarizes "Seven Survival Skills" that he believes students need in order to be effective in the knowledge age. He arrived at these by interviewing managers, business developers, and CEOs. They include the following abilities:

- Engage in critical thinking and problem solving
- Collaborate across various networks and lead by influence
- Be agile and adaptable
- Demonstrate initiative and entrepreneurialism
- Communicate effectively both orally and in written form
- Access and analyze critical information
- Demonstrate curiosity and imagination (p. 67)

Notice how closely his recommendations match the projections made by the National Center on Education and the Economy in Figure 4.1. Competence in research, development, design, marketing, and sales require all of the survival skills Wagner suggests as essential.

Skills Students Need in Order to Function as Intelligent Citizens

The spirit of democracy in the United States has long depended on effective education. This was articulated early on by Thomas Jefferson when he said, "If a nation expects to be ignorant and free, in a state of civilization, it expects what never was and never will be." (Monticello Web site: http://www.monticellocatalog.org/200168.html).

John Dewey also addressed concerns about developing people competent to function democratically. He dedicated an entire book to the theme, *Democracy and Education* (Dewey, 1916/2010).

The issues and goals formulated by the Educating for Human Greatness group introduced in Chapter 2 have a similar thread, though they are dealing with contributions to community in general. Here are two of their previously mentioned goals:

- *Identity*—Help students learn who they are as individuals with unlimited potential, develop their unique talents and gifts to realize self-worth and develop a strong desire to be contributors to family, school, and community.
- *Integrity*—Develop honesty, character, morality, and responsibility for self.

Many others have addressed this issue. For instance, Costa and Kallick (2008) have researched and taught "Habits of Mind" as part of a "thinking" curriculum, and again, they reflect the theme explored so far. They list the following Habits of Mind on the Institute for Habits of Mind Web site (http://www.instituteforhabitsofmind.com/what-are-habits-mind):

- Persisting
- Thinking and communicating with clarity and precision
- Managing impulsivity
- Gathering data through all senses
- Listening with understanding and empathy
- Creating, imagining, and innovation
- Thinking flexibly

- Responding with wonderment and awe
- Thinking about thinking (metacognition)
- Taking responsible risks
- Striving for accuracy
- Finding humor
- Questioning and posing problems
- Thinking interdependently
- Applying past knowledge to new situations
- Remaining open to continuous learning

While all the lists vary, there is a very strong overlap. At the core is the notion that students need to leave school equipped with a set of capacities and skills for functioning effectively in a complex world. Insofar as society spells out a set of standards that need to be addressed by education, those capacities and skills should be front and center.

Skills Students Need for Living in a World Steeped in Technology

We now explore the skills and capacities addressed above from the perspective of the world into which students are moving. It is a high-tech world in which every student has access to an enormous amount of information and opinion. This has to be sorted, interpreted, assessed, evaluated, and used. While operating in this world, students need to be centered and have some self-control, because it is very easy to get caught up in a wave of activity initiated by others and fostered by crowd momentum. This flow of information is accompanied by a massive expansion of contacts, mostly online, but many will be translated into "live" interactions. Students need to assess both the people and organizations with which they network and the manner of making connections. In the course of all of this, emotions will be engaged and passions aroused. Students need to monitor and regulate themselves so that they can function in a healthy way in a partially live and partially virtual world. And throughout it all, students are framing and developing their own interests and ways of being in the world. Are they victims or leaders? Are they pursuing their dreams or supporting the interests of others? Are they becoming isolated or capable of working and thriving in community?

Success in the videotech world, both in terms of prosperity and democracy, depend more and more upon the development of the sorts of skills outlined so far. Marc Prensky (2009) has deeply explored the link between technology and what this generation of students needs, and has produced a list of skills that individuals must master in order to survive successfully in the knowledge age. Notice again the concurrence between the skills that have been called for above and Prensky's list of "Essential Skills for the 21st Century":

1. *Knowing the right thing to do.* This means that students have to know how to behave ethically, think critically, set goals, make good decisions, and have good judgment.
2. *Getting it done.* By this he means that students will have to know how to plan, solve problems, be self-directed, assess their own work and capacities, and engage in multiple ways of learning something.
3. *Doing it with others.* This requires that students are capable of leading, communicating and interacting with others, programming (interacting with machines), and interacting globally and with other cultures.
4. *Doing it creatively.* Students will have to know how to adapt, think creatively, "tinker and design," play, and express their unique identity.
5. *Constantly doing it better.* Students will have to develop the capacity to reflect, be proactive, take manageable risks, think long term, and continually improve and learn.

Prensky also notes that these are similar to Covey's (1990) "seven habits of highly effective people." In fact, while these capacities are essential for the knowledge age, it should be clear that these sorts of skills and capacities have been called for by many thinkers and researchers years before technology came of age. Technology, however, and the powerful forces that drive a new type of economy are making these skills more relevant and essential.

THE EXECUTIVE FUNCTIONS OF THE HUMAN BRAIN

There is an interesting and powerful common thread to all of the recommendations we have looked at so far. They are all expressions of potential capacities with which every student is actually to some extent endowed at birth. Neuroscientists describe them in terms of executive or integrative functions of the human brain (Fuster, 2003; Miller & Cohen, 2001; Miller & Cummings, 1999), while cognitive scientists talk of higher order functioning and metacognition (Dunlosky & Metcalfe, 2009; Krasnegor, Lyon, & Goldman-Rakic, 1997; Lyon & Krasnegor, 1996). They represent capacities that are essential to employability, ownership, leadership, and citizenship.

There are a variety of overlapping ways to describe executive functions, and they mesh well with the skills we have been describing as essential to working, reasoning, and making decisions in the complex, knowledge-based world of the future. Christine Temple (1997) includes the following:

- The ability to plan ahead and organize behavior across time and space in order to fulfill goals and intentions
- The ability to shift strategies and adapt to changing circumstances
- Planning, decision making, directed goal selection, and monitoring of ongoing behavior
- Self-awareness, empathy, and social sensitivity

The term *executive functions* also refers to personal drive, planning, purposeful action, and effective performance (Boone, 1999). And Denkla (1999) points out that executive functions are central to higher order cortical operations that connect attention and memory. They represent the ability to integrate and combine an almost infinite number of brain functions at a given moment in time and space (Fuster, 2003; Goldberg, 2001; Miller & Cohen, 2001).

Executive functions are required whenever someone has to shift his thinking or behavior in order to respond to change. So these functions are invoked when someone is able to use effective search strategies. Search strategies require recognizing essential patterns, classes, or categories that are used when someone has to search for and recognize specific solutions. These skills are also critical to recognizing roles and functions and knowing how to respond to those (Miller & Cummings, 1999). Here the brain combines emotions, sensory detail, self-regulation, working memory, and inhibition.

At the heart of executive functions is "the ability to maintain an appropriate problem-solving set for attainment of a future goal" (Pennington, Venetto, McAleer, & Roberts, 1999, p. 586) which is also called *working memory*. Working memory refers to the ability to maintain plans and programs in mind or "online" until needed in order to complete a specific action or plan over time. Working memory also allows an individual to override an automatic response and shift problem-solving strategies to an alternate solution when needed. While the specifics of executive functions are still being explored, clearly they can be seen to be at the heart of decision making and the control strategies and processes described above.

WHAT DOES THIS MEAN FOR EDUCATION?

The research on executive functions sends important messages to educators. The first central message is that the sorts of skills and capacities and thought that leaders and experts are calling for are essentially the same sorts of skills and capacities with which all children are potentially endowed. Thus children come biologically equipped to develop the skills and capacities that will be needed. The key is to ensure that the processes and conditions in the world of education nurture, strengthen, and develop those skills and capacities, and do not suppress them.

Executive functions do not develop automatically and to the same extent in everyone. Although much has been said about how these functions develop more completely (anatomically) during adolescence (Restak, 2001; Sylwester, 2002, 2007), these capacities must be a part of the learning environment from day one. Choices, puzzles, and solving problems, along with decision making offered by the natural approach to learning we will unfold in the rest of the book, are critical to developing the student and citizen ready to handle the knowledge age. Education must shift to include teaching that develops higher order capacities by including the following:

- Skills must be continuously developed and refined in the course of pursuing personally relevant goals.
- Logical thinking and problem solving needs to be applied daily in pursuit of real-world outcomes.
- High-quality real-world knowledge is called for and continuously demonstrated.
- Intuition and creativity are valued and explored as a way of life.
- Flexibility and adaptability are practiced and seen as essential.
- The role of emotions and ethics are studied, applied, and understood.
- Maintaining relationships both at home and with individuals from different worlds is valued and practiced.
- Learners are being prepared for technologies that have not yet been developed and for solving problems we have never before encountered.

The second central message is that executive functions need to be called into play in order to help students achieve high academic standards. Content and higher order functioning work together and support each other. Resnik (2010) is moving in this direction when she shows that in the course of instruction, "We now try to teach students the metacognitive capabilities of self-monitoring and self-management of learning" (p. 186).

So it is not a matter of piling a huge additional burden onto educators and students. Rather, it is a matter of grasping how people develop and learn naturally, and teaching with that sort of learning in mind, so that these different "standards" can develop in parallel. To repeat, high academic standards can be generated at the same time as higher order thinking is being developed.

Where to Begin? Rethinking Standards

The first step is to frame standards the right way. They have to embrace this expanded set of skills and capacities. And they have to provide adequate treatment of academic material in a world in which there is so much information and such rapid change that coverage is literally impossible. One solution is to ensure that all standards are framed in terms of a set of big ideas and a philosophy that grasps the concept of interconnectedness. Marion Brady (2007), for instance, has suggested that the core curriculum should be systems theory. And the curriculum framed by the state of South Australia (2001) called SACSA attempts to resolve the problem by combining what it calls Learning Areas with Essential Learnings. The Learning Areas are: English, arts, society and environment, health and physical education, mathematics, science, design and technology, and languages. The Essential Learnings refer to understandings, capabilities, and dispositions that address personal and intellectual qualities, not bodies of knowledge. They are intended to broaden the options for students as well as enrich the lives of all members of the larger society.

> Essential Learnings form an integral part of childrens' and students'
> learning from Birth to Year 12 and beyond. They are resources which
> are drawn upon throughout life and enable people to productively en-
> gage with changing times as thoughtful, active, responsive and commit-
> ted local, national and global citizens. (South Australia, 2001, pp. 1–2)

Within the SACSA Framework, five Essential Learnings have been identified:

- Futures—develop the flexibility to respond to change, recognize connections with the past, and conceive solutions for preferred futures
- Identity—develop a positive sense of self and group, accept individual and group responsibilities, and respect individual and group differences
- Interdependence—work in harmony with others and for common purposes, within and across cultures (Freire, 2000).

- Thinking—be independent and critical thinkers, with the ability to appraise information, make decisions, be innovative, and devise creative solutions
- Communication—communicate powerfully

The Impossible Tension

The problem is that the skills called for cannot be developed by way of transmission or direct instruction using a two-dimensional medium. These skills must be experienced! Dr. William Spady states, "One-dimensional thinking is to 'know something.' Three-dimensional thinking is to know something and be able to apply it in context under conditions that reflect real life" (quoted in Engel, 2009, p. 15).

It is simply not possible for direct instruction and the transmission model, embedded in its massive infrastructure, to generate the sorts of outcomes that are needed. In short, emerging collective goals for education are simply incompatible with the meme that drives the way that education currently operates.

Interestingly, not only the designers of video games, but also the educational theorists who look to video gaming as a source of renewal for education, understand this fact. One of them, James Paul Gee (in the foreword to Shaffer, 2006), writes as follows:

> Here's the sad fact about that old-time school content, all those facts and equations on the tests: We have known for years now that most of the kids who can pass these tests—physics or social studies tests, say—cannot actually apply their knowledge to the real world. (p. x)

Gee continues connecting the future of education through gaming:

> These games are . . . "augmented by reality." Kids go back and forth between the virtual world and real world as they play. When they redesign a city as urban planners, it is their city. They can walk the streets of their town in both real space and in the virtual world. . . . They come to see the real world in a new way. (p. xi)

Some of this may well be an overstatement because it is not clear that skills developed in the world of gaming automatically transfer to other aspects of the real world. However, the world of gaming understands and designs on the basis that there is more to learning than practice and rehearsal, and more to teaching than transmission, classroom management, and testing.

At present, the long-held view of learning and teaching is in conflict with a world that is being shaped by forces that cannot and will very likely never again conform to a past reality.

The temptation to believe that students can learn the higher order skills called for by so many of the authors we have quoted thus far, only if they practice and memorize the fundamental essentials of math, literature, science, and other subjects independent of broader higher order social and survival skills, is deeply flawed. Our point in this book is not to ignore the fundamentals of any subject. Our point is that there is a different way to teach this generation, raised with technology.

Where Do We Go from Here?

What would a school look like if it was built around social environments and interactions that took for granted student choice, initiative, collaboration, and responsibility for learning?

A powerful look at what schools need to look like is presented in a book by Frank Kelly, Ted McCain, and Ian Jukes entitled *Teaching the Digital Generation* (2009). And we present our own version using two schools—an American and an Australian in Chapters 16–18.

When we look at Jake and Dan (introduced at the beginning of Chapter 1), we begin to see how neither technology by itself, nor traditional teaching focused on memorization, replication, lack of meaning, and mastery of a very limited and predetermined curriculum, is meeting student needs. We can also see that society as a whole, along with educators and parents, all need to have a new understanding of what it means to learn.

We need a more powerful model and belief in human capacity and greatness. In society's effort to "fix" things it has focused on disability instead of possibility. Research in Positive Psychology (Csikszentmihalyi, 1990/2008; Fredrickson, 2009; Seligman, 1990) is pointing the way. Any new meme must include and focus on what human beings are capable of becoming (Alexander, 1990; Begley, 2007; Doidge, 2007).

If there is another meme for education, what does it look like? Can it be described in a way that can be understood and implemented without falling into confusion and failure? For the answer, it is essential to have a deeper understanding of how people learn naturally and what that implies for creating the education that is needed.

Part II

WHAT IS NATURAL ABOUT LEARNING?

CHAPTER 5

The Perception/Action Dynamic: The Foundation for Learning from Life

In the earliest period of infancy, for instance, the prefrontal lobes develop parallel to the growth of the sensory-motor system. . . . If, however, the child's environment does not furnish the appropriate stimuli needed to activate prefrontal neurons . . . the prefrontals can't develop as designed. The cellular growth itself becomes compromised and faulty.

—Joseph Chilton Pearce (2002, p. 47)

IF EDUCATION IS to properly access technology, and prepare students for the knowledge age into which they are being born, then a much deeper understanding of how students interact with the world and learn needs to permeate the entire system. That deeper understanding provides the foundations for an alternative approach to instruction that meshes with the way that students themselves are wired.

THE PERCEPTION/ACTION DYNAMIC

Learning is supported by brain circuits linking perception and action.
—Meltzoff, Kuhl, Movellan, & Sejnowski (2009)

We begin with the fact that in order to survive in, and adapt to, the world, all human beings are constantly engaged in a dance of perception and action. They have to gather useful information about their environment and themselves using their senses (perception); and based on this information, they have to manipulate their environment, and themselves, in a way that is advantageous to them (take action). This is the basis of the way in which every one is continuously adapting to his or her environment.

To make this real, think of being in a car driving to work. As you observe yourself you will notice that you are constantly scanning your surroundings for any clues and changes that may affect you. "Is that car too close to me?" "Can I make that curve?" "Why is that guy speeding up?" are perceptions continuously impacting how you respond and what you do. This entire process is totally automatic and essential to your survival.

In fact, experience can be defined as the constant and continuous operation of perception and action. The problem is that the amount of information and the number of stimuli is vast, much greater than even the superb human brain can deal with. That is why field theorists such as Arthur Combs (1999) talk about the perceptual field. So the brain (more properly, the brain/mind) is constantly looking for patterns within the field—for ways in which all the input is organized (Restak, 2001). At the same time, the brain constantly searches its own repertoire of patterns of response—ways to act. Pattern perception is usually so obvious as to not be noticeable, but every aspect of our lives is framed in sets of patterns. For instance, your car, other cars, roads, sidewalks, the setting (ranging from buildings to trees), the speed at which one is traveling, overtaking, stepping on the brake, turning the steering wheel, and every other aspect of your driving are all patterns—ways of organizing experience. And we perceive them and apply them as we move around in the world. Michael Hayward, of the University of California at San Diego, puts it this way, "Perception and action in the real world form the foundation for cognition" (1998, p. 3).

Scientists from many different disciplines are now shedding more light on what Maturana, Varela, and Paolucci (1998) called "the biological roots of human understanding." The interplay of perception and action is central to life itself. Some researchers are confirming that the two processes deeply interact, with neither being passive. Noe (2004) writes that perception *is* action. Other neuroscientists frame all brain processes in terms of many levels of perception and action, all of which interact (Fuster, 2003). Yet other scientists (Hurley, 2006) show that the entire body participates in the interplay of perception and action, as we describe in the pages to follow.

Let us begin with the understanding that there is a continuum of perception and action, ranging from the very simple and almost instantaneous to much more complex processes that include intention and thought.

Most basic is what we call the *perception/action dynamic*. At its most elemental, the perception/action dynamic occurs below the threshold of consciousness and is as simple as an eye blink that occurs spontaneously in response to dust in the air or a bright light. The response is automatic and executed by the body itself.

But just above this level, individuals engage in perception/action by interacting with their world in ways that deal with immediate needs by way of familiar patterns and routines including the recognition of categories and stories. There is some awareness of what is happening and some decision making (how to respond). The perception/action dynamic plays out every moment of every day in adults and children alike. It can readily be found in schools.

An Example—The Perception/Action Dynamic in Elementary School

When we watch young children in the very early grades, we see dynamos of activity. All children have an explanatory drive that sparks their search to understand how the world works (Gopnik et al., 1999) and this can appear unorganized and chaotic.

We recently watched a video of a brilliant preschool teacher named Maria Moore, who almost intuitively grasps this dynamic. Initially, her teaching is not so much focused on reading and math as separate subjects, but rather, on how children are being immersed in environments that teach them to master new habits, patterns, and routines. She and her fellow teachers know that young children have to master basic patterns that include how to act in relationship with others, control their impulses, see and recognize what is happening around them, recognize more complex patterns (ranging from how people interact to recognizing geometric figures), understand stories, and differentiate between all kinds of animals housed in the science room next door. And these teachers also know that the way to help their students grasp these patterns is to guide them through their moment-to-moment experiences. As we watch Maria on the video, we observe her giving students opportunities to make discoveries, make manageable decisions, notice things, sequence actions, observe, and focus. And she does this with patience, consistency, and repetition, and by constantly taking time to garner their attention for things that matter most. In fact, much of what she does is closer to herding cats than training children to do as she says.

Because children are immersed in a world filled with almost infinite possibilities, mastering routines is very important and happens very much like some aspects of language acquisition. Children have to have the same and similar experiences repeatedly over time and within a context until patterns are mastered. They need consistency until the essential patterns become natural for them. And, like language, the acquired patterns of response and behavior are not ends in themselves but contribute to the larger purpose of engaging with others in a world that makes sense. And in time the children do settle down. They grasp stable patterns and routines such as reading time, how to find their books and name tags, where to sit, when, and why. At the same time, they may have questions and continue to explore and to wonder why.

Maria doesn't think of their behavior in terms of good or bad. So she doesn't appear to ever punish the students (though she can be quite direct and relentlessly repeat herself when supporting acceptable behavior and eliminating what is unacceptable). Most of the time she asks students respectfully if they recall what is needed and where they need to be. Maria is calm, focused on one child at a time (she pays total attention to each child when they talk), helps them solve problems and even explain their actions.

What Is Actually Happening?

Biologists and neuroscientists are telling educators that perception and action are not separate. Each is part of the other. And even more dramatically, perception and action and pattern recognition and the forming of new patterns are all taking place at the same time and use and affect the whole body, brain, and mind. As Alva Noe (2004) explains, "Perception is not a process in the brain, but a kind of skillful activity of the body as a whole. We enact our perceptual experiences" (p. 2).

Maria intuitively knows that the children in her class are little perception/action beings governed by the dynamic that is essential to life itself. They are like little space creatures who have landed on this planet and are trying to figure out where they are and how things work. So they rarely sit or stand still. They see, they sense, they hear, and they want to touch, explore, and find out what it all means.

These children are literally "embodying" their experiences (Gibbs, 2007). Cognitive scientists and neuroscientists therefore talk about "embodied cognition" (Lakoff & Johnson, 1999; Thompson, 2007; Wiedermann, 2004). The bodies and brains of the children are being organized on the basis of what is happening to them. Little by little, the constant interaction with consistent patterns shapes how children act, react, and respond to the world around them and who they become, and prepares them for further development. And in the course of this they are utilizing and developing their brain and executive functions (Zelazo, Carter, Resnick, & Frye, 1997).

And play is an essential part of learning. Here students can make up rules, develop their social skills, practice using language, experiment with new ideas, and solidify their understanding.

The dance of perception and action takes place throughout life. Brains and bodies are made to engage with experience. Every aspect of life calls for perception and action. It is how living things biologically adapt to their environment in significant ways over time (Fuster, 2003; Huttenlocher, 2002; Varela, Thompson, & Rosch, 1991).

The Role of Emotions

One of the major research findings of recent times is that emotions color every aspect of a person's functioning. Thought and emotion and movement all interact. As we mentioned in Chapter 1, one source of this new understanding comes from Candace Pert (1997) who identified what she called "molecules of emotion." Some of these molecules are secreted whenever people think. This is confirmed by another neuroscientist, Antonio Damasio (1999), who talks about "the feeling of what happens." (The nature of emotions, and the relationship between emotions, feelings, and the body, is actually very complex. For a very thorough exploration of some of these issues see Roald, 2007.)

What does this mean? It means that the perception/action dynamic is always colored by emotions, though emotional intensity can vary greatly. Parents and educators need to know that children's emotions are powerful and pervasive, and are more developed than intellectual understanding. And yet young children (and, unfortunately, many children of all ages) tend to have very little control over their emotions (Lazarus, 1999). So working with and protecting the emotions of all students is critical.

The Emotional Coloring of Perception/Action: Two Examples

Example 1. The mother of a very active and social boy called us recently to say that her son was coming home every day crying and saying he hated school. He had a new teacher who had established a behavior modification program in her class. Everyone had to behave acceptably, and "acting out" meant that they had to stand on either an orange or red circle (depending on how severe the misbehavior). Her son reacted with anger to this system so the mother spoke with the teacher who didn't understand the problem. "Your son is fine," she said, "he is always on the green (safe)." "You don't understand my son," fired back the mother, "he loves his little friends and he hurts when they are being punished." In this example, the teacher simply did not grasp the emotional currents that were present in the children she was punishing and in the little boy who was their friend. And what she did had a huge impact on his perception of, and reaction to, his entire school experience.

Example 2. Watching Maria's class, we see one little girl drag an embarrassed-looking boy to the teacher in order to tell her that he spit on his book. Maria calmly asks him why he did that. He says that he doesn't know why. Maria responds by making the book, not his actions, the object. "We all love our books, don't we?" The boy and the little girl who brought him nod their heads solemnly. "So we want to take good care of them, right?" More nods. "OK, why don't you both go back and clean that book?" Notice that her responses are diverted from the boy and are nonjudgmental. Hurt feelings or feelings of guilt can overpower children by deflecting their ability to observe and interact with things outside of themselves or sideline appropriate patterning. Here, Maria entered into the entire event in a way that was intended to reshape the way that both children perceived the situation. And she did so by calming their emotions as well as by maintaining her own calm emotional state.

It is important to note that it is not only what Maria says that matters, it is how she says it. It is her tone, relaxed demeanor, and the genuine warmth captured in her remarks that are being "read" by children whose emotional systems are very acute. And because these children are watching her all the time (similar to an adult driver watching the road and what other drivers are doing), this little incident also taught them something about adults, school, and, most of all, who they are.

Building Habits

As we note above, eventually the brain and body develop and establish patterns in the form of small units of behavior that can be used more or less automatically. The repeated, orderly, and predictable interactions have become habits and frames of reference that represent automatic ways of interacting with life. We rarely think about these reflexive or automatic behaviors, but use them hundreds of times a day. Here are some simple examples: washing hands before a meal, looking both ways before crossing the street, checking the weather on your smart phone in the morning. Sometimes the habits have an element of automatic problem solving:

Perception: "It is too dark in here" /Action: Turn on the light
Perception: "I am running late"/Action: Speed up.
Perception: "It is cold outside"/Action: Pick up a coat.
Perception: "This is not a good road"/Action: Look for another route.

This can be seen with students over and over again:

> Perception: "I need a pen"/ Action: Searches for it or asks to borrow one.
> Perception: (College student) "Where is my class?" / Action: Asks someone or looks it up.
> Perception: "The teacher is looking at me" /Action: Puts one's head down to avoid notice.

All of the above are coherent patterns that have been acquired over time. These patterns then determine how efficiently and effectively, or (the opposite) how ineffectively someone interacts with everyday life. In fact, it is fair to say that people are "trained" to perceive and act in thousands of more or less automatic ways that contribute to a world that makes personal sense. Most of these are culturally specific. A world that does not make sense is frightening to children. A friend of ours who grew up in an alcoholic family put it this way: "I cried for order and there was no order."

Educators spend an enormous amount of time and energy, usually in terms of "classroom management," trying to cope with this natural dynamic that is biologically a part of all human beings. That is understandable because the dynamic can play havoc in classrooms. The problem is that most attempts made from a TDI perspective call for suppression and control of the dynamic. The bottom line, however, is that teachers cannot stop the perception/action dynamic; they can only channel it. That is why the alternative we suggest is that classrooms be places where students are respectfully, personally, and meaningfully engaged or challenged.

For parents and educators, the balance between establishing appropriate actions and habits, while at the same time allowing for new learning sparked by personal needs to explore and engage with all sorts of exciting experiences, is a difficult one.

THE PERCEPTION/ACTION DYNAMIC IN ADOLESCENCE

Our illustrations so far have dealt with young children. But the perception/action dynamic operates in all people and at all ages. For instance, when adolescents are bored, in general terms we know what is happening. Boredom is a mind state (see Chapter 11) that indicates a lack of interest and involvement. The perception is that "this (whatever it is) does not relate to anything I want or need." Given this perception students *will* take action of some sort no matter how undesired it may be by the teacher.

Here are some of the responses most teachers (and former students) recognize as emerging from boredom. Student perception: I am bored. Possible actions: Write on the desk; day dream; read favorite books or magazines under the desk or hidden in some way; bother someone or whisper to friends; fall asleep. When transferred into the age of technology the above behaviors can be translated into: texting or e-mailing friends; playing with one's iPod or iPad; playing games with apps on a phone or going online; all of the other behaviors described above.

These responses are those that we do not want to see. But adolescents are just like their younger peers. When they are interested and motivated, they are much more likely to persist and persevere and dig more deeply into what they are working on. That is precisely what happens with students who, though they may fall asleep in school, spend countless hours seeking to improve their results and performance in video games.

Students want to be engaged and involved, and they need good habits that help them manage themselves. Teachers need to recognize that the perception/action dynamic *will* express itself and that this need is natural. This is also true of adults who also seek to amuse themselves in any number of ways, some of which may not be indicative of "good behavior." For example, experienced teachers may walk out of a workshop in order to answer their cell phones or chat online on their laptops while involved in meetings and conferences.

THE PERCEPTION/ACTION CYCLE

The dynamic as described so far reflects the foundation upon which we can build an understanding of how people learn. There is much more, however, because it is quite a distance between reflexively responding to life and the many more complex processes that lead to deep learning. For instance, humans interpret situations, make conscious decisions based on evidence and preference, use language, and can abstract their experience. Humans use concepts and categories that organize objects based on an almost unlimited number of characteristics, and express themselves in terms of metaphors like "an ocean of emotion" or "hot under the collar" and symbols such as "$" to stand for wealth (Lakoff & Johnson, 2003).

But even though human beings develop complex vocabularies, master many skills, and acquire masses of information, and even though their thoughts and actions become more sophisticated, perception and action are always involved. The next state of the continuum is one in which the many momentary and largely unconscious perception/action events become subsumed into a more complex perception/action cycle (Fuster, 2003) that is characteristic of more complex problem solving. The cycle automatically jumps into action when people are faced with situations that need to be addressed and resolved in the course of everyday life.

> The perception/action dynamic and the perception/action cycle constitute the foundation of natural learning. The perception/action dynamic is largely reflexive and usually occurs outside of the field of awareness. The perception/action cycle is used for recognizing and solving everyday problems and incorporates the perception/action dynamic.

The perception/action cycle differs from the perception/action dynamic in that the cycle includes time to make sense of what is happening, gather new information or knowledge, and make decisions that address a given situation. However, it also naturally includes the kind of short-term, seemingly instant reflexive decisions that we have described as the dynamic.

The Perception/Action Cycle in More Detail

Let us see how the dynamic and the perception/action cycle might work together in real-world events that involve everyday problems and puzzles. Take a moment to recall the last time you had to solve a problem as an adult. How did you deal with it? This is what we think took place:

- The situation challenged or interested you in some way, and there may have been a sense of confusion or uncertainty.
- As you delved into it, you clarified it to some extent. You recalled what you already knew or understood, and you represented or structured the problem in some way. The clarification may have been instantaneous or emerged over time.
- A more specific question or questions formed.
- With them in mind, you thought about some options.
- If you needed additional information, you searched for it.
- You then made a decision, devised a plan, and did what you decided would solve the problem—you took action.
- Afterward you found out how well your solution worked—you got feedback of some kind.
- The process might then have been refined or altered if necessary.

We go through this process an almost endless number of times during any day, year, or lifetime. It happens when we are caught in traffic and figuring out the best way to bypass the situation, solving a financial dilemma, or stopping a leaky faucet. Every time we experience a problem, we have the opportunity to gather new resources, think about it, frame it, and take action. This is the perception/action cycle at work. If our actions meet with success (or failure), we have the opportunity to add new information and/or understanding. We learn something. So right at the heart of natural learning is the process of dealing with everyday problems and adapting to the world around us. Even those experts researching problem solving and decision making are now looking at what is sometimes referred to as "naturalistic decision making" (Zsambok & Klein, 1997).

Yet natural as this process is to every human being and every culture on the planet, it tends to be largely disregarded and removed from the controlled and fragmented kind of learning that formal, traditional education favors. Schematically and simply, the process looks something like Figure 5.1.

In essence, experience leads to questions such as: What is it? What do I know about it? What do I do with it? Then decision, planning, action, and feedback follow, and some type of learning results.

Although at a very simple level, an infant is constantly immersed in this natural process. It is always solving problems. That is why Gopnik and her colleagues describe infants as "scientists in the crib" (1999). Lying safely in its crib, an infant observes and is fascinated by an object (perceives), reaches for it, gets feedback from how it feels and how the object responds, kicks it again and again (acts), and attempts to control what happens. In the course of repeated journeys through the cycle it discovers something about what the object does and how it can be manipulated. On the basis of this simple exchange, brain cells (neurons) fire together in order to represent the new insight in the form of a very simple knowledge network, one that future experiences will expand upon. This process is at the heart of how all people deal with problems and inadvertently learn from life. It provides a common platform for understanding others and our selves.

> As a result of acting, an individual gets feedback and that feedback provides guidance about how to act next time. Thus, to the extent that any person responds to feedback, every interaction can lead to changes in the capacity of that individual to respond to what is happening and to act and/or perform more intelligently (get what they want). In short, they learn and the entire process is natural.

FIGURE 5.1. Perception/Action Cycle

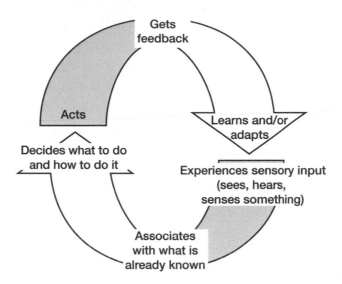

An Everyday Example of the Perception/Action Cycle

Think of the last time you were caught in traffic. You used your senses (vision, movement, sound, and so on) and recognized that there was a problem (*perception*). You looked at your choices: "Do I stay here or are there surface streets I can use that are less likely to be congested?" You then made a *decision*. If you were unsure of alternative available streets, you chose to stay in the car, fume, listen to the radio, call a friend, or do a relaxation technique (*action*). Action was followed by results that provided information on how well your actions worked (*feedback*). Perhaps, on reflection, you decided on the strategy you would use in the future whenever stuck in traffic. If, after you arrived at your destination you didn't process this event by looking up alternative streets on a map, asking a colleague about alternative routes, or looking at alternatives on the Web, then you may have bypassed an opportunity to acquire new and useful knowledge. On the other hand, if you decided to take immediate action and left the freeway, you would have gotten immediate feedback on your decision to take a risk.

The entire process is so natural that most of us use it but never recognize it as a possibility for powerful learning. In effect, the perception/action cycle is a constant flow of recognizing needs and solving small and large problems in order to function successfully in everyday life. Human beings are fantastic problem solvers, something that becomes very evident when adults reflect on all the decisions they have made during the course of a day.

The world of videotech makes use of both the perception/action dynamic and the perception/action cycle. In order to see this more clearly we need to explore a little more of the science behind the perception/action cycle.

CHAPTER 6

The Science Behind the Perception/Action Cycle

Parents soon find out that young children are natural learners. They are like explorers or research scientists busily gathering information and making meaning out of the world. Most of this learning is not the result of [direct instruction] teaching, but rather a constant and universal learning activity as natural as breathing.

—Angela Engel (2009, p. 9)

THE PICTURE THAT we painted in the last chapter is still not complete. That is because the perception/action cycle involves the whole person at multiple levels and in multiple ways. Neuroscientist Antonio Damasio (1994) spells this out more formally:

1. The human brain and the rest of the body constitute an indissociable organism.
2. The organism interacts with the environment as an ensemble: the interaction is neither of the body alone nor of the brain alone. (pp. xvi–xvii)

Every child is, in fact, a "whole" child, surviving by adapting to its world.

At this point we are still not addressing learning in school although the implications become obvious. We are in essence building the foundation for showing what schools need to build upon and what videotech engages readily.

THE ORGANIZATION OF THE BRAIN THROUGH
THE LENS OF PERCEPTION AND ACTION

In the course of behavior, the two hierarchies [for perception and action] are engaged in a cybernetic cycle of dynamic interactions with the environment that I have termed the perception action cycle.

—Joaquin Fuster (2003, p. 74)

As we mentioned in Chapter 3, a more precise and exciting description of perception/action, grounded in the organization of the brain, is described by neuroscientist Joaquin Fuster (2003). He suggests that the overall organizational principle for the entire brain is based on twin hierarchies of perception and action. Each operates from a very simple and modular level to a very complex and integrative level, and at every level perception and action "communicate" with each other along the way. His approach meshes perfectly with the emerging cross-disciplinary synthesis that is beginning to explain natural learning and that we have been tracking since we first presented our 12 Brain/Mind Learning Principles in 1991 based on a meta-analysis of research across disciplines. We have revisited these principles over time (Caine et al., 2009) in light of continually growing research in cognitive and neuroscience, and we briefly summarize them here because they shed light on the processes involved in the perception/action cycle.

The central notion is that each person is an integrated living system. That means that body, brain, emotions, and mind are all involved in learning. Our approach, therefore, has been to synthesize research across many disciplines, ranging from neuroscience to cognitive psychology, for the purpose of eliciting a set of useful and accurate principles of learning.

In our view, such principles need to meet four basic criteria:

- The phenomena described by a principle should be universal. A Brain/Mind Learning Principle must be true for all human beings, despite individual genetic variations, unique experiences, and developmental differences.
- Research documenting any specific principle should span more than one field or discipline. Since a learning principle describes a system's property, one would expect validation and confirmation from research across multiple fields and disciplines.
- A principle should anticipate future research. It should be expected that emerging research will refine and confirm each principle. For example, much of the brain research on the links between emotion

and cognition was published after we first formulated our principles (Caine & Caine, 1991).

- The principle should provide implications for practice. As a minimum, learning principles ought to provide the basis for an effective general framework to guide decisions about teaching and training and help in the identification and selection of appropriate methods and strategies.

The 12 Brain/Mind Learning Principles are as follows:

1. All learning is physiological.
2. The brain/mind is social.
3. The search for meaning is innate.
4. The search for meaning occurs through patterning.
5. Emotions are critical to patterning.
6. The brain/mind processes parts and wholes simultaneously.
7. Learning involves both focused attention and peripheral perception.
8. Learning engages both conscious and unconscious processes.
9. There are at least two distinct types of memory.
10. Learning is developmental.
11. Complex learning is enhanced by challenge and inhibited by threat associated with helplessness and/or fatigue.
12. Each brain is uniquely organized.

These principles are totally compatible with research on perception/action. Human beings use the capacities revealed by the Brain/Mind Learning Principles as they interact with life. Fuster has developed an elegant model of brain functioning that integrates all the aspects of learning expressed by the principles.

HOW THE CORTEX DEVELOPS

According to Fuster (2003), perception and action operate together in the brain to literally "weave" together skills and knowledge on the basis of ongoing interaction with the environment. In Figure 6.1 we unpack the core elements of this process in a summary based on Fuster's work. In the summary we describe what happens to an individual in the everyday operation of the perception/action cycle. We also indicate some of the qualities of the experience that an individual might have. It is important to remember that the interaction between the sensory and motor cortex is more or less instantaneous and totally integrated. For the sake of clarity we have artificially separated the two.

What Figure 6.1 confirms is that the entire body, brain, and mind are involved, even while there is order in how the cortex or outer layer of the brain organizes and stores information and deals with ideas and actions. In the previous diagram we separated perception and action. The following is intended to clarify the diagram and clarify the hierarchical organization of the cortex.

- At the "smallest" and most discrete level, perception involves sensory input, and action consists of simple acts associated with that input.
- These fragments of sensory input and actions are integrated into larger wholes.
- Emotions, mediated in part through the limbic system and through a vast ocean of neurotransmitters, come into play at every level.
- Social interactions and the entire physical context are involved, calling into play "mirror neurons" (see Chapter 7) and the larger perceptual field.
- Associations are made with prior experiences and memories, engaging such regions of the brain as the hippocampus and the association cortices.
- There are higher levels of functioning that involve ideas and imagination and planning and decision making, largely driven by the prefrontal cortex.

Thus the brain acts in terms of an up-and-down hierarchy of parts and wholes, what Ken Wilber (2001) calls a "holarchy." A holon is something that is simultaneously both a part and a whole. A holarchy is a hierarchy of holons. On the one hand, various regions and areas have specialized functions. On the other, much of what is in the brain is integrated into neural or knowledge networks that come together for "in-the-moment" perception and action. It is important to emphasize that we are talking about a natural process that simply exists for all human beings. This is a process that operates in everyday life, and in school where real life is the invisible curriculum. Acknowledging how natural all this is will help show how to improve education by making use of both the principles and perception/action in teaching.

Notice also the continuous role of choice, decisions, and actions. These are the powerful forces that develop the executive functions.

FIGURE 6.1. P/A Summary

Sensory Cortex

Lowest Level. Sound, smell, sight, taste, and other sensory impressions are processed in specific areas of the cortex largely at the back of the brain.

Implications: Novel situations and new problems usually involve a physical encounter.

The Primary Association Cortex. Almost instantly the brain takes the sensory information and combines it into a "whole."

Implications: Through the action of their senses, and based on previously established categories, individuals make initial sense of what is in front of them or what they are experiencing. They recognize features and aspects that come together "as a whole."

The Secondary Association Cortex. Again, spontaneously and naturally, these regions of the cortex (many regions linked to the rest of the brain and body), integrate past experiences (memory) and emotional data, to conceptually organize and integrate the experience in a way that makes sense.

Implications: Individuals begin to identify what they are experiencing with their senses. What they recognize depends on their own past experience, knowledge, and present emotional state. At this point they spontaneously ask questions and need answers.

The Prefrontal Cortex is activated when an individual needs to make a decision or take action. This area is also called the Integrative Cortex because in order to do the above, the brain accesses and integrates all the internal and external data available.

Implications: Once individuals have questions they need the opportunity to find appropriate answers that matches their question or situation.

The Executive Functions of the Prefrontal Cortex are engaged when a personally meaningful question is asked and action is needed to act or solve a problem.

Implications: Perceptions include understanding the need for time lines, planning, order, logic, documentation and clarification.

D E C I S I O N

Motor Cortex

Lowest level. Deals with simple movements, from the changing of eye-gaze direction to moving toward or away from objects. As an individual encounters something new (which raises curiosity), the pupils dilate, there are chemical changes in the body (and brain), the body moves forward or backward.

Actions

Basic movements are coordinated into simple actions. If curiosity persists, then the individual will move in a way that reflect a natural need to act on what is being experienced.

Programs

Basic actions become coordinated into coherent programs the individual applies to any given situation. At a higher level, the elicited actions will include such steps as further reading, online research, experimenting with ideas, or working on projects.

Plans

Planning here is regarded as a motor activity. All of the above are involved in making coherent plans of action in order to address a specific situation, answer a question, respond to a particular situation, or solve a problem.

Once questions have been raised or actions are needed, the individual plans how to go about finding something out and producing something.

Concepts

The individual is able to conceptualize and implement new understanding in some form. Actions include making a plan, establishing time lines, systematically finding solutions, negotiating, documenting new knowledge and ideas. New learning may result.

AN EXAMPLE THAT BLENDS LIFE AND SCIENCE

In this section we follow a child naturally experiencing what is described above in the summary of the perception/action cycle and give our interpretation of the event and the Brain/Mind Learning Principle that applies. Ultimately, the organization and phases of the perception/action cycle are experienced by anyone solving a real-world problem of personal interest or importance.

> Every child is always immersed in an ocean of experience governed by the senses and involving action. The child is awash in sensory impressions and constant small actions. ["All learning is physiological"—Principle 1.]

Within this ocean, every now and then, the child comes across and focuses on something new that fascinates him—a first firefly glowing as dusk settles, or a first view of a shooting star. Perhaps it is something more mundane, such as an interesting-looking pebble or shell on a beach.

> Attention is sparked by novelty. Perception and action interact as the child focuses attention. Everyone is continuously immersed in a perceptual field, and constantly selects a part of that field to attend to and act on. ["Learning involves both focused attention and peripheral perception"—Principle 7.]

Regardless of what it was, chances are that the child first tried to figure out something about the object or experience. She did this automatically by connecting it to something she had already experienced—to a similar object, or knowledge stored in memory.

> The explanatory drive kicks in, and the brain/mind automatically searches for associations to what is already known. ["The search for meaning is innate"—Principle 3.]

If the object or experience was truly exciting, the child decided to investigate further. And now questions rose like soap bubbles. "Where did it come from?" "Why did it do that?" What do I need to do?" "Where can I find out more? "What did that to it?" "What is it called?" "Why is it . . . ?"

> The emotions are more fully engaged. ["Emotions are critical to patterning"—Principle 5.] They are "actor-centered adaptive questions" driven by the ongoing search for meaning.

The questions might not have been clearly expressed, of course, and pointing and gesturing served very well, with an implied request for someone to help with the investigation.

> The questions may be implicit and not be fully formed. Meltzoff
> et al. (2009), for instance, note the deep interconnectedness
> between language and movement, all of which takes time to de-
> velop. ["Learning is developmental"—Principle 10.]

The questions and the actions that followed belonged to the child alone. These ongoing questions addressed a personal need. If the child felt safe, motivated, and empowered by those around him, further exploration would follow.

> Intrinsic motivation and safety propel the child to "research"
> the phenomenon and gather information. ["Complex learning
> is enhanced by challenge and inhibited by threat associated with
> helplessness and/or fatigue"—Principle 11.]

There was, however, a need for a knowledgeable adult to answer questions of the very young directly. With luck, and when a little older, home and the adults in it provided resources as well as answers. Adults also provided the means for figuring out more about what was needed and pointed out how to follow where imagination led.

> The child might seek or need some guidance. One way that a
> mentor might help is by guiding the child to think about and
> process his experience. Deep processing is a key both to memory
> (Craik & Lockhart, 1975) and to discerning patterns and form-
> ing concepts that may require reflection and/or time to discern.
> [Two Principles apply: "Learning engages both conscious and
> unconscious processes"—Principle 8; and "The search for mean-
> ing occurs through patterning"—Principle 4.]

Again, with luck, the "expert" did not provide complete answers but rather managed to make the child more curious. In addition to providing some essential information, that individual (expert) asked even more questions and pointed out things the child could do or research with friends or by herself. And there was usually another strong social element to the process as the child connected with friends, shared with others, tried things out, got information, imitated elders, and generally grew into the subject matter in question.

Learning is a social process that is both direct and indirect. Informal learning and relationship with others feeds understanding (Bell, Lewenstein, Shouse, & Feder, 2009). [Two Principles apply: "The brain/mind is social"—Principle 2; and "Complex learning is enhanced by challenge and inhibited by threat associated with helplessness and/or fatigue"— Principle 11.]

If continually encouraged, and motivation persisted, the child both came to understand more and decided to do something more concrete. Perhaps the child decided to collect distinctly different rocks, sorting various types according to weight, color, size, and shape. Or perhaps the child decided (with help from an adult) to put fireflies in a glass jar in order to observe how they behaved differently during the day. We have all seen children persevere in learning to ride a bike or skateboard or practice some sport for hours at a time.

Even very young children have some capacity to make choices, plan, and act, all of which are aspects of the brain's higher executive functions. There is a constant ongoing synthesis of experience at different levels of a hierarchy, culminating in the integrative prefrontal cortex. ["The brain/mind processes parts and wholes simultaneously"—Principle 6.]

With question(s) constantly in mind, and sometimes changing, the child experimented in many ways with many things with widely differing results. Perhaps the rocks changed color when they were dry, or perhaps the fireflies stopped showing flickers of light. The results of the child's actions provided critical information and ongoing feedback. And the entire world was the child's oyster as he observed, tried things out, remembered, asked questions, made plans and decisions, applied understanding, and generally came to perform more effectively.

Actions have consequences. Experiments produce results. This is the feedback that informs the questioner and leads to understanding and competence. ["Learning is developmental"—Principle 10.]

Once a product of some kind was created, (say a collection of rocks) or a skill mastered (say working out how to keep rocks wet to maintain their color), it was probably presented or displayed somewhere or somehow. Perhaps this gave someone else the opportunity to respond to what the child did, or gave the opportunity for someone more expert to point out through challenging questions how something did or did not work, or required more refinement in language, calculation, observation, or detail. If this feedback was from a caring adult who took the time, demonstrated or modeled a better approach that helped the child refine her ideas and recognize more expert work, then the feedback resulted in new learning. To be useful, however, the feedback needed to be relatively instant, objective, and respectful, and linked to the child's interest.

> **Ongoing feedback throughout the experiences and on any final product is essential for continuous learning and refinement of skills. Note also that the social nature of the process is ongoing, as is motivation.**

Chances are that this entire experience did not occur in a linear or one-step-at-a-time sequence. The child was often distracted, followed other interests, and was involved in other, unrelated events. But if interest persisted, then the child came back to the same or similar questions or actions. And even though there are different tiers of perception and action and different stages along the way, it all points to the fact that the whole child was involved. Senses, movement, the whole body, emotional reactions, relationships with others, the physical environment, prior memories, thoughts and beliefs, expectations, and state of mind contributed to and had an impact.

The whole child was involved all the time.

This entire process was natural (though not effortless). Rarely was the child *made* to do the things he did, even though at times work became intense and required much practice. The questions asked were personal because they mattered to the child and focused directly on what he experienced through his senses.

And although some things need to be taught directly (how to use scissors or differentiate between permanent markers and those that can be erased) this entire process can be short-circuited in many ways when adults take over and control what happens. The remarkable fact is that many adults observing children can easily misunderstand or simply miss all this learning. The ongoing activity might just look too "messy" and disorganized and appear as though nothing is happening, when in fact the brain is unbelievably busy organizing itself in ways that reflect its real-world experiences.

THE CENTRAL ROLE OF QUESTIONS AND DECISION MAKING

One factor was constant at every stage of the process. The child had to ask questions and make decisions. Countless questions. Countless decisions. And one of the central weaknesses of most education is the extent to which asking questions and making decisions is taken out of the hands of learners. The issue is, then, what sorts of questions and decisions matter most?

There are many ways of defining and categorizing types of decisions and types of questions. In our view, the most useful term that we have come across is the notion of actor- or learner-centered adaptive decisions, and its counterpart, actor- or learner-centered adaptive questions. In essence, these are decisions and questions that matter to the person making or asking them. They are personal and important (Goldberg, 2001).

Actor-Centered Adaptive Questions

Actor- [student-] centered adaptive questions sustain the perception/action cycle because they emerge out of the individual's intrinsic need to know more or act on something of significance to that individual. These questions result in what Fuster (2003) calls *Adaptive Action* (p. 165). *Actor-centered adaptive questions* therefore are questions that lead to adaptive decisions and hence action.

Adults live in a world filled with actor-centered adaptive questions and decisions. They include determining the best way to get to an important meeting, how to anticipate costs, or how best to communicate with someone important. These kinds of questions and the resultant actions, which are the hallmark that drives the perception/action cycle for all human beings engaged with everyday life (including students outside of the formal curriculum), rarely make it into the traditional classroom. It is almost as though the entire adult community has made the decision that these kinds of questions are not important to learning. Yet they represent the gateway to the development of the brain's executive functions.

Consider, for instance, the question: "How many miles is it from the earth to the moon?" This could be a question asked by a teacher to a student for whom the issue is totally irrelevant. However, it becomes an actor-centered adaptive question when someone is engaged in a project or personally meaningful quest where the information is important (adaptive) to one's course of action (not just something memorized as a fact). It may be asked, for instance, in the context of a project about the cosmos selected by the student in which he is very interested.

It is perhaps safe to say that every fact and formula that students are given to memorize by well-meaning teachers, was initially developed by someone who had asked an actor-centered adaptive question. Einstein, Edison, Galileo, and Madame Curie are only a few among many.

Actor-Centered Adaptive Decisions

Actor- [learner-]centered adaptive decisions are the decisions that have to be made in the course of the perception/action cycle and that matter to the actor. They are the results of thinking about questions or dealing with situations that address a personal need. And they engage the prefrontal cortex and open the door to higher order thinking guided by executive functions. They are decisions that are made when a person is in an ambiguous situation and has to work out a path of action for herself. The individual is, in fact, free to decide among any number of options. This sounds easy but is rarely so because the questions that drive the need to act often result in disequilibrium. We just have to look at the questions and decisions made by great scientists following a failed experiment or the questions raised and decisions that have to be made by an adolescent after experiencing rejection for the first time.

Having to make decisions of this sort is absolutely indispensable to the development of the capacity to adapt and flexibly interact with a changing world and such decisions propel the perception/action cycle. These questions and decisions are also essential to invoking and developing the executive functions. Actor-centered questions and decisions are actually two sides of the same coin most of the time.

Questions Asked by Others and Decisions Made by Others

Well-intentioned educators often assume that their questions are the best ones, and the ones that matter to students. The issue here has nothing to do with the quality of the question; it has to do with how much the student cares about it. If the right relationship between student and teacher exists, then in the course of Active Processing (defined in depth later) the teacher will ask the sorts of questions that invite the student to think in such a way that the student takes ownership of the questions being asked. Otherwise, no matter how well framed the question, it will not energize the student's self-motivated pursuit of understanding and competence. It will not be a learner-entered adaptive question.

Questions asked by others usually feel imposed because the person being asked is not invested in a personally relevant way. Questions imposed by others represent the foundation for countless multiple-choice exams and result in answers that can easily be found on any search engine. An example might be a question that depended on a student having memorized the number of miles from the earth to the moon (238,700 miles from center to center). This information represents effective and stable patterns everyone can count on. But notice how the answer ends any further questions and, in particular, does not engage higher order thinking. There is no need to wonder how someone figured out the distance or what the distance might have to do with fuel consumption for space ships or how the distance might impact direct or indirect landings on the moon. Because the answer has been found to a question someone else thought to be significant for a reason or purpose not yet understood, it all ends there. That is, of course, unless that person asks another question.

If there is a purpose for finding meaningless answers, the student is usually motivated by issues related to power or obedience like pleasing someone else, or getting a grade, or preparing for an exam. All of us have memorized countless amounts of facts we ultimately did not use or apply to real life.

Similarly, if a teacher decides what a student must master, then even if the subject (from the point of view of an outside observer) is the "right" one, the decision will not be the student's. And so, even if a teacher is acting with the best of intentions, the student is likely to comply rather than engage the perception/action cycle in ways that we describe in depth in later chapters.

A great example is telling students that they must make a decision to study harder if they want to get into college, when college is still years away. The ability to project into the future calls on executive functions that usually develop in later adolescence. This is obviously an attempt to motivate the student by a caring adult. But the meaning and purpose is heard but not registered as meaningful by the student. The students may decide to act because they fear punishment if they don't comply (not doing something the adult obviously cares about), or because they want to please the adult asking for the decision to work harder.

The Perception/Action Cycle Ultimately Opens the Door to Higher Order Thinking and Functioning

As the child introduced previously pursues the answers to his own actor-centered questions over time, some very interesting things could happen and shape who he becomes as an individual. Examples include how to follow a train of thought, take initiative, do some experimenting, and express imagination and new findings in any number of ways. With support from a well-educated and knowledgeable adult, there would be the opportunity to acquire vast amounts of information as he masters new vocabulary, identifies physical characteristics, notes similarities and differences (such as the fact that it takes six legs to qualify as an insect, or that a magnifying glass can be used for almost an infinite number of purposes), and groups or organizes findings. Most of this additional learning would be "embedded" in the many iterations and phases of the perception/action cycle as the child also acquires new ways to function in the real world.

And with a knowledgeable mentor and challenging projects and puzzles, the child would have the opportunity to discover that knowledge doesn't come to us one subject at a time that small things are always part of some bigger idea, that big ideas include critical elements, and that it takes lots of practice to master some things. The child would have many opportunities to grasp that one does her best work when efforts are challenged and supported, and worst work when threatened or scared. Our learner would have opportunities to discover that ideas sometimes come only after they are left alone for a while; that some things take time and others can be done quickly and in a hurry. Our young learner could have grasped the fact that practice is important for some things and that other things can be remembered even if experienced just once.

Conditions for Learning Are Not Always Ideal

Many factors could interfere with the natural process described above. If circumstances were not favorable or adults didn't listen or gave instant answers that ignored the child's deeper questions, learning would have occurred, but would be of a different type. It is then entirely possible that the child would come to believe that learning is hard, boring, or only happens when controlled by adult direction (Dweck, 2006).

Can this process then become a foundation for more formal learning environments? The answer is a resounding yes! Examples where knowledge can be expanded using the perception/action cycle include exciting physics classes where assumptions are challenged by real-world experiments, building and constructing experiments for a science fair, and entry into all sorts of competitions from fiction writing to documentary filmmaking. But getting there is an immense challenge.

CHAPTER 7

Perception/Action Learning

Goal-directed behavior depends on the continuous operation of the [perception/action] cycle at several cortical levels simultaneously. The more automatic and routine behaviors will be integrated at lower levels. . . . More complex and novel behaviors will bring in the cortical areas of association [prefrontal cortex].
— Joaquin Fuster (2003, p.108)

I N THE PRECEDING chapters we introduced the ongoing dance of perception and action in life that plays out as people bump into and solve numerous problems in everyday life. Both the perception/action dynamic and the perception/action cycle are natural, innate processes that may or may not lead to actual new essential skills or knowledge. Learning that does result can be very deep, but is usually incidental (though some purposeful learning may take place).

GOAL-DIRECTED PERCEPTION/ACTION LEARNING

Goal-directed perception/action learning is different. We will simply call it *Perception/Action Learning* (P/AL). It deals with situations where an individual intentionally sets out to master something new or gain additional expertise. Learning to play golf, play an instrument, use new software, or invest in the stock market all involve a clear intention to know more or become more proficient.

And something else is necessary. P/AL makes use of experts and of guidance or instruction. P/AL requires focus, effort, modeling, and practice. So while it makes sense to talk about the perception/action dynamic and perception/action cycle as independent of instruction, this is not the case with P/AL.

Definition: Perception/Action Learning is purposeful learning. Proficiency requires involvement over significant periods of time as individuals intentionally set out to solve problems of their own choosing, acquire skills, and master subject matter that means something to them. Purposeful learning of this kind is grounded in, makes use of, and goes beyond the perception/action cycle.

We are now also in a position to define *natural learning* as used in this book. Natural learning integrates the perception/action dynamic, the perception/action cycle, and Perception/Action Learning. (See Figure 7.1.)

The challenge, now, is to see how the perception/action cycle is used in an effective, purposeful, educator-facilitated learning environment that engages the integrative functions of the brain. The world of videotech shows the way, and this is also an introduction to a teaching model for a new kind of education.

How Mastering Video Games Taps Into Perception/Action Learning

There are several ways that natural learning plays out as young children, adolescents, and adults master video games.

Connection to past experience: Play itself is natural (Panksepp, 1998), and game playing emerges very early in a child's life. So while video games are a genre of their own, they link into an entire world of past experience of playing games, even in those who are quite young. And both children and adults come across video games in the course of their immersion in everyday life, just as the child above came across something new that was interesting.

Questions: Initial, entry level questions emerge, usually in the form of "Let me try that" and "Wow, how did that happen?" While the sorts of questions that are asked are similar, each person's reactions and questions are personal. They are actor centered and "owned" by the newcomer to this type of experience.

Learning processes with in-the-moment feedback: The game is structured to be interesting and enticing with specific goals spelled out. The setting begins with an understandable scenario, often involving a

FIGURE 7.1. Natural Learning

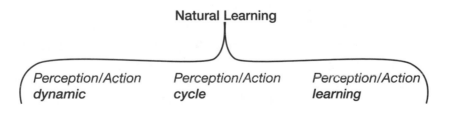

primal plot (saving friends, finding the treasure, killing the enemy, preserving the superiority of a closely knit group, and so on). In-the-moment feedback is continuous. Players are interested, engaged, and motivated, and those inner responses are strengthened by other factors such as competition and the thrill of winning.

Problem solving and processing: A wide range of problem-solving skills is employed. They include, but are not limited to, detailed observation of a scene with a view to discerning clues; devising and testing strategies for moving, acting, and responding; trial and error; calling on strategies that have worked in other situations; alternating between focusing on the big picture or the immediate situation; and using out-of-the-box thinking to see if nonobvious steps work.

Practice and rehearsal become natural: While the reasons for participating vary (and will be discussed in Chapter 10 on motivation), players are like the young child above. They keep going and persist over hours, days, months, and years in getting better. The better learners use what Ericsson (2006) calls "deliberate practice." This is mindful practice in which game players pay attention to and focus on what they are doing so that they gain more from each step that they take. Some dip in and out, as they move between different aspects of their lives. But many keep coming back.

The process is social: Video gaming tends to be a very social process, even though much gaming occurs in the privacy of a home or bedroom. Gaming is "in" and players are supermotivated by peers and adults they respect who spend time with video games and invite them to play. In fact, the more sophisticated games can lead to the formation of an immensely strong peer group bond among those who play. So players tend to text each other, compare notes at school and elsewhere, visit Web sites, offer online advice, and generally interact on multiple levels, with gaming at the core. In this way many game players are immersed in what are called "communities of practice" (Wenger, McDermott, & Snyder, 2002).

Coaching, guidance, and mentoring: Expertise abounds within this social networking. More advanced players offer hints and suggestions. And while there may be nothing called a "course in playing a video game," a great deal of instruction is available as people turn to others for assistance. Some players become de facto guides, mentors, and coaches for others (even though they would not use these terms).

Actor-centered adaptive decision making accompanies every step: At every stage of the process, the player asks questions of personal interest, and makes decisions about where to go and what to do next. Some of the time there may not be much personal awareness or, indeed, much personal control. Some people become addicted and overdo game playing (Clark, 2006; Schlimme, 2002). Others do what their peers do. So there is an enormous need for game players to take charge of their lives and develop their executive functions. Nevertheless, they make decisions that (from their point of view) serve their needs.

Varying degrees of expertise is the result: The dance of perception and action permeates the entire process. The entire process calls for recognition, awareness, new perceptions, decisions, actions, feedback, response to new situations, implementation of new skills and remembered moves, and the growth of richer and richer knowledge networks (see Chapter 8).

This is Perception/Action Learning in operation. It feels good to learners because it is so natural, even though there can be immense frustration along the way when success does not come easily. No one has to "make" kids or adults take all the steps they take, though they can learn how to perform better and benefit from someone else's expertise.

Where P/AL Is Used

The general processes and the overall pattern is familiar to anyone who has become proficient in any field of endeavor. Athletes participate in their sports, gather knowledge, practice, receive guidance, gain feedback, socialize with others in a variety of ways, and improve. This is how anyone learns to play golf or tennis.

Artists may seem to be different from athletes, but artists also follow the path of purposeful Perception/Action Learning as they gain mastery and improve. Some field of art, encountered during life experience, excites the budding artist. He will pursue an interest, learn to observe, try things out, find coaches or mentors, produce an artifact or perform, deal with feedback, and so on. The artist "lives" this process and engages in it over and over again.

The general pattern described above maps very well onto the ways that most adults pursue other interests such as working with antique cars, painting, developing expertise in photography, jewelry making, playing an instrument, or sculpting. And if we take a bird's eye view, this is the way that people master their various professions.

It is important to repeat that the cycle has organization but is not linear. Also, there are cycles within cycles, some long term and some short term, and the perception/action dynamic is functioning throughout as individuals have basic, often unconscious and reflexive responses based on earlier learning or when sparked by fears or survival issues. In fact, the general set of procedures is deeply familiar to every single one of us because this is the way in which we all have acquired the skills and competencies and knowledge that we bring to bear in the course of everyday life.

DIVERGENT PATHS IN TEACHING

For educators looking for instructions on how to teach anything one step at a time with tight controls and connections to traditional environments, the more natural learning approach can appear at first to be careless and frightening.

The first time this realization surfaced for us was in an elementary school near Sacramento, California, where two teachers had merged their classes in order to create a larger community of approximately 60 children. Students were encouraged to master the curriculum by studying how things actually worked in a miniature city they created. A reward poster for the capture of "the big bad wolf," for instance, was evidence of their explorations of what the police did. They studied how libraries worked, how firemen worked, and how all sorts of community organizations operated. Math, science, reading, and history were naturally embedded, and these students were motivated and learning in documentable ways. This was truly natural learning in action.

The principal who had been observing these teachers was so impressed that she suggested that the rest of her teachers observe the class for about 2 hours. She hired a "roving sub" to take over classes for teachers who were observing. In the observed class, students were working in highly motivated groups, testing ideas, creating products using writing, reading, creating displays, and applying math. All of them were sharing their work and thinking with each other. The two teachers were continually interacting with students, providing input and processing. They did this by asking challenging questions, pointing out where things might need additional precision. Excellence of all types was the unspoken benchmark for everyone.

Yet most of the observing teachers were not able to see how to reproduce the natural or organic process they were observing. They asked the "natural learning" teachers to tell them or "teach" them what to do. They wanted clear directions.

The result was frustration on all sides. The two teachers who were doing it had never thought about how to teach other teachers. They had organized their teaching after visiting workshops, visiting leading educators such as Lauren Resnick, and studying the Brain/Mind Learning Principles. At that time no one had spelled out what we are attempting to do in this book. Because of a general lack of clarity many of the "observing" teachers began to believe that their highly successful colleagues were actually holding out on them, while the teachers who were using natural learning were also frustrated because they were unable to articulate the ways in which they had organized the learning around student-generated questions and projects.

Can Perception/Action Learning Be Systematized?

A combination of research findings and experience suggests to us that teaching with natural learning in mind can be taught, but that the process is challenging and needs to be understood in some depth. The place to begin is with a grasp of goal-directed Perception/Action Learning (P/AL).

Below we begin to clarify the elements that both research and experience indicate must be in P/AL. We believe that many efforts at a more naturalistic approach to education have failed or proven inadequate primarily because they did not incorporate or fully address or identify all of the elements below. Because the process is not linear, any and all elements can occur in multiple ways. However, it seems to us that they are *all* essential. We introduce them here in a very simplified way. Most of them are based on the general practices and procedures introduced above as we described the way that video gamers tend to learn. And all of it emerges out of, and is compatible with, Fuster's summary and the Brain/Mind Learning Principles in Chapter 5. Here are the critical elements of Perception/Action Learning:

- Learners need to encounter a lifelike, real-world event as an experience that has personal meaning and significance, which garners their attention, and which triggers personal interest and relevant and personally meaningful questions. We call this event a *Multisensory Immersive Experience*.
- There should be opportunities and time for learners to automatically search for and make initial associations and links to prior knowledge.
- Actor-centered adaptive questions must be allowed to surface (What do I do now? How do I solve this problem? What do I do next? What is most important about this? What do I need to know more about? How do I want to investigate this?).

- With those questions in mind, learners have opportunities to gather information, do research, interact with others—both peers and mentors—solve problems, try things out, seek coaching and guidance, and repeat and practice regularly in order to acquire knowledge, insight, and skill.
- All these actions will result in real-time feedback of many sorts. There may be responses from experts or peers. Teachers and peers may ask questions or make suggestions. The focus can be on every aspect of the process, from mastering skills like writing and the ability to communicate well to content specifics. From this point of view, even no feedback (in the sense of no response) can serve as feedback in some cases.
- The feedback is processed by the learner. It will either confirm the learner in her beliefs about her work, or will consolidate a way of behaving, or will lead to shifts in how the learner perceives some aspect of her work and will allow for changes and additions.
- There should be some learner product or performance. Doing and producing in the real world is an indispensable aspect of Perception/ Action Learning. It can begin in the early phases of the cycle or be initiated a substantial way through. But it must take place. It includes planning, organizing, sequencing, and appropriate attention to detail and essential steps and skills.
- A final product or service is produced for summative assessment using performance of some type.

There is more, and it will be unpacked in more detail, beginning with the example we introduce in Chapter 9. As presented here the cycle seems to be sequential and clear-cut, but it's actually more complex because the perception/action dynamic is always operating, and different cycles interact.

It should also be noted that there are many, many peripheral learnings. Sometimes a learner will find a tangential question to be of interest and will pursue that; much of the time incidental comments or issues are introduced into the conversations and the processes; and to a large extent some additional capacities (such as concentration) or skills (such as some aspects of problem solving) are being developed.

> **The important point is to get a feel for how natural learning functions. In fact, it bears much resemblance to what is known as the "scientific process" and the final requirement for most PhDs—the dissertation.**

Personal Reflection

As you reflect on the differences between the learning processes associated with traditional teaching and what we have described so far, ask yourself the following questions:

- Where are the experiences within a classroom that trigger interest and authentic questions?
- Where are the opportunities to make learner-centered adaptive decisions and to choose real paths of action?
- Where are the opportunities to search for information that is personally relevant?
- Where are the opportunities to display, present, or act out what has been learned?
- Where is the ongoing feedback that continually builds on the students' sense of what is needed and how to expand both thinking and expert application?
- How are students engaged in a passionate pursuit for personal mastery?
- Where is the sense of camaraderie experienced with fellow seekers?
- Where are the opportunities to explore unique skills and shape their identity?

Almost all of this is absent from traditional schooling. For instance, when we ask today's students what kind of decisions they are allowed to make in the course of academic learning in school, they often look at us with blank faces. Given a chance to rate their opportunities to generate questions using a scale of 1 to 10, when asked if they have genuine choices about what to study or how to go about it, students inevitably choose 0 or 1. It is almost inconceivable to them that learning anything in school should involve their own choices and ideas.

Similarly, ask students in any class why they are studying what they are studying and after looking at you as though you are a bit mad, they will respond that they are doing it *because their teacher told them* to do it or because they have to do it *in order to pass a test or get a grade*. Their own motivation, enthusiasm, and effort to find unique solutions to personally relevant questions are rarely engaged. (The same incidentally holds true for teachers forced to teach the standards using standardized instruction.)

The answers to these questions will reveal where the Perception/Action Learning is actively engaged and where it is suppressed. And they provide a first look at how education needs to function.

In the course of our interviews with Jake and Dan (introduced in Chapter 1) we asked Dan what he was studying in school. He said they were studying Lewis and Clark's expeditions (this actually required some coaching because he only half remembered their names). He said that they were reading about this and "studying it." We know his teacher and she is highly motivated. She was attempting to have students actively connect with their textbooks and other writing by having them create an "interactive notebook." Her technique was to have them transfer parts of the text to their notebooks and add their own comments.

One of us asked Dan if he had ever ridden in a canoe. His eyes lit up as he mouthed "no." He was then asked if he could imagine himself going into the untamed West and what that might look like. How did Lewis and Clark survive? What did they have to do day in and day out in order to cope with the treacherous and dangerous terrain and threats from animals and Indians? Dan became animated for the first time. We were making the "stuff" exciting and real. And that was just in conversation.

Where to Go From Here?

The perception/action cycle and purposeful, goal-directed learning are processes that are inherent in every single human being. We have all become who we are by virtue of those processes. They literally are second nature.

> And so perhaps the most peculiar aspect of the entire attempt to improve education is the struggle to implement a learning process in schools that is part of the biological and psychological endowment of every student and every teacher.

Yet many of the practices of direct instruction and most of the factory-like and prison-like procedures that are used to organize many schools actively suppress the learning capacities and processes that are the key to substantially raising standards and improving student performance and engaging and developing the executive functions.

The next step in understanding teaching with natural learning in mind is to revisit the outcomes of learning. Most important is to grasp the deeply networked nature of all useful knowledge.

CHAPTER 8

Goals and Outcomes: Building Rich Neural Networks Requires Real-World Knowledge

Our experiences in the world build patterns in our mind, and then the mind shapes our experience of the world (and the actions we take in it), which, in turn, reshapes our mind. Concepts are never set and finished. They are like a large tree that always seeks to rise higher (i.e., attain more generality) but that must always send into the ground deeper roots (i.e., return to embodied experience).

—James Gee (2007, p. 91)

IN CHAPTER 5 we discussed the problem of being caught in a traffic jam, and how this experience included the perception/action dynamic and cycle. In the end we suggested that the entire experience provided an opportunity to find optional streets, learn about time required for a detour, and even learn about fuel consumption differences between waiting in traffic and taking an alternate route. These actions, and the possible learning that followed, provided more than new information. The experience and knowledge changed the brain in the form of expanding existing networks to reflect any knowledge added. This leads to an important fact. The iteration of perception/action leads to the acquisition and expansion of knowledge networks.

Neural networks develop in the brain as neurons (brain cells) connect with each other through delicate fibers called dendrites and axons. Stimulated by experience, they set in motion an electrochemical process whereby cells begin to "communicate" with each other. And on the basis of ongoing perception and action, brain cells (and body) reorganize themselves. This capacity of the brain to change is called neuroplasticity (Cozolino, 2006; Diamond & Hobson, 1998).

Guided by biological capacities, limitations, and constraints, all organisms are influenced and shaped by their experiences. Gerald Edelman argues:

> Smaller parts form heterogeneous components which are more or less independent. But as these parts connect with each other in larger and larger aggregates, their functions tend to become integrated, yielding new functions that depend on such higher order integration. (quoted in Doidge, 2007, p. 295)

That is why Varela et al. (1991) argue that living *is* cognition. They put it this way: "We lay down a path in walking" (p. 237).

KNOWLEDGE NETWORKS

Imagine the immense capacity of billions of brain cells and trillions of networked connections all lighting up in patterns representing thoughts and sensory interaction with the environment. Knowledge "resides" in these neural networks— vast webs of interactive neural links. As Fuster (2003) puts it, "There are no systems of memory, but there is the memory of systems . . . of neural systems, that is."

A wonderful analogy for these networks can be found in how the World Wide Web organizes itself. On one level the Web is interconnected and massive in content and information. Yet within this immense network of connections are "nodes" or "pools" organized around specific concepts, information, and topics. The entire process is vast yet orderly. Search engines like Google find topics or critical words that lead to an entire series of related networks and massive amounts of knowledge housed in individual Web sites.

Similarly, no unit of knowledge or concept in the brain occurs in isolation. Experiences continually expand and build relationships between different ideas, concepts, and modes of action. This has far-reaching implications for our collective understanding of memory and teaching.

Students are far more likely to remember something that is networked to things they already know or understand. Learning anything by rote is relatively ineffective. Dealing with subject matter that relates to something personal and meaningful to students is a much better way for them to remember (Greene, 2010).

Take, for example, the word *house*. Think about that word. In most cultures the word automatically brings to mind something with a roof, a floor, windows, and doors. And if you think of each of these items separately, you will automatically bring to mind a range of additional features (e.g., you might think of a metal or wooden window). So every category or concept or idea or procedure is networked in multiple ways. At some general level, the meaning that you give to the word *house* is shared by millions of other people.

Now dig deeper. This time, think of your own *experience* with houses. Begin with the one you grew up in. What do you recall? Any impressions? Memories? Feelings? Can you recall the people that lived with you in your home or visited? Events? Celebrations? What about the furniture? Appliances? Can you recall rooms and colors and decorations?

Even though we have asked you to recall individual items, everything that you experienced is related to your unique definition of *house*. This includes famous buildings such as the White House, houses you have admired, the one you are living in now or hope to own. Your concept of house may also include knowledge about construction, mortgages, heating and flooring, and experiences you have had with such issues. Perhaps you visited some famous houses or houses of historical figures. Perhaps you learned how other cultures lived by watching a program on TV.

The list of what one can know really goes on and on and is virtually endless. And notice how much of what *house* means to you derived from layers upon layers of experiences including prior reading, TV programs (e.g., *Little House on the Prairie*) and perhaps academic information acquired about houses that played a role in history such as Jefferson's house, Monticello.

And then the concept can be expanded to include its possible metaphorical and symbolic meanings. Here are just a few of the many examples that might come to mind: "Don't bet against the house," "a house divided against itself," "courthouse," "houses of parliament," and "house one's tools."

Thus concepts and ideas and procedures can grow and change and expand and morph and connect with other concepts and ideas and procedures endlessly.

Perception/Action Creates and Expands Knowledge Networks Through Multiple Iterations

Your knowledge or cognitive network for *house* was generated through many opportunities to engage perception and action, which over time included the following elements:

- Sensory input
- Associating new understanding with what you already knew
- Actor-centered questions that engaged emotions in terms of personal wants and needs ("How does that roof stay up?") and decisions ("Let's paint the outside in beige and white.")
- Reading, researching, practice, modeling by others, and the play of imagination (decorations and remodeling), and thinking through abstract concepts and ideas
- The activation of simple routines and small knowledge networks in the course of larger remodeling projects such as how to handle lunch every day, whether to hire someone to do the more skilled work, how long and when to work, and so on
- Getting feedback in the form of results that you had to live with and subsequent conclusions that you reached or new insights that you had ("OK, so it really does pay to repaint the house often in this weather.")

At times you found yourself caught in the perception/action dynamic, acting unconsciously and reflexively (perhaps concerning an issue of fear or survival). At the same time you employed the perception/action cycle, solving problems as they came up as a part of living. At other times you set out to master something specific or work on a specific skill or goal (P/AL).

These knowledge networks have certain characteristics:

- They are often called "assemblies" or "cognits" (Fuster, 2003) in that a number of neurons together represent associated features.
- There is synchronous or nearly synchronous firing of the neurons that represent the network.
- They are "coincidence detectors" (Fuster, 2003, in that they are activated when something happens in the outside world (or is thought of or imagined) that calls on that network. So networks are activated by both sensory associations and by internal imagery (such as daydreaming or abstractions).

Some connections are very tenuous, some strong but limited to basic visual or sensory information. Networks can also deteriorate over time or never properly form because of environmental factors such as air pollution (Dugandzic, Dodds, Stieb, & Smith-Doiron, 2006), malnourishment, or environmental poisoning such as that from mercury or lead (Langford & Ferner, 1999). These environmental factors may be equally as harmful as lack of more formal education or absence of practice and repetition. (One could easily speculate that simply keeping children mentally and physically healthy and fit by outlawing any and all dangerous human encounters and pollutants could improve educational standards in and of itself.)

QUALITIES OF KNOWLEDGE NETWORKS

Even though all knowledge is networked, networks can vary according to how rich or impoverished they are, according to how much of the Perception/Action Learning Cycle is engaged in building them, and according to how much people actually take charge by way of their own Perception/Action Learning. In fact, networks inevitably contain other networks so the possibilities are enormous (Fuster, 2003).

There is a vast difference between the sort of knowledge that can simply be recalled and recited, and the sort of knowledge that can be used in the real world in the course of making decisions that matter. For the purposes of education, it helps to think of three different qualities of knowledge networks: *surface knowledge, technical/scholastic knowledge,* and *dynamic knowledge.* We call them *levels of knowledge* (Caine & Caine, 1991, 2001; Caine et al., 2009).

Surface Knowledge

Surface knowledge is largely limited to memorized facts and procedures and shallow understanding that require very little activation of the different aspects of P/AL. Many techniques for improving memory tap into emotions, visualization, and collective action. However, there is very little higher order thinking, problem solving, complex action, and exercise of the executive functions. The result is the acquisition of information that is great for trivia questions but may also result in very little depth of understanding and virtually no capacity to apply the knowledge in adaptive and ambiguous situations in the real world.

We have asked literally hundreds of individuals the following question: "Why did you study?" The answer was: "For the test." We then asked: "What did you do after the test?" The answer in chorus was always: "Forget it."

In the words of the philosopher Alfred Whitehead (1929), this type of learning results in "inert" knowledge. These surface knowledge networks are not useless. They are just insufficiently networked to be useful outside of the environment in which they were developed.

There is an exception. Sometimes memorization *is* important in schooling. Core facts and routines may need to be memorized in the course of more complex learning because they act as rails to run along. The huge failure of much of traditional education, however, is to assume that memorization is the *final* outcome, when it is primarily useful as a process in a much more complex endeavor.

Technical/Scholastic Knowledge

Technical/scholastic knowledge has more depth than surface knowledge because it includes deeper understanding. It involves a grasp of key concepts and competence that incorporate relatively structured skills and procedures. Developing this type of knowledge engages many more aspects of P/AL because problem solving is involved, more meaningful social relationships are involved, and more complex decisions and more deliberate practice and questioning are called for. These are the processes advocated by Resnick (2010) in her work on the Thinking Curriculum. Technical/scholastic knowledge may be formed in conversations with others and involves topics about which people feel quite strongly. Yet mastery of ideas and the ability to express and communicate them often fails to transfer into increased real-world competence. That is why there is such a divide between understanding something in theory and being able to use it in practice. As the bumper sticker says, "Don't believe everything you think!"

A good example of the limitations of technical/scholastic knowledge can be seen in media literacy courses where students study advertising and advertising techniques. Students can examine how advertising is constructed to influence the viewer, while at the same time fail to understand how their own actions are being influenced by the very same advertising. The latter progression in thinking would be an example of dynamic knowledge.

Dynamic Knowledge

Dynamic (or performance) knowledge is knowledge that can be applied in the real world, in both planned and spontaneous and ambiguous situations. It is the sort of knowledge that we described earlier in this chapter and illustrated by the complex notion of "house." Dynamic knowledge cannot be acquired without the constant involvement and interaction of many layers of both perception and action, some of which take place in real-world environments. This is the basis of the emphasis by Dewey (1938/1997) and so many others on experiential approaches to learning. Examples range from what Roger Schank (1992) called "goal-based scenarios" to in-depth project-based learning (Edutopia Web site, http://www.edutopia.org).

> A person with dynamic knowledge has "made sense" of something to the point where it can be used and applied spontaneously in the everyday world. Making sense of something occurs through the ongoing operation of the cycle as one interacts with the environment, focuses on some things and picks up other things directly or indirectly, talks to people, asks questions, uses new vocabulary, designs products and processes, makes decisions, and is confronted by the feedback that results when something is applied through application to real-world contexts.

Over time, learners can develop the capacity to take personal charge of acquiring dynamic knowledge. Through many opportunities to make choices, act, and gain feedback, an individual is able to develop the ability to monitor herself and take charge of her own learning. These capacities are governed by executive functions of the human brain introduced in Chapter 4.

Layers of Dynamic knowledge

Of course, not all dynamic knowledge is equal. An individual may have a limited capacity to function in the real world with true excellence. We can get a clearer understanding of this by comparing the knowledge networks of an adolescent learning to drive and an experienced race car driver.

Not only would the race car driver have more (cognitive) information, but the race car driver would have had many experiences that required the development of both driving skills and knowledge acquired in the pursuit of his own needs or interest. Motors, driving surfaces, fuel differences, how to drive under all sorts of conditions, how to control emotions under stress, and many other things would all have been connected to experience. Note the sorts of factors that lead to the increase in dynamic knowledge listed here:

- Recurring needs to respond to different situations, calling for attention and focus
- Decisions that needed to be made
- Consultation with experts on a multitude of matters
- Feedback in the moment as the result of decisions made and actions taken

- Coaching and mentoring
- Multiple opportunities for deliberate practice, with more feedback
- Exposure to more information, new ideas, and alternative strategies and processes
- Constant integration of all these factors in the process of developing greater proficiency

As a result of the new action taken, the race car driver's neural networks expand and are reorganized. The connections in the brain relate intimately to the knowledge the driver accumulated. This is the way in which expertise develops.

Something else happened. The driver developed the ability to flexibly apply his knowledge in his work. Our adolescent would have very little of what shaped the expertise of the race car driver (though he might acquire other sorts of knowledge). His experiences driving around the neighborhood, the courses or guidance he received from instructors, the book he may have read, watching an instructive DVD, or studying and passing a test, would do very little to help in many difficult driving situations. Almost all of us can recall driving with an inexperienced driver who made terrifying decisions, especially under pressure. The adolescent learning to drive has little information and limited experience. In effect, he simply does not have the variety of experiences or the multiple iterations of the Perception/Action Learning Cycle that are necessary for the development of expertise.

A wonderful example of the application of such expertise can be seen in the way that pilot Sully (Chesley Burnett) Sullenberger landed the U.S. Airways Flight 1549 plane in the Hudson River on January 15, 2009. On takeoff from La Guardia Airport the plane was struck by a flock of birds, stalling both engines. Although lacking power and still at a very low altitude, the pilot dealt with all the available landing options, glided his jet into the Hudson safely, avoided breakup, and made it possible for every passenger and crew member to be saved. It helped that the pilot was also a glider pilot, had worked extensively on airline emergency preparation, and had experience as an expert military pilot.

All real-world competence is similar in this respect. A basketball player, a research scientist, and a financial adviser all read the environment, take action, and adjust to current situations based on understanding and assessment of what is happening and what is needed. So real-world competence always requires a blend of perception and action in which specific ideas, skills, and processes need to be applied and related to different situations and contexts. And all of it, both the learning and the application, continually engage the perception/action cycle at the many layers identified by Fuster (2003).

SCHOOLS VERSUS VIDEOTECH

We return again to why videotech seems to register so much more with students than their schoolwork: It is not just the nature of the subject matter; it is the extent to which natural learning is or is not taking place. As we point out elsewhere in this book, almost all schooling tends to suppress many of the elements that are natural and biologically based elements of the Perception/Action Learning Cycle.

The result from the present system is that students develop relatively impoverished networks—inert knowledge or surface knowledge—for most of the standards. This surface knowledge consists of memorized facts and routines with little understanding and almost no practical value in terms of using the information in context.

When we look at the processes and actions involved in the world of videotech, we see complex knowledge networks forming. In the world of videotech, even if the content is harmful or has no redeeming qualities, there are many more levels of engagement. Here is a list of actions that students engage in:

- Talk to and compete with each other in games that they purchase or find online
- Focus attention, often for hours at a time
- Interpret situations and make appropriate decisions resulting in immediate feedback
- Become emotionally involved at a visceral level
- Change physical locations and move about (say to each other's houses)
- Access masses of material in the outside world that support what they are doing (movies, magazines, international experts, Web sites, and more)

The result is that students develop much more complex networks for the "curriculum" of videotech. They understand it at deeper levels and take it into their lives and use it. They gain a feel or "felt meaning" (Caine & Caine, 1991) for the world of games and the Web, something that cannot be acquired without a lot of complex experience. And that is why so much of what they learn in the world of videotech becomes dynamic knowledge, the sort of knowledge that can be used to navigate through other and ever more complex video games and technology. Every game played provides the opportunity to become a better player and thus develop learner capacity. In effect, the world of videotech harnesses much, much more of their natural biological basis for learning than school does. No wonder it has more of an impact on them.

Educators have assumed that going from a small knowledge network (such as the periodic table of elements, initial practice for a math formula, breaking writing into segments, and so on) to mastering the ability to apply knowledge when needed is a sequential, one-step-at-a-time process beginning with the pieces. This is the assumption that underlies countless lesson plans and much of direct instruction. But the research on natural learning shows that understanding and mastery do not work like this.

THE CHALLENGE FOR EDUCATION

The essential problem of schooling is that most of the perception/action cycle and most of P/AL is suppressed or excluded from school "learning." That means that the networks that are formed are insufficiently connected, and the quality of the knowledge that is acquired is quite limited.

If we are serious about genuinely raising standards and preparing students for the knowledge age, we have no choice but to acknowledge the importance of natural learning. The problem is that, although many educators have attempted to teach in ways that are compatible with this research, the current meme does not allow such teaching to flourish.

The perception/action cycle and P/AL are at the core. Because the perception/action cycle is something with which every child is endowed, it follows that every child has a host of natural learning capacities. The key to upgrading education significantly is to start working with all those capacities—and no child need be left behind.

Is there a role for direct instruction? Of course there is. The problem is that education has created a false dichotomy between experience-based learning and direct instruction. Nothing in the Perception/Action Learning Cycle supports this dichotomy. Rather, the full operation of P/AL calls for the inclusion of facts, data, concepts, and skills through the use of coaching, explanations, practice and rehearsal, and sometimes even memorization—in the context of a fuller, more meaningfully engaging experiential approach. We deal with this blend of approaches in depth in our book *Seeing Education in a New Light* (Caine & Caine, in press)

Many great educators, philosophers, and others have advocated an experiential approach to education, such as those mentioned earlier. Indeed, one of the great swings of the pendulum in education has been between those who favor education that includes hands-on or life experience and those who do not.

The world of videotech is so successful because it understands and capitalizes on much of what children and adults do naturally. Yet that world is quite limited. It does not do nearly enough to help children mature because only the most sophisticated games (Shaffer, 2006) support the sorts of higher order, self-monitoring functions that need to be developed. And most of the content translates only into the online environment, but not into other real world activities.

The challenge for education is to harness the power of natural learning and do so in a way that helps students master essential standards and take charge of their own learning and their functioning as mature individuals. Technology in all its forms is here to stay. Videotech needs to be embraced, incorporated, and transcended. If education is to raise the bar and teach for in-depth understanding, let alone real-world competence, it has to rise to meet this challenge.

CHAPTER 9

Side by Side: Traditional and Perception/Action Learning

*As the prospect of being an all-knowing teacher fades into the past, educators are beginning to understand that they must make the transition from teaching their students to learning **with** their students and even learning from their students.*

—Ted McCain and Ian Jukes (2001, p. 121)

OUR GOAL IN this chapter is to begin the journey toward a different kind of teaching by introducing practices that are built with the play of perception/action in mind and that demonstrate natural learning in action. In our view it provides a structural foundation for those practices mentioned in Chapter 7 and elsewhere in this book such as project-based learning, self-directed learning, challenge learning, and others that function (whether knowingly or not) by engaging more of the perception/action cycle for the purpose of reaching a goal. It is, in fact, tapped by many of the modes used by good teachers but can be exploited by them much more effectively when they consciously and consistently leverage the natural learning power of the perception/action cycle. It is similar to much of the work being done in connection with the development of expertise in the "real" world (Leonard & Swap, 2005).

We do this by introducing, in a schematic way, Perception/Action Learning (P/AL). It is important to recognize that in schools P/AL calls for a sophisticated project-based approach. The goal is always twofold. We want students to master content by way of experiences that motivate them and simultaneously challenge them to use higher order thinking skills reflective of executive functions. Despite its fluid nature and multiple options, this teaching demonstrates and holds to parameters, which are consistent with those spelled out in Chapters 5–7.

In order to contrast traditional teaching with instruction based on natural learning, we provide below two separate examples for teaching the digestive system to fifth graders. One uses traditional instruction (TDI) and the other uses Perception/Action Learning (P/AL). Both examples focus on the teacher as "guide" with profoundly different assumptions and results.

TRADITIONAL INSTRUCTION

We provide here a traditional lesson plan that takes place within a traditional context, follwed by suggested student assignments. The standards spell out what students need to know about digestion. The teacher introduces this topic at the time scheduled. It is handled in short blocks of time—say 40 to 50 minutes. The material consists of a textbook and teacher presentations. Other issues that students are interested in are largely ignored.

With the above in mind, here is a prototype of a more or less typical approach:

- The teacher introduces the topic and refers to the appropriate chapter in the text.
- The teacher gives a lecture, accompanied by a PowerPoint slide show, on the digestive system.
- After the lecture is over, the class is directed to read and discuss each segment, one at a time, over one or more class periods.
- The teacher asks students factual questions that address information to be found in the text or lecture. If the answer is incomplete, she explains clearly what the student needs to know in addition.
- At the end of the lesson, she hands out the study guideline for homework.
- She says that there will be a test next Friday.

Here are examples of suggested assignments that have students explore how the digestive system breaks down food:

1. Provide a definition for all the vocabulary words.
2. Outline the function of the digestive system.
3. Provide examples of the different types of nutrients.
4. Differentiate and give examples of nutritious and nonnutritious foods.

5. Define and compare mechanical and chemical digestion.
6. Illustrate the parts of the digestive system and state the function of each part.
7. Explain how nutrients get into the blood.
8. Create a healthy diet for a weeklong trek into the mountains.
9. Determine the effectiveness of different weight loss programs into usable forms for cells.

Instructions for a Way That the Teacher Can Cover the Standards More Comprehensively

Instructions for the teacher might include the following:

Step 1. *Explain* to students the purpose of the study guide you prepared for them. They are guides that you have prepared that will help them complete the assignment.

Step 2. *Explain* to the students and help them see how their study guide can be used as a map to find the information that will help them complete their assignment. Their study guidelines should be "user friendly," not intimidating.

Step 3. *Tell* the students that the best way to use the study guidelines is to set them next to whatever source they are studying, such as their textbook, worksheets, or notes. They are to use the study guidelines the way their parents would use a map in order to get where they want to go in the car.

Step 4. *Tell* them that the central concept for the lesson should be at the top of the page. They are to focus on this as the key idea for the assignment (as opposed to meaningless assignments like "Chapter 24," "decimals," or "World War II").

Our Commentary

This is a well thought out and highly structured approach. It strives to produce intellectual understanding of the concept and processes of digestion by calling on students to work through the material in several different ways, some of which involve a little of their own thinking and some of which is an attempt to connect with the real world. There is even a little problem solving, as in the challenge to devise a healthy diet for use in the real world.

Note, however, the consistent references in the teacher instructions to *tell* and *explain,* as well as the absence of many of the features that activate the Perception/Action Learning Cycle. Little or nothing is organized to trigger student interest. There is little provision for student actor–centered adaptive questions. Physical engagement is limited to writing and drawing. No provision is made for social interactions in the course of study. Most information is given, with no provision for research. And the same path is to be followed by every student even though they may act in some individual ways (habits of study or doing things right away or procrastinating). What is ignored here are personal preferences or unique skills students could apply to some aspects of the topic. The most profound absence involves personally relevant questions that could motivate students to research, find unique data and solutions, plan, engage in social interactions and communication, and find alternative perspectives. All of these could call on the development of the executive functions by inviting higher order thinking that engages the need for planning and decision making that relate to their personal interest in digestion and call on real-world applications and solutions.

PERCEPTION/ACTION LEARNING

What follows is not a formula, nor are the parts spelled out ahead of time. What guides the entire approach is the teacher's "feel" for how the Perception/Action Learning Cycle is best activated and continually engaged. The curriculum standards and disciplinary details self-organize through teacher and student use of ongoing formative and summative assessment that we call *Active Processing*. Active Processing by the teacher is ongoing and occurs throughout the experience. In order to do this the teacher must have the standards and essential skills "internalized" and must continually think and act in terms of eliciting excellence (Chapter 18).

The context is substantially different from the one described above. The topic of digestion would be dealt with during a flow of interest that a class is following, and would occur at an opportune moment in this flow, based on the current progress and interests of students. There would be long blocks of class time. And, while teachers may have their own preferred text, the bulk of information and material would be found from other individuals and experts or a host of possible Web sites and other digital sources.

Beginning with an Introductory Multisensory Immersive Experience (MIE)

The teacher knows that students need an initial direct, real-world experience of digestion. So students are asked to bring their lunch to class (if this is to occur before lunch) or save some of their food if the class is after lunch. The teacher also has some bread or crackers for students who don't have anything when they gather for the Multisensory Immersive Experience.

Without saying anything about digestion, the teacher asks the students to put some food in their mouths, but adds quickly, "Don't swallow it! Just observe." Then, as they simply sit there with food in their mouths, he asks them to notice what is happening.

"Are you feeling the food get wet? Do you know why this is happening? Don't answer and don't swallow—just notice what you want to do with it.

"OK, now notice how you automatically want to chew. OK, go ahead and chew the food, but don't swallow! Do you understand why you are chewing? Don't answer, just notice.

"OK, put your hand on your throat and swallow. What just happened? And what happens to the food now? Where did it go?"

Sensory processing. Students talk about what happened to them, what was odd or great, what happened to the food while it was in their mouths, and so on. It is at this point that the teacher asks students what they wonder about (a truly creative teacher who has a great relationship with students can make this into a mystery to be solved).

Actor-centered adaptive questions. The main objective of the immersive experience is to raise actor- [student-]centered adaptive questions. All the student-generated questions are put on the board, no matter how silly. With the help of the students, the teacher narrows the questions down to ones they can research and that the teacher knows will ultimately include the standards.

For example, "Why do we eat three times a day?" may be turned into "Why do we eat?" The teacher can also volunteer questions such as these: "What happens between the time we take in food and it exits?" "Anybody have an idea of how the liver fits into all of this?" "Who wants to research the role of the liver?" If no one wants to research the liver the teacher makes a note to include this later in processing when it becomes relevant to student-generated research. "OK, so we know where some of it ends up, but what does our food really feed?"

Note that questions can arise which deeply engage individual students. A student with dietary problems or diabetic or obesity issues or students who care about the food available to the poor, different ethnic diets, and a host of other issues are lying just under the surface. The art of the teacher, in part, is to find a way to allow students to select those personally relevant questions in their research and process their results in terms of the essentials on digestion. However, that is not difficult when students report back on what they have found in their own research and discuss and debate discrepancies.

Planning, organizing, and doing research and skill development. Students decide what they want to research and whether to do this alone, as a pair, or as a group. Their interests and research questions determine how groups are divided. Timelines are also established by everyone, with built-in flexibility in case they need to be extended or shortened. Students agree on a few resources they want to investigate and spell these out. The use of vocabulary and articulation of what has been learned is strengthened when they report back to each other and the class. Technology is used widely as are interviews with experts.

From time to time students gather and the teacher asks questions for either a small group or the whole class (Active Processing). "So, who found a description of the digestive system?" "Anybody come across the difference between nutritious and nonnutritious food?" "Anybody come across the difference between mechanical and chemical digestion? Can you explain it to us?" "What is stomach acid made of? What does it do, and how does stomach acid respond to stress?" "How does this relate to our other questions?" Most teacher questions will emerge out of student comments and research results and will inevitably connect to standards. When the teacher sees that students have problems with the questions or that some information can be helpful to everyone, she gives an explanation or brief "lecturette." The same holds for practice of vocabulary or pronunciation. But everything is done to support *students'* work and *their* questions and research.

Findings can be reported verbally, in writing, and in a multitude of ways provided that every type of documentation uses the correct vocabulary, spelling, and grammar and essential concepts, facts, and skills accurately. All work is in the students' own language as they provide their own, personal explanations. The teacher makes certain that the digestive system is talked about in a myriad number of ways while using the correct vocabulary at every possible moment.

Creating a product that requires use of new learning. Finally, the new knowledge has to be applied in some fashion. For example, the teacher might propose, "Let's imagine that we are going on a weeklong trek into the mountains. What kind of food would be best? Why?" Allow students an opportunity to discuss, debate, defend, explain, and so on.

As another example, students could create a model of the digestive system using varying materials and doing it to scale. Or students may combine to write a report for their state or federal representative and even embark on political action, if that was the direction of their interest. This could easily expand into in-depth understanding of how bureaucracies, the legal system, and government work.

Formative and summative assessment are handled with ongoing Active Processing. Active Processing is essential and nonnegotiable. Throughout all this student-generated learning, the teacher continually challenges student thinking, hidden or unarticulated assumptions, and mastery of concepts and accuracy. Periodically, the teacher has students reflect on how well they are working together as a team. Being inclusive here is critical to establishing and maintaining a positive relationship among everyone and to making certain that all are contributing. Participation is never just for the purpose of "getting the grade." It is critical to learning and essential for student empowerment as learners. Computerized and other forms of individualized tutoring need to be incorporated as needed for skill development and agreed on by both teacher and student. For example, some students may need help pronouncing and recalling new vocabulary. Software for this may be available. If writing skills are inadequate, students may need to visit a learning center or work with software that targets their writing problems.

Formal feedback. Final products are essential to this process. Public demonstrations, presentations, models, or documentations of all kinds are made available with attention to use of vocabulary (both written and spoken), and include the ability to answer spontaneous questions from experts or novices, using the appropriate language and concepts.

Technology is infused throughout. The use of technology is required everywhere. The Multisensory Immersive Experience can be direct and hands-on as in the example above or may include great videos or an interactive game or Web site. All are possibilities as long as they represent real-world applications of the topic to be investigated and are capable of creating student interest and motivation to know more. This is where the work of great video producers and makers of sophisticated video games can be immensely helpful.

The Natural Inclusion of Executive Functions of the Human Brain

Notice how this type of teaching allows for constant feedback while students acquire academic excellence. And at the same time, they need to develop what we have identified as knowledge age learning skills in Chapter 4. Teachers need to see these skills in tandem with academic mastery. Recall that the teacher must nurture these capacities and that they can only be mastered through actual application:

- Set goals
- Plan ahead and manage time effectively
- Solve problems
- Make effective decisions
- Delay gratification
- Monitor and regulate their own emotions
- Work with others
- Adapt to a changing world
- Learn how to learn
- Deal with details as well as the "big picture"

These are skills that invite higher order thought processes, all essential to the world they will be facing as successful adults. This instructional approach can therefore be used as a doorway to self-knowledge and understanding oneself. And it is the primary way in which academic excellence and knowledge as well as knowledge age survival skills can be developed simultaneously.

The prefrontal cortex is designed to become myelinated (the axon is covered with a fatty insulation that speeds up communication between neurons), and anatomically mature after puberty. Recall that the prefrontal cortex is essential for higher order thinking and decision making. The best way to enhance these capacities is for students to have to make learner centered adaptive decisions—and begin to take charge of themselves—even when they are very young.

Thus the key to harnessing the natural learning capacities of students is for the entire world of education to be infused with processes that engage Perception/Action Learning throughout their years in school. In essence, then, education is organized around experiences that include the parameters of P/AL in which the high-level content is embedded.

WHAT CHANGES WITH THE PERCEPTION/ACTION LEARNING APPROACH?

When Perception/Action Learning is used, the thrust and dynamic of instruction is essentially turned on its head. The reason is that the learning of the learner, and not the teaching of the teacher, drives what happens. It also allows students to engage in learning that is actor centered, similar to great inventors and researchers.

Note, however, that the bulk of material dealt with in the traditional approach will also be dealt with here. In fact, it is dealt with in much more complex, interactive ways, which is one reason why the learning is deeper. Note also that there are even some small overlapping processes. For instance, in the traditional approach the teacher asked students to prepare a diet for a weeklong trek in the mountains. The critical difference is that, in the second approach, the projects emerged out of student interests and were genuinely selected by them. The difference between teacher-driven and learner-driven education lies in who gets to choose and decide—really. In the course of this exploration, the students are almost certain to come across information and issues of which the teacher was unaware, and so the teacher is also a visible learner in the process. This actually enriches the questions that she asks, and helps to ensure that questions are introduced in such a way as to propel the learning further.

The Role of the Student Shifts Fundamentally

- The entire process calls on students to be more self-directed and to participate fully as decision makers.
- Working with groups or alone becomes natural and is based on student needs and preferences and the nature of the task.
- Students become much more responsible for maintaining an orderly and supportive community.

The Role of the Teacher Shifts Dramatically

The job of the teacher is to dynamically facilitate the Perception/Action Learning Cycle through ongoing questioning and engagement using Active Processing. Feedback, both formative and summative, and reflection on feedback needs to be embedded in and included throughout student research and projects. There can be more formal feedback in the form of assessment by people who are competent in the field (including the teacher but also parents with expertise, online references, and experts). Doing a brief "drill and practice" on all the new vocabulary is not out of place but should usually be fun—done to a song, poem, or ditty, which students can collaborate to create or create in teams and perform for each other. Reading and resources in the form of books and articles or research summaries or commentaries need to be made available. Reading of all types is encouraged but not forced. This is where teacher modeling and assumptions become critical.

Note that teacher input and guidance is rarely absent. There will be times when a teacher pulls the class together in order to emphasize important points, discuss new concepts, or refine specific skills. There will be times when teachers set limits or parameters for what can and cannot be done. All of this, however, is done in the service of students and the larger process and supports the playing out of goal-directed Perception/Action Learning engaging each student.

Through all this, teachers need to be prepared to learn new things from students as students research their questions, and teachers need to develop a sense of comfort and even celebrate with students that they are sometimes learners together. In effect, everyone becomes a learner. Students learn from each other and from sources of their own choosing.

The Structure of the School Community and Operations Changes Profoundly

As learning becomes more in-depth and more dynamic, traditional constraints of time and space need to be relaxed. For instance, students move more freely in classrooms and in the school, projects and activities spill into private times and sometimes other classes, and the student community begins to monitor its own functioning.

Thus the key to harnessing the natural learning capacities of students is for the entire world of education to be infused with processes that engage P/AL throughout their years in school. In essence, then, education is organized around experiences in which the standards are embedded and expertise is continually encouraged by feedback from others and teacher expertise. The physical structure needs to allow for all this to happen.

Making It Work

Great teaching is a highly demanding art and skill. For instance, just mastering the core process of this more natural approach is complex, and yet there is more. The reason is that a student is *not* a blank slate or an object like a computer. As we have demonstrated, all the individual characteristics of human beings play a part in learning including emotions, relationships, physical context, and state of mind.

A way needs to be found to make all of this manageable. We take our guidance from the simple words of neuroscientist Joseph LeDoux (1996) who points out that the brain has a "high road" and a "low road." There is a way of working with people that taps into and engages their higher order capacities for learning. And there is a way of working with people that suppresses their higher order capacities and diminishes their learning. The key to the enhanced power of the P/AL is to understand and engage the high road. We turn to that next.

Part III

THE BODY/MIND
CONNECTION

CHAPTER 10

Motivation: The Engine That Drives Perception/Action Learning

So are the goals of rigorous learning and having fun incompatible and mutually exclusive? I think a great many teachers and academics believe this, and resist any efforts to make learning fun, passing the same pain down, generation after generation, as an academic rite of passage. That's absolutely absurd.
—Marc Prensky (2006, p. 85)

ONCE WE ALLOW student questions and quests to drive the course of how they want to approach a subject or broad topic like "digestion," an entirely new world opens up.

The nature and quality of those questions are influenced not only by the Multisensory Immersive Experience, but by the students' personal search for meaning guided by connections they have made to their own lives. Questions such as "I have a brother who has diabetes and he can't have sugar, can I study why?" or "Why do some people get fat and I can't gain weight?" The teacher has to take the time to narrow down some of these questions by way of consensus or agreement. But once students ask their actor-centered adaptive questions, allowing them to pursue their questions becomes essential. And once they do that, they very likely move beyond the teacher's own expertise. Letting go of this kind of control can be very hard.

The goal is to release and then channel student interest and energy. The Multisensory Immersive Experience begins the P/AL phases and its primary purpose is to generate student-centered adaptive or personally relevant and meaningful questions. Actor-centered questions are still largely related to a specific discipline, but they allow the students to find "their way" of investigating using a topic or theme. The teacher is there to support the students, as are all the materials and experts available in life and technology.

As the other steps essential to natural learning emerge, intrinsic motivation must be maintained. All aspects of the process serve this goal, including immersion in the topic (modeling by others, coaching, Internet search, expert opinion and knowledge, and so on), creating a product of their own that represents and incorporates new learning, and getting feedback.

> Moving students throughout the phases of P/AL can't be forced or controlled by a teacher, though it can be guided and facilitated, and keeping students motivated becomes one of the teacher's biggest challenges. This is delicate work.

JUST WHAT IS MOTIVATION?

What is it that makes someone training to become a fireman strap on a 30-pound suit in the sweltering heat, carry equipment that weighs another 75 pounds, and run up two flights of stairs or make it on to a roof of a high building? What makes a researcher go back again and again to the lab and continue an experiment that keeps failing? And how does a politician pick up after a failing election or losing a fight for critical legislation?

Whatever it is that keeps anyone going to break old limits and is against the odds requires a certain spark. That spark emerges out of a belief in oneself and a love or fascination with something that links to a personal goal or purpose. Motivation is the engine that propels the perception/action cycle and consists of the stirrings within an individual that direct behavior toward an important, meaningful goal. Natural learning makes use of this spark wherever and however it emerges for a student.

Motivation is the general term used to describe the totality of the factors that propel a student toward or away from a course of action. P/AL is driven by the wants and needs that a student has. It is reflected in responses to such questions as "What do I care about doing?" and "How strongly do I care?"

There is a vast amount of research on motivation, and many theories to explain it (Petri & Govern, 2003). We cannot possibly do justice to this body of research, and yet motivation is so important that we cannot ignore it. The key, for us, then, is to focus on some of the essentials.

For the purposes of natural learning, the most important distinction is the difference between *extrinsic* and *intrinsic* motivation (Ormrod, 2010).

Kinds of Motivation

Extrinsic refers to factors that make or compel or drive a person to act in some way largely independent of personal choice or meaning. This is what tends to happen when decisions are not actor- or learner-centered adaptive decisions and are made for the student, which we referred to as "decisions made by others" in Chapter 6. Something or someone outside of the individual uses influence, control, or coercion to ensure that something is done a certain way.

Extrinsic motivation means that meaning and understandable purpose reside with someone other than the learner. These external inducements are relatively immediate and direct. They largely consist of some tangible reward that follows an action or a punishment that is also relatively immediate and concrete or tangible. When students don't want to do what teachers insist they must "learn," extrinsic threats or rewards can induce behavior and produce results of a certain kind. This is how teacher-determined assignments tied to grades and tests tend to work.

Intrinsic motivation is internal, personal, meaningful, and adaptive. It refers to the urges, persuasions, and forces, including personal wants and needs that come from inside a person and lead to actor-centered adaptive questions and the resultant personal decisions and actions (Zuckerman, Porac, Lathin, Smith, & Deci, 1978). The difference is in the word adaptive, which refers to a personal need to find a solution or answer. Learners are therefore driven by their own desire or need to know (recall the introduction in Chapter 6 of actor-centered adaptive decision making).

Use of Motivation

Here is an example of the contrast: A parent in a teacher education program at the University of Florida complained bitterly about a new behavior modification program that had been implemented in her child's school. "She loves to learn and wants to find out all kinds of things and now they give her M&Ms every time she gives a right answer. She hates it and I am really angry!" Here, the innate joy of learning was actually suppressed by the use of candy as a reward for learning.

We need to be clear that it often takes a combination of intrinsic and extrinsic motivation to maintain motivation. This is not about "either-or," but more about "more or less." All of us have been pushed or pulled into taking some action or having an experience we initially didn't want, only to become motivated to do more of it. That is why the tension between the two types of motivation has been examined in some depth in recent years (Cameron, Banko, & Pierce, 2001; Deci, Koestner, & Ryan, 1999). The challenge is to find the right balance, and to use extrinsic motivation on occasion to elicit and trigger intrinsic motivation.

Of course, coercion by way of a promised reward or punishment that bypasses student's deeper intrinsic motivation can be used in cases where noncompliance means danger for a student or other. It can also be used where necessary in order to manage and maintain some routines, such as turning the lights out in order to save energy. Looking both ways before crossing a street or washing one's hands after going to the bathroom are also common examples of routines that initially require extrinsic motivation.

If the relationship between the person requiring an action and the student is positive and strong, students can often comply because they want to please that individual. A mother recently gave a perfect example of deliberately pressuring her son to play soccer. He was extremely hesitant and resistant, only to discover he loved it and wanted to sign up for soccer camp after experiencing it first hand. This also provides a clue for teachers who may have to "reward" initial effort in order to get some students to try doing something new or challenging.

The indispensable central point is that Perception/Action Learning (P/AL) requires that students be self-motivated as much as possible. Why? Because intrinsic motivation ensures that all phases of the cycle will take place, from the initial experience to final feedback. Intrinsic motivation is also vital for the development of higher order functions such as planning, analyzing one's actions, and making intelligent decisions. Actions propelled by reward or punishment, controlled by an external authority, tend to invite compliance instead of thought, reflection, the need to deal with consequences, critical debate, and intelligent questioning. It is clear, however, that P/AL can be sabotaged or diverted at any time. We address that in some detail in the next chapter.

WHAT MOTIVATES STUDENTS INTRINSICALLY?

The key for educators is to see that some immensely powerful inner wants and needs naturally drive learning and that these are accessed through Perception/Action Learning (P/AL). We discuss below several ways that this type of natural learning can access intrinsic motivation. We treat them as separate for the sake of clarity. However, they all overlap and connect with each other as they play out in life.

The Search for Patterns That Connect

Every one of us is innately driven to make sense of our world by finding what Gregory Bateson (1979) called "the pattern which connects." The search for patterns lasts throughout life, and it begins at birth.

> We seem to have a kind of explanatory drive, like our drive for food or sex. . . . We see this same drive to understand the world in its purest form in children. Human children in the first three years of life are consumed by a desire to explore and experiment with objects. (Gopnik et al., 1999, pp. 85–88)

Natural learning, with its emphasis on inquiry, research, modeling, experimentation, and reflection, is grounded in the "pattern-making abilities" of all students. At the same time, explanations from teachers, experts, the Internet and texts are also important because they assist students in finding patterns that are central to their understanding.

The Power of Purpose and Passion

Much of the advice provided in the world of self-help, therapy, management, and human resource development is based on the fact that purpose and meaning are crucial to peak performance. "Begin with the end in view" is one of author Stephen Covey's seven habits of highly effective people (1990). James Hillman (1996) reaches deeper. He writes that "what is lost in so many lives, and what must be recovered: [is] a sense of personal calling, that there is a reason I am alive" (p. 4).

The rigor, persistence, and perseverance of great inventors, thinkers, entrepreneurs, and others are testament to the power of purpose.

The beauty of P/AL is that, by working with authentic student interests and choices, it naturally taps into this basic drive.

The Joy of Creativity and Problem Solving

"Getting it" really is thrilling. The sheer pleasure and joy of insight is so great that it is intrinsically motivating and keeps people going and even reaching for almost impossible heights.

> Like other human drives, that explanatory drive comes equipped with certain emotions: a deeply disturbing dissatisfaction when you can't make sense of things and a distinctive joy when you can. (Gopnik et al., 1999, p. 162)

Thus the chairman of Procter and Gamble, John Pepper, explained that business needs schools to nourish: "Basic thinking skills, a sense of discovery and the thrill of success. When students experience these, they will certainly want to learn more" (quoted in Hirshberg, 1999, p. 43).

Great scientists in their research, great artists in their creativity, children at their play—all experience aspects of this state. It is sufficiently compelling, often, to replace other basic needs. It is one of the most powerful motivators in the human repertoire. The joy of creativity has much in common with the state of flow, described in the next chapter, when people get so pleasurably involved in exploring the task at hand that they even lose sense of time (Csikszentmihalyi, 1990/2008).

And the opportunity to frequently experience the thrill of insight is a core aspect of this approach to learning.

The Joy of Connecting and Working with Others

Social networking alone attests to the ongoing need and joy of connecting with others. Science tells us that this need to connect is fundamental to life itself: "We are an intensely social species, deeply dependent on one another for our very survival" (Gopnik et al., 1999, p. 23). Going further than physical survival, much of the way that we all think and learn is grounded in relationships with each other. Siegel (2001) puts it this way: "The mind emerges from the activity of the brain, whose structure and function are directly shaped by interpersonal experience" (p. 1). The social nature of learning is further explained in terms of situated cognition introduced in Chapter 1 and expanded in Chapter 14.

The interaction between people is very subtle and much of it is nonverbal. In their attempts to explain this connection, some scientists speak of a "mental state resonance" (Siegel, 1999, p. 70) when people are in a type of alignment. This is very important in therapy, for instance. Such an alignment permits a nonverbal form of communication to the client that she is being "understood" in the deepest sense. She is "feeling felt" by another person. This attunement of states forms the nonverbal basis of collaborative, contingent communication.

In essence, most students relish the opportunity to belong to a group and to work with others (Damasio, 2003; LeDoux, 1996, 2002; Siegel, 1999). Part of our identity depends on establishing community and finding ways to belong (Boleyn-Fitzgerald, 2010). It has been called the "contact urge" (Brothers, 1997, p. 7).

Natural learning makes ongoing joint ventures possible, and the simple fact of working on them with others is often intrinsically motivating.

The Sense of Self-Efficacy

Self-efficacy, a concept attributed to Alfred Bandura (1997), refers to the belief that people have about their own effectiveness. The more personally effective people believe themselves to be, the more they are motivated to act—and to learn.

> Perceived self-efficacy influences the level of goal challenge people set for themselves, the amount of effort they mobilize, and their persistence in the face of difficulties. Perceived self-efficacy is theorized to influence performance accomplishments both directly and indirectly through its influences on self-set goals. (Zimmerman, Bandura, & Martinez-Pons, 1992, p. 665)

Learning in the ways we describe makes regular accomplishment possible. At the same time, it offers students multiple opportunities to reflect on their processes and accomplishments and this, in turn, develops the capacity to self-regulate and so perform at higher and higher levels.

WHAT ARE THE INDICATORS OF INTRINSIC MOTIVATION IN THE LIVES OF STUDENTS?

There are several indicators of high intrinsic motivation in students, though the entire context needs to be taken into consideration (Ormrod, 2010). We list some examples here:

- Increased attendance, without reminders or threats or rewards
- Voluntary work on projects and assignments after school hours
- Persistence over time, even when an assignment or project seems difficult
- Unprompted and relevant questions from students
- Continuous work on a task or project when teachers leave the room

When the two of us work with a school, we ask teachers to leave their class periodically to conference with us. In some classrooms, the teachers can leave a room without students being disturbed or distracted from what they are doing.

In one case when the teacher left the room, the substitute teacher did nothing but walk around playing the mandolin. Most students barely noticed. They were working in groups to solve a math problem that focused on discovering the most parsimonious way to design streets for a new city—streets that would reach the most buildings at the least cost. Although one or two asked where the substitute played (he explained that he regularly played at a local restaurant) they were only being polite and almost immediately turned back to what they were doing.

Since that time we have observed this reaction often in classes where students are deeply immersed in a problem that fascinates them (so they are intrinsically motivated). A different reaction occurs when students are primarily extrinsically motivated through teacher explicit direction and control; when the teacher leaves or is replaced by a substitute teacher, chaos tends to ensue.

EXTRINSIC MOTIVATION RULES IN TRADITIONAL EDUCATION

Traditional education has given us externally defined and controlled behavioral objectives and teacher-designed rules, rubrics, strategies, and benchmarks. The teacher controls both the information to be mastered and the rewards or punishments meant to encourage students to do what is required of them. This has shown up most recently in the design of *pacing guides* (written schedules displaying the alignment of concepts, topics, and skills related to a particular curriculum to be addressed over a defined period of time) and packaged programs that dictate what and where the teacher instructs and how students need to perform.

Why should all of this matter? Perception/Action Learning requires teachers and educators to stimulate and ignite the inner world of students so that they want to ask their own unique yet appropriate questions, make tough decisions, persevere and persist with their inquiries and their practice, and generally move toward mastery or expertise that includes higher order functions. The kind of prescriptive teaching described in the previous paragraph does not encourage higher order thinking and problem solving to develop.

Note that the P/AL approach is far from laissez faire. Schools, parents, and the community do spell out much of what students need to master, including academics, social skills, and self-regulation. Finding the way to blend student self-determination with the needs of the community is a central problem that education needs to solve. This is what Perception/Action Learning is designed to do. But in order to make that possible, we need a clearer view of the obstacles that have been erected that so much get in the way.

A Bit of History—The Mirage That Sideswiped Educators

How did schools become so convinced of the merits of extrinsic motivation?

Schools were not first. A number of factors were in play, grounded in the beliefs and practices already established in industry and 19th-century educational practices. But the advent of behaviorism in psychology played a leading role. From the point of view of formal research, we can trace the beginning to the famous experiments by the Russian scientist Ivan Pavlov. Pavlov had demonstrated that a dog could be conditioned to salivate by ringing a bell every time he was brought food. By combining the ringing of the bell with food for a number of instances, the dog began to salivate even when there was no food. Because of the animal's association between bell plus food, he "learned" to salivate to the bell alone. This became known as *classical conditioning* (Ormrod, 2007).

This experiment unleashed a torrent of research and led to a more advanced process called *operant conditioning*, the father of which was B. F. Skinner (1971/2002). Where classical conditioning (Pavlov) has to do with pairing conditions and shaping a new behavior, operant conditioning has more to do with what reinforcer follows a particular action. Skinner's book *Walden Two* (1948/1976) provides an excellent example of the utopian dream that suggested what a world filled with "modified" individuals might look like. The research ultimately led to *behavior modification*, which is pretty much what its name suggests. It is a way of modifying behavior, either eliminating unwanted behavior or increasing the likelihood that a more desired behavior occurs. In schools it serves as the foundation for countless behavioral approaches to maintaining discipline.

Think back to the perception/action dynamic, which we defined as largely reflexive and occurring below the level of awareness in Chapter 5. It refers to habitual ways of acting and habits that are hard to change. Negative examples include automatically responding with inappropriate anger and violence, or being late all the time, or even positive actions that may or may not be appropriate in a given situation. Another example can be found in the world of personal finances. Both saving and spending money have their place, but both saving and spending as reflexive responses at the expense of logic or reason can be destructive. Literally thousands of actions occur automatically as habits that seem to be beyond one's ability to control. Behavior modification can sometimes be used in these circumstances to program in other reflexive behaviors.

The fascination for educators was as obvious as it was bizarre. All learning could be reduced to changes in behavior. Indeed, the stronger versions, sometimes called *radical behaviorism*, contended that mind did not matter. And all teaching could be reduced to manipulating conditions that changed behavior by applying a combination of externally introduced rewards and punishments (this is a vast subject covered in most basic psychology texts such as Ormrod, 2010). The external controller decided, therefore, whether a behavior was desired or not. This led inexorably to programmed instruction, also initially developed by Skinner (Ormrod, 2010).

We have dealt with the subject at some length even though psychology itself has advanced, because behaviorism has had, and continues to have, a profound impact on how educators—and the broader community—view motivation and how they define learning. Whenever there is a proposal to pay students to learn, or to treat learning as their "work," or to hold educators accountable based on student test scores, then an underlying theory of motivation is being invoked, a theory grounded in behavior modification and belief in the role and power of reward and punishment.

What Could Be Wrong with This Picture?

In a paper presented in 1970 entitled "Two Views of Motivation," Art Combs pointed out the fundamental limitations of Pavlov's experiment (Richards, in press). Combs suggested that in the end Pavlov had found a magnificent way to develop a pretty useless dog. The dog ended up behaving in inappropriate ways (salivating for no reason), doing something that was unnatural and that served no purpose other than that which served Pavlov's experiment.

Combs also pointed out that in order to achieve this useless behavior Pavlov had to first separate the dog from all other dogs, thus separating him from social contact with his own species. He also restricted the dog's movements so that it could not behave in any way other than intended by the researcher, and he prevented any other stimuli to enter the experimental conditions and potentially confuse the dog. This was taken to such an extreme "that the Czar, who was very interested in the problem, had the whole square around the laboratory that Pavlov was working in covered with tanbark so that the rumble of the wagons going over the stones should not disturb the dogs in the laboratory" (Richards, in press, p. 71).

The question that was totally off the table with Pavlov and all the research that followed was "What did the dog want?" While this seems to be an absurd question, in effect the question that is totally off the table so often in schools is what students want or care about. In other words, what students want is often treated as irrelevant. Thus in *Walden Two* Skinner suggests that his approach is the perfect answer to creating successful people and a healthy community. Individuals are randomly reinforced to become bakers, construction workers, or farmers who are (according to Skinner) content with their lot. It all sounds ideal until the end when the reader realizes that the "programmer" (in this case Skinner) is really playing God.

We are not suggesting for a moment that conditioning does not work or questioning the fact that it can be very useful. Clearly, human beings can be programmed to a significant extent. Recall our earlier discussion on the perception/action dynamic. Behavior is often biologically "programmed" guided by survival needs. Once established, these behaviors become inflexible and applied with limited regard for appropriate fit. And there are situations (particularly therapeutic situations) in which behavior modification is quite potent and helpful.

The larger point is that behaviorism, and behavior modification, are a totally inadequate foundation for education in the knowledge age. Not only does it fail to explain most of what happens when people learn, it also leads to the disregard and suppression of enormous reserves and capacities that students have and upon which educators can rely.

A Corollary of *Walden Two*

Just imagine for a moment that a teacher can control students to such an extent that students do not talk with each other, listen only to what the teacher says or wants them to hear, read only what a teacher prescribes, and do all this at the same time and in the same way, and that they can be made to do so with enticing rewards or punishment. Imagine further that it is possible to eliminate outside influences and sources of information (cell phones, e-mails, the World Wide Web, books, other students, other adults) and thoughts about a personally challenging situation, puzzles, and interests. And imagine further still that all these "behaviors" and responses can be rewarded with candy, pizza, grades, praise, and prizes whenever they do the right thing, and punished by means varying from low grades to public embarrassment when they do not do exactly what the teacher or adult wants or do not perform in exactly the right way. This is a perfect way to kill initiative and creativity, breed conformity, drain energy, and generally dull the minds and weaken the motivation of students. It is also a definitive way to prevent students from mastering skills essential to the knowledge age (Chapter 4).

Yet for far too many educators, parents, politicians, and researchers, that scenario sounds not only familiar but describes the theoretical foundation for what they believe is required in order to achieve and "learn" in school.

There is nothing new in our discussion of behaviorism, and its limitations have been dealt with for decades. We use it to show that the core belief in the primacy of extrinsic motivation still pervades education and that higher order thinking and behavior cannot happen without choice and making decisions that matter. This does include appropriate behavior, but there are many other ways for students to master their behavior, as we point out in the rest of this book.

Fortunately, other branches of psychology have emerged that explore a more complex view, one that includes the role of emotions and higher order thinking. In more recent times, many of these ideas have been either acknowledged or embraced by cognitive psychology and, even more recently, by neuroscience. These developments have impacted every aspect of the functioning of a human being, including motivation. Our Brain/Mind Learning Principles document these changes.

HOW IS PERCEPTION/ACTION LEARNING DIFFERENT?

The theory of natural learning tells us that perception/action is intrinsic to life itself. Children come equipped to make sense of life experiences and how they experience life shapes them (brain and body).

P/AL is based on the fact that the energy for learning is already there, driven by all the aspects of intrinsic motivation described above. And this limitless reservoir of energy to act and to learn is accessible to educators and education. So the task of educators is to understand how all this works and then guide and shape the experiences that students have and the learning that then becomes possible. Children and students are literally motivated to learn from the moment they are born. We have to guide their opportunities and choices but, for the most part, we don't have to "make" them learn.

The bottom line is that an enormous amount of student energy for learning is simply waiting to be ignited. However, the process is intricate and complex because it is so easy to suppress student enthusiasm, even with the best intentions in the world. The more complex, more education-specific Guided Experience Approach that we introduce in Part IV of this book is our way of tapping into the extraordinary unused reserves of motivation and energy of most students. But there is more to be addressed before we get there.

CHAPTER 11

The Optimal State of Mind for Learning

Whenever I go to school I have to "power down."
—A student (Prensky, 2006, p. 10)

Complex learning is enhanced by challenge and inhibited by threat associated with helplessness and/or fatigue.
—Principle 11 (Caine & Caine, 1991)

JAMES AGGREY (http://knol.google.com/k/leadership-prospective#) tells the story of a man who finds a young eagle. He places the eagle in the barnyard among his chickens. Here the eagle learns to behave like a chicken, pecking for food on the ground. The eagle basically believes that he is, in fact, a chicken. A naturalist visits the man and upon observing the eagle he asks why an eagle, capable of so much more, behaves like a chicken. He then takes the eagle out every day in order to help him remember that he is in fact an eagle, capable of flight.

This is of course an allegory but in terms of capacity for learning, human beings fit this allegory comfortably. Could it be that most humans are the equivalent of eagles who too rarely use their capacities to learn and lead, and instead act like lower, less developed beings filled with fear and scrounging for their bit of turf? Could it be possible that beings, who are smart enough to create robots and fly into outer space, do not yet understand themselves? In our view, the brains/minds of most of us are vastly underused.

We can get closer to solving this puzzle when we have a better grasp of the interaction of emotions, motivation, cognition, and performance.

MIND STATES

A person's inner state, or state of mind, is the total pattern of activation of the brain, involving body, cognition, and emotion, at any point in time (Siegel, 1999) and is influenced by the totality of the conditions in which one finds oneself (LeDoux, 1994, 1996, 2002). Much has been written about states of mind (Conlan, 1999), including the nature of mindfulness (Langer, 1997), contemplation and contemplative states (Wilber, Engler, & Brown, 1986), the nature of consciousness and states of consciousness (Alexander & Langer, 1990; Kihlstrom, 2007; Velmans & Schneider, 2007), the connections between consciousness and the brain (Gazzaniga, 1988, and see generally the *Journal of Consciousness Studies*), and the links between speed, depth, and range of functioning (Claxton, 1997).

Like motivation, the inner state of learners is a topic that can never be adequately covered, in part because so many factors are involved. These include environmental factors, economic and personal debt forces, the use of drugs, diet and physical health, fatigue and emotional health, addictions of all types, and both short- and long-term stress.

Educators encounter a wide variety of mind states in their students and in themselves. This represents a major challenge. Even though teachers may focus on specific academic work, teaching itself must deal with the fact that anyone may be impacted by factors that cannot be identified or whose origin remains a puzzle.

And yet we have to deal with the issue because, for practical purposes, a state of mind represents the degree of energy, the range of possibilities, the type of focus and engagement, and other capacities that the learner brings to a task or situation. All of these impact the perception/action dynamic, cycle, and learning. For instance, any of the above factors can affect someone's level of patience, quality of thinking, and mental focus and concentration.

Recall that at every moment of every situation, the perception/action dynamic is operating, as we show in Chapter 5. Joaquin Fuster demonstrated that, in principle, the entire body, brain, and mind are involved in the perception/action cycle. Three points became critical:

1. The brain/mind is taking in the entire field of awareness surrounding an individual and influences how that person responds.
2. The focus of attention constantly shifts, and can be riveted, based on initial interpretations of a situation.
3. There is always action of some kind, though even inaction is a type of action.

And the entire process is influenced by a person's state of mind.

This issue is vital for education to address because a central goal must be to expand rather than diminish the overall functioning of students, educators, and all others who impact the system. With an appropriate mind state, learning can be enthusiastic, expansive, creative, rigorous, and ongoing. Without an appropriate mind state, learning is easily sabotaged or simply dropped.

Fortunately, while there are many factors over which educators have little or no control, there is much that they can do to reduce mind states that sabotage learning and nurture mind states that enhance learning.

This can be done in the short term (where states may be transitory) and in the long term (where they become more predictable as personality traits; see Dweck, 2000).

To understand how educators can facilitate mind states that enhance learning, take time for some personal reflection. Recall a time when you felt despondent, apathetic, and disinterested. Perhaps you felt that a task was just beyond you. Or you simply did not care about whether it was completed or not. Now contrast this with other times such as when you felt totally empowered, when things appeared to fall into place. Or you may recall a moment of insight that left you breathless after thinking or working on something important to you. Perhaps there were less exciting moments when you were lost in a world that held your attention and focus, where time almost stood still. Perhaps your empowering moment involved executing a physical skill like swimming at a top speed or building a cabinet that truly impressed you and others. And now ask yourself about the extent to which the two different types of inner feelings are fairly constant in your life.

Question: What were the differences in your thinking, motivation, and actions? And what was the impact on your capacity to persevere with learning anything?

We contend, based upon experience and research, that there is an optimal state of mind for learning. We have called it *Relaxed Alertness*. It is one where learners feel confident, competent, and motivated.

In essence, then, teachers can help facilitate a state of mind in which learners feel confident, competent, and challenged to act. And they can help avoid and neutralize mind states involving learner helplessness, hopelessness, boredom, and fatigue.

THE BRAIN'S TWO OPPOSING TENDENCIES—
THE HIGH ROAD AND THE LOW ROAD

The two alternative states that we describe above can be formalized in terms of the notion that the brain has two opposing tendencies—a high road and a low road (Goleman, 2006; LeDoux, 1998). In his research Joseph LeDoux has fleshed out pathways of fear in the brain and has mapped the link between the experience of fear, the secretion of neurotransmitters and hormones, and the ways in which different brain regions function under different environmental conditions.

> LeDoux points out that there are two major pathways in the brain: One can access higher order functions that are conscious and rational, the other is largely below the level of awareness and results in what we have described as the reflexive and automatic survival response. He refers to these two roads as simply the "high road" and the "low road."

His well-known example of how the survival response works, involves someone walking in a forest. Suddenly that person becomes aware of something curled up close ahead on the ground. It is a snake. Most people who fear snakes will stop in their tracks ("freeze"), their heart rate will increase, and their blood pressure will rise. Their pupils will dilate and nonessential functions like digestion will slow down. The body is preparing for a fight or to run away. But other people are different. And their reactions and internal states differ.

The brain initially sends basic information from the senses to the auditory and visual thalamus. Here the brain will pass on the information along two paths. Part of the information will go to the cortex where basic memories and facts about snakes are processed. These include childhood memories of encounters with snakes, verbal memories that allow the person to connect to the word *snake,* and impressions gleaned from stories and movies. At the same time, for some people, the emotional center of the brain, the amygdala, is blasting out an emotional response of "emergency!" This signal from the amygdala sets into motion an entire physiological reaction that is immensely quick and bypasses all sorts of important information and data. Time is a critical variable. The way of the amygdala is the low road—fast and reflexive. The high road, which allows someone time to access a more rational or thought-out reaction, takes more time. In a very real sense the high road is hijacked by the brain's response and initiation of the low road.

The high road can be readily accessed by other people who know and like snakes or find themselves in an environment where they feel safe (e.g., accompanied by a herpetologist). Their responses are more likely to be ones of curiosity or, in the case of those who love snakes or all animals, ones of wonder and excitement.

This introduces us to the essence of the high road. Accessing the higher or more integrative functions of the human brain requires learners to be in a positive mind state, one that involves challenge but does not dwell in fear or helplessness. This and related research has led us to conclude that learners experiencing a sense of confidence, competence, and positive motivation most readily access the high road.

The other side of the coin is a drive to survive. The drive to survive is obvious during a natural disaster or in an emergency. In fact, that drive is in play to some extent everywhere. Infants have it when they enter the world, parents have it as they seek to protect their families, businesses feel it in tough economic times, and as we will see in the next chapter, it permeates the world of schooling and education. Students of all ages, teachers in their classrooms, administrators who are responsible for the people in their care, and all the others who play a role in education can potentially be in survival mode.

The path between the low road and the high road is a continuum. There are degrees of fear and helplessness associated with survival, and there are degrees of higher order functioning. The diagram in Figure 11.1 on the next page depicts the nature of the continuum and how it impacts P/AL.

Another way to put this is that the brain is somewhat like a grid that uses electricity. The parts of the grid that require the most energy take energy from the grid at large and put other functions in a state of "brownout." In terms of the brain, if it becomes a question of survival, sparked by fear, helplessness, or extreme fatigue, then energy is taken from the "higher," slower processing, or more integrated areas—the prefrontal or integrated cortex housing executive functions—in order to strengthen those areas responsible for ensuring what the brain interprets as physical survival (Sapolsky, 1998). This doesn't mean that one area is more important than another, only that different areas perform different functions and nature will first see to physical aspects of survival housed in the lower brain areas. In very subtle or not so subtle ways, mind states affect and are affected by the play of the grid.

Researchers

Many researchers have anticipated the mind state continuum in one form or another. We briefly discuss the work and thinking of some of them here. We

FIGURE 11.1. High Road and Low Road

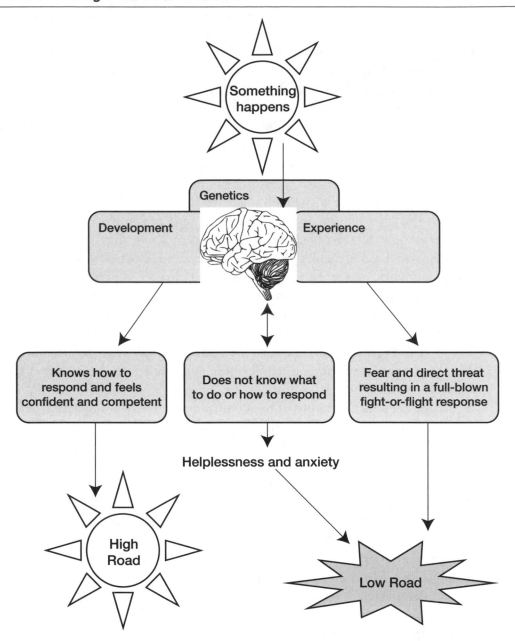

can only approximate what might or might not cause a particular reaction or interpretation for any one individual. But we do know that in general self-efficacy grounded in confidence and mastery, as well as a positive, well-regulated, and healthy physical environment are essential to traveling the high road.

Paul MacLean. Neuroscientist Paul MacLean's triune brain theory was perhaps the first to elaborate on the physiological aspects of such a continuum (Corey & Gardner, 2006). MacLean suggested that the brain developed three deeply interconnected but functionally different regions that evolved in successive stages over time.

> Have you seen the fish squirm and wiggle in the heron's crop as it is swept along to be slowly peeled away by burning juices? Have you heard birds cough themselves to death from air-saccultitis? Have you risen in the night to give them cough syrup? Have you seen the cat play with a mouse? Have you seen cancer slowly eat away or strangle another human being? The misery piles up like stellar gases tortured by a burning sun. Then why, slowly, progressively, did nature add something to the neocortex that for the first time brings a heart and a sense of compassion into the world? Altruism, empathy— these are almost new words. Altruism—"to the other." Empathy— "compassionate identification with another individual." . . . In designing for the first time a creature that shows a concern for suffering of other living things, nature seems to have attempted a 180 degree turnabout from what had been a reptile-eat-reptile and dog-eat-dog world. (MacLean, 1978, pp. 340–449)

While the linearity of MacLean's approach has been questioned, the underlying pattern seems to be remarkably robust.

1. The ancient reptilian brain, and the first to evolve, deals with biologically programmed (reflexive and unconscious) functions as well as primitive emotions that involve some aspects of fear or aggression and sexuality (Panksepp, 1998).
2. The limbic system, which is in the center of the brain, including the amygdala and hippocampus, deals with more sophisticated aspects of fear and anger and is also the seat of many social emotions.
3. The higher and most recently evolved centers of the brain, which he called the "neomammalian brain" and which largely consists of the neocortex, houses the cognitive, rational, and higher order functions.

MacLean contends that an individual's state of mind (our term) is indicative of the region of the brain that predominates. The most basic, reflexive responses of the reptilian brain prevail in times of fear and alarm; the emotional reactions of the limbic system prevail when one experiences arousal and vigilance; and the higher order functioning of the neocortex is contingent on being calm and engaged. This view maps perfectly onto Perry's continuum

FIGURE 11.2. Perry's Continuum

MIND STATES

CALM AND ENGAGED

- The most active part of the brain is the *cortex* (houses the executive functions of the prefrontal cortex).
- One can think in abstract terms (metaphorical, logical, or symbolic) and can access multiple types of higher order thinking.
- One is able to deal with long-term goals (longer time horizons) and planning, self control, and mastery over emotional reactions.

AROUSED/VIGILANT

- The most active part of the brain is the *subcortex and limbic system.*
- One can focus on concrete learning tied to practice and performance of known information gathered by expert others. *Concrete aspects* of learning are the primary focus and may include:
  How much time is needed
  How many words are required
  Performing for purpose of replicating a skill or recalling correct answers
  Performing for explicit extrinsic rewards
  Dealing more with isolated facts than integration of thought and understanding.

ALARM

- The most active parts of the brain are the *limbic system and the midbrain.*
- One is emotionally charged. Thinking is inflexible and very concrete.
- One can only think in terms of enforced learning (enforced by someone else) involving narrowly defined pre-specified goals tied to specific outcomes.

FEAR

- The most active parts of the brain include the *midbrain and brainstem.*
- One is limited to reflexive/reactive thinking.
- Learning is limited to satisfying immediate needs driven by feelings of urgency.

TERROR

- The most active part of the brain is the *brainstem.*
- One is almost totally reflexive with little or no awareness present.
- One has no sense of time or connection to what is happening.

(Figure 11.2), and is in harmony with Maslow's general approach, two other theories we introduce below.

Joseph LeDoux. LeDoux, among many, has shown that the pathway of fear ranges from a full-blown fight-or-flight response to more subtle variations. In essence, if a person is not overly frightened, some complex and higher order mental and emotional processes can be accessed and the person can handle most situations with moderate comfort. As LeDoux (1996) notes, "No matter how useful automatic reactions are, they are only a quick fix, especially to humans. Eventually you take control. You make a plan and carry it out" (p. 176).

LeDoux also suggests that there is a difference between anxiety and fear. He defines *anxiety* as a state that results when there is a concern over what might happen, whereas *fear* is a reaction to a specific and immediately present situation. Someone experiencing an uncomfortable sense of anxiety is worried about what *might* take place as a result of what they did or didn't do. Some examples include not having completed a promised project others are relying on, being unprepared to present work to fellow students and/or experts at a scheduled feedback session, having procrastinated or put off essential required tasks tied to an agreed-upon deadline, or being asked to demonstrate some competency that has not been mastered. It is also present when people find themselves in long-term situations for which they are not prepared; an illness of a loved one or being in a dysfunctional relationship are two of many examples.

Anxiety impedes performance because it limits the capacity to be fully creative, explore possibilities that go beyond everyday expectations, or act decisively in unfamiliar circumstances. The reactions to, and consequences of, both fear and anxiety tend to be unpleasant but differ in degree.

Bruce Perry. Bruce Perry's (2000, 2003) work with trauma patients also corroborates the existence of a continuum. He has documented how fear accompanied by a sense of helplessness engages the brain and body differently from other mind states, and shows that these differences result in a coherent set of emotions, perceptions, and actions. He summarizes what happens to the brain and behavior when fear and threat associated with a sense of helplessness and/or fatigue predominate. Figure 11.2 illustrates how a safe and empowered environment allows individuals to access higher order functions housed in the prefrontal or integrative cortex of the brain (executive functions). This happens most readily in what he calls the "calm and engaged" mind state. This state is fundamentally different from mind states of "arousal," "alarm," "fear," and "terror." He has documented how each state is accompanied by activation of specific brain areas and how those areas determine access to cognitive capacities. We have taken the liberty of summarizing his conclusions in Figure 11.2.

It is important for educators to note that Perry distinguishes between an active response (*hyperarousal*), which results in individuals acting out aggressively, and a passive (*dissociative*) response, which results in withdrawal and disinterest. We all recognize daydreaming as a natural and often pleasant phenomenon. But individuals in the lower levels of the passive continuum are predominately in a world made of daydreams and when in alarm, fear, or terror, lose contact with (are dissociated from) reality.

Identifying a student in the passive or dissociative state can provide a challenge for teachers. Teachers tend to identify and seek help for the defiant student who acts out aggressively, but they can often fail to notice or recognize students who "behave" but do not engage.

The Psychotherapeutic Connection

A group of scientists and philosophers called Gestalt theorists at one point held much sway over a more holistic view of mind and life. The word *Gestalt* means "the whole thing." While many thinkers and researchers were focused on identifying idiosyncratic characteristics, a bit like focusing on one tree, Gestalt theorists were focusing on how the trees acted together to prove that there was a whole forest. They foreshadowed this time when we are beginning to put the pieces together and science is beginning to see more of the "whole" brain and human being (Pessoa, 2008). The Gestalt theorists did not have the benefit of neuroscience research but provided a holistic perspective that some neuroscientists are now using and validating (Fuster, 2003; Greene, 2010).

Gestalt thinking deeply influenced humanistic thought or what became known as humanism. The reason it is important to recall leaders in this movement is because from the beginning they envisioned a path of development that closely resembles the continuum we are discussing here. Additionally, they saw human beings as integrated "wholes," not as machines or in terms of parts that needed fixing. They did not separate out body, mind, and cognition but looked at how the whole person functioned and was affected by experience and the environment. Three major figures need to be considered: Abraham Maslow, Art Combs, and Carl Rogers.

Abraham Maslow. A fountainhead of much that is agreed upon about human motivation and capacity is summarized in the work of psychologist Abraham Maslow (1954, 1968) and his hierarchy of needs. He contended that

> One set of forces clings to safety and defensiveness out of fear, tending to regress backward, hanging on to the past, afraid to grow, . . . afraid to take chances, afraid to jeopardize what he already has, afraid of independence, freedom and separateness. The other set of forces impels him forward toward wholeness of self and uniqueness of self, toward full functioning of all his capacities, toward confidence in the face of the external world at the same time that he can accept his deepest, real, unconscious self. (Maslow, 1968, p. 46)

FIGURE 11.3. Maslow's Hierarchy of Needs

In essence, he argued, basic needs have to be satisfied before more complex needs can be dealt with. Figure 11.3 shows our version of the original model of Maslow's hierarchy.

There are two main points to be made here. First, and once again, we see the connection between taking care of the most basic functions first because they ensure survival. He called these "deficiency needs." And second, we begin to gain a sense of the sorts of additional capacities that are available to people once safety has been established. These occur as "growth needs," which involve the higher levels of the pyramid and are only activated when an individual has passed beyond many fears. Such an individual is largely free to respond more realistically and openly to life. A truly self-actualized person possesses a greater level of awareness. Maslow himself noted that the hierarchy is dynamic and the dominant need is always shifting, and that a single behavior may relate to several needs.

Arthur W. Combs. Arthur Combs was a perceptual psychologist who believed that understanding individuals' beliefs about themselves and others would provide the greatest insight into their actions. He adopted the Gestalt view that bypassed the notion of conscious and unconscious. Instead, he preferred the concept of a "perceptual field" that constituted the reality or awareness experienced by any individual at the moment of action. A person was either aware or not aware of something. Things were either in focus or below the level of awareness.

> The perceptual field is the universe of naive experience in which each individual lives, the everyday situation that . . . each person takes to be

reality. No matter what we are told, our own perceptual field will always
seem real, substantial, and solid to us. . . . So strong is our feeling of
reality with respect to our perceptual field that we seldom question it.
(Combs, 1999, p. 21)

In terms of our present discussion of the continuum, Combs insisted that
the field of awareness became smaller or more constricted under conditions of
fear and anxiety. When a person feels threatened there is a narrowing of the
perceptual field. This means that the range of what can be perceived is limited,
as is the capacity to be flexible and adjust to what is needed. One of the reasons why frightened people do not respond as expected is that they literally do
not grasp cues or see what seems to be right in front of their noses.

In the context of education, Combs and Snygg (1959) argued:

As long as teachers insist on forcing material that, from the students'
perspective, has no relevance to them or their lives, education will be
an arduous process. Teachers must get to know their students, because
the motivation to learn is inside of them, in their phenomenal fields and
phenomenal selves.

Carl Rogers. Carl Rogers, also known as the father of Person-centered
Therapy, believed in what he called the "fully functioning person." Thousands
of therapists practice his approach to therapy, which is based on the idea that
individuals are capable of solving their most difficult problems if and when
the appropriate conditions exist. He spelled out three conditions: empathy,
congruence, and positive regard. *Congruence* referred to a sense of coherent
honesty—there was little difference between what that individual said and
actually did—and *positive regard* referred to a deep respect between client and
therapist. He later took this perspective into education where he documented
profound individual changes and learning in students in his book *Freedom to
Learn* (Rogers, 1969), based on person-centered education.

All three of the above perspectives shared the belief that human beings
could "grow" and develop naturally into intellectually competent, compassionate, healthy, happy, and productive human beings, given the right conditions and relationships.

Others

Although we don't have the space to deal with them here, many other
theorists have explored human functioning in terms of stages and a continuum that allowed for the development of and access to increased capacities.

Examples include Jean Piaget (1976, 1977), Benjamin Bloom (1956/1984), Hans Selye (1956, 1974), Lawrence Kohlberg (1984), Ken Wilber (2001), and Alexander and Langer (1990).

WHAT DOES A POSITIVE MIND STATE LOOK LIKE IN A CLASS OR SCHOOL?

If positive conditions can affect a student's capacity to learn, what would such improved functioning look like?

Here is an illustration, framed in terms of what is called positive affect. *Positive affect* is a mind state accompanied by a mild increase in positive feelings brought about by common everyday events. These feelings include moments of contentment and joy, interspersed with hard work that is intrinsically motivating (Ashby, Isen, & Turken, 1999). Individuals learning in such environments show an increase in the higher order capacities we have been identifying as part of the executive functions:

- Have better working memory
- Have better episodic memory (memory for events)
- See more options for solving problems
- Are more flexible in their thinking
- Are more competent in dealing with social relationships (helpfulness and sociability)
- Have greater verbal fluency (give more innovative examples)
- Have better decision-making abilities

When a person experiences positive affect, neurotransmitters that affect learning are stimulated. For example, the neurotransmitter dopamine is stimulated sufficiently to stimulate acetylcholine. Acetylcholine stimulates the hippocampus, which is the gateway to forming new memories.

A similar but higher intensity experience of the high road is the "state of flow," a state of concentration that is both pleasant and productive, as researched and described by Mihaly Csikszentmihalyhi (2008). Factors that contribute to this state include the following:

1. Clear goals and immediate feedback
2. Opportunities for acting decisively that are relatively frequent and matched by one's perceived ability to act
3. Merge of action and awareness so that there is a clear focus of mind

4. Concentration on the task at hand so that irrelevant stimuli disappear from consciousness and worries and concerns are temporarily suspended
5. A sense of potential control

We synthesized the approaches described and found the patterns shown in Figure 11.4. In essence, there is a cluster of factors that induce the low road, and another cluster that induce the high road.

Notice that the conditions that invite the low road can also sabotage the perception/action cycle and PA/L.

NEXT STEPS AND A WORD OF CAUTION

As a practical matter, educators need a way to get a handle on all of this. As we mention above, we coined the term *Relaxed Alertness* as a way of describing the optimal state of mind for deep learning (Caine & Caine, 1991; Caine et al., 2009). It consists of low perceived threat and high intrinsic challenge and motivation. In this state, students and educators feel competent, confident, and motivated. We expand upon this in some detail in Chapter 16.

This does not mean that the goal is for students to just "feel good" at all times. Learning needs to be rigorous and challenging. As pointed out in Chapter 9, there will be times of frustration and anxiety, problems that seem to be too difficult, and so on. Learning must also be accompanied by genuine and explicit feedback and conditions that support what students are attempting to accomplish. Feeling challenged and empowered through documentable behavior and actions appreciated by others whom students respect is what we are after. The task is to help generate the overall states of mind that make it possible for students to do the following:

- Make effective decisions
- Handle difficult situations
- Work with others
- Monitor their own emotions
- Think in the long term as well as the short term
- Solve problems
- Be flexible and adaptable
- Combine intuition with rigorous thought
- Generally and regularly function at the high levels that are absolutely indispensable for genuinely high standards

FIGURE 11.4. Summary of Conditions That Invite the Low Road or High Road

Some conditions that contribute to a sense of helplessness and invite the low road	*Some conditions that contribute to a sense of confidence, competence, and motivation and invite the high road*
• Absence of control • Fatigue • Meaninglessness and absence of purpose • Externally imposed deadlines unrelated to one's personal interest, abilities or talents • Pessimism about personal abilities and outcomes • Absence of support	• A sense of personal control • Health and rest • A sense of meaning and purpose • Manageable tasks and projects • Meaningful parameters, even if strict • Positive attitude • Belief in one's capabilities • Resilience (ability to bounce back from adversity) • Support
POSSIBLE RESULTS	POSSIBLE RESULTS
• Rebellion or disinterest • Concrete thinking • Fragmented thinking • Poor effort or performance • Reversion to stereotypic behavior (reflexive) • Inability to perceive success as process • Short time horizons (can't see long-term implications) • Distracted • Anxious	• Focused thinking • Capacity to deal with abstractions • Taking reasonable risks • Expanded effort • Ability to work with ambiguous situations • Dealing with interconnected concepts like ecology and systems thinking • Long-term planning • Self-control

As our exploration of future needs demonstrates (Chapter 4), every learner needs to master more of these higher order capacities. The tragedy of the current system of education is that so much of what is done in the name of education elicits the low road, and therefore sabotages higher order functioning and powerful learning. We examine that issue in the next chapter.

CHAPTER 12

How the System Engages
the Low Road

Threat rigidity is the theory that an organization, when perceiving itself under siege (i.e., threatened or in crisis), responds in identifiable ways: Structures tighten; centralized control increases; conformity is stressed; accountability and efficiency measures are emphasized; and alternative or innovative thinking is discouraged.

—Brad Olsen and Dena Sexton (2008, p. 15)

TRAVELING THE HIGH ROAD is not as simple as it may seem. No teacher or educator lives and works in isolation. Each is part of the larger system. And almost all the workings of the larger system serve to drive students and educators down the low road. The power of the system to influence and keep things at this level cannot be underestimated.

THE BIG PICTURE

We have synthesized the work of the researchers mentioned in the previous chapter in order to create a schematic for educators that addresses the interaction between motivation, mind state, and cognition.

For this purpose we have created what we call the "Access V" (see Figure 12.1). The low road is at the bottom of the "V," the high road is at the top.

We have given each mind state a number for the sake of clarity even though divisions are not clear-cut. The primary point is that the bottom of the "V" refers to mind states largely driven by fear of failure and most likely to result in compliance (doing what they are told). The center of the "V" represents a transitional state that involves more choice and initiative. The top of the "V" indicates the potential for higher order thinking and functioning.

The "V" clearly meshes with Maslow's theory, as described in the preceding chapter. However, we have inverted the pyramid because one's capacity

FIGURE 12.1. The "V"

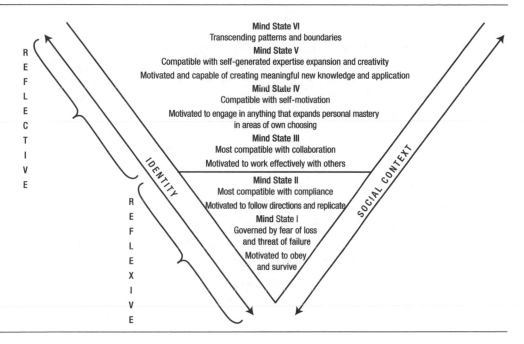

to learn expands with the conditions we have indicated. Although the number of individuals arriving at the highest level of human functioning may be the smallest when it comes to the general population (Maslow's model), the capacity to think and function at this level is directly in relationship to the greater degree of freedom and challenge provided by one's environment.

It is easy to see that the "V" is relevant beyond the classroom. Of course, there is often a need for orderly, systematic procedures. Indeed, they are sometimes crucial to a sense of safety. However, when there is a bureaucratic, standardized process, driven primarily by coercion and the absence of intrinsic motivation, this process can easily generate a mind state of fear and helplessness and can trigger the survival response at almost every level of the system, from classroom to boardroom. Notice how motivation at the bottom of the "V" focuses on obedience and fear of loss or threat of failure. So much of teaching and the current emphasis on testing ends up here. Unfortunately, almost the entire system, from students to teachers to most administrators, has become convinced that the only way to reach "high standards" is to use coercion that triggers fear of failure as the motivator. This is beautifully articulated in an article by Brad Olsen and Dena Saxton (2008) entitled "Threat Rigidity, School Reform, and How Teachers View Their Work Inside Current Education Policy Contexts." Much of education generates and then follows the path of survival, of contraction, of doing what is necessary to get through the day and to get through life.

> [T]hreat rigidity occurs in a number of similar ways: by centralizing and restricting the flow of information, by constricting control, by emphasizing routinized and simplified instructional/assessment practices, and by applying strong pressure for school personnel to conform. (Olsen & Sexton, 2008, p. 14)

On the other hand, there is a dynamic system that calls for and utilizes intrinsic motivation, allows for choice and personal decision making, and so generates self-efficacy and releases what Lozanov (1978) called the "hidden reserves" and underused capacities of the brain/mind of staff and students.

Although we have been talking in stark, black-and-white terms, the situation is clearly much more complex than we have so far described. For instance, if a person is highly self-motivated and truly wants to perform well or achieve something, and also has a sense of self-efficacy, then he may not walk the low road, irrespective of what the system does. For that person, the overall process might contribute to personal challenge and hence contribute to his ability to access both creativity and higher order functions. Similarly, some students love the more traditional approach and thrive in it because they have mastered the demands of grades and high-stakes testing in the course of doing what the teacher requires. They feel confident and competent in the tightly structured format that for many other students leads to boredom and indifference. And, as we have seen with highly motivated waves of immigrants, some students and their families may place a high value on "acquiring" education no matter how it is delivered in order to help them survive and succeed in a new country, and they bring this riveting intrinsic motivation to bear on learning in any school setting. Moreover, mind states flow into each other and shift according to a wide range of circumstances. For example, a student motivated by the need to comply will follow directions (Mind States I and II) but may also be motivated to connect with others (Mind State III) as in the case of sports or social networking.

In general, however, education is best served by the high road. It is a path of expansion, of creativity, of setting out to make a difference. It is important for seeing interconnectedness, thinking beyond the concrete and in the long term, and performing in ways that engage executive functions. And in everyday terms, it is the state characterized by a sense of confidence, competence, and motivation to learn and be motivated to accept a challenge.

> A mind state does not ensure higher order thinking and application of expertise, but these cannot happen without the appropriate mind state and the motivation that comes with it.

WAYS IN WHICH THE SYSTEM INDUCES THE LOW ROAD

Unfortunately, public schools and current policy consistently and systematically generate the low road by inducing mind states most compatible with compliance and obedience. *The low road is real.* Here we review the sorts of perceptions that result in the low road (see Figure 11.4 in the previous chapter) and then explore some of the ways in which they are created by the traditional education system. The low road drives perception and action as a practice that leads people to experience the following conditions:

Loss of control

Meaninglessness and an absence of purpose

Absence of support

Burdened by inappropriate time pressures and the need to produce
    largely meaningless (to the person) results

Disconnectedness and an absence of relationship

What is most important is that under these conditions higher order functioning is sabotaged.

For many years we have watched the power and force of the traditional model with its persistent focus and emphasis on using threat to "improve" student learning. No matter what the original intentions may have been, what actually happens cannot be ignored. For example—and this has repeated itself in one form or another across the country—at a workshop in Wyoming we were puzzled by an apparent lack of participation in a process we had designed for maximum participation. Before the day was over a group of teachers we had been watching came up to us and quietly told us that they loved what we were showing them but they had been here before. Other very exciting and well-meaning consultants had worked with them previously. But each time, after they had felt some hope, the district extinguished any and all efforts to accommodate what they had learned. "It isn't you," they told us, "but after you leave, they tell us that there is only one bottom line and that involves test scores." No time is ever given for teachers to implement anything else besides teaching that would directly impact testing. Like all sensible human beings, they dared not deviate from direct instruction.

Now we are going to examine some of the specific ways in which the traditional education system leads to the low road.

Standardizing Teaching

America has always been seen as one of the most creative and productive countries, the question of equity and noble intentions notwithstanding. And yet a dominant thrust of many "reform" efforts is to standardize teaching (Ravitch, 2010). As we mentioned before, this is found in highly structured pacing guidelines and materials that direct what teachers should say and do in specific classes on specific material. It is reinforced by administrators who proudly proclaim that they know precisely what every student will be studying no matter where they are in the district and who walk corridors and peer into classrooms to enforce standardized practices. When this happens, teachers are literally not permitted to adjust what they do to respond to the needs, abilities, and responses of individual students, whether or not the students seem to understand what is being "taught"; they may not respond to the varying enthusiasms and crises that occur when 30 young people are pulled together in different situations and contexts; they may not take more time or less time to work on specific issues, whether students have mastered the material or not. In short, many teachers are deprived of the capacity to manage their classrooms and relate to, and work with, individual students and fellow professionals, even though they are being held accountable for the results. So there is loss of control, loss of relationship, the burden of time pressures unrelated to student needs, and an absence of meaning because there is no opportunity to connect materials to the issues that students care about.

Is it any wonder that teachers avoid taking risks and revert to doing what is best to save their skins? And that students respond accordingly?

And, most important of all, *Newsweek* reports (Bronson & Merryman, 2010) that for the first time creativity in the United States has declined. We predicted that when standardized teaching and the emphasis on testing was first introduced.

Note also that standardized instruction ignores the world of technology almost totally. Computers and other tools may be used, but usually as ways of contributing to a tightly structured process tied to the old meme of transmission/direct instruction (TDI). Today the problem is even more drastic as we add the divide between "wired" students who are connected in multiple ways to a world online that can give them more information and motivation than any classroom confined by a school environment. Thus, in addition to an entire world of resources being kept out of the classroom, most students are disconnected from the world in which they feel at home. Sometimes, of course, this disconnection is quite appropriate. However, the wholesale barricades set up against the world of videotech are not warranted.

The Abuse of Standards by Fragmenting Knowledge

We have addressed this issue to some extent in Chapter 4. Some core standards, in the sense of a moderately prescribed curriculum, make perfect sense. Students do need to learn to read; they do inhabit the world of videotech; even in a multicultural world, the culture of their lives is important to master, and so on. The issue of what to include is a large one, and we cannot discuss it here.

The critical point for our purposes is not with the concept of having standards but with what is done in the name of high standards. Here, for instance, is a perfectly understandable example from the Common Core Standards (http://www.corestandards.org) that are now being adopted by many states. These are for reading informational text in Grades 9–10.

Key Ideas and Details

1. Cite strong and thorough textual evidence to support analysis of what the text says explicitly as well as inferences drawn from the text.
2. Determine a central idea of a text and analyze its development over the course of the text, including how it emerges and is shaped and refined by specific details; provide an objective summary of the text.
3. Analyze how the author unfolds an analysis or series of ideas or events, including the order in which the points are made, how they are introduced and developed, and the connections that are drawn between them.

Craft and Structure

4. Determine the meaning of words and phrases as they are used in a text, including figurative, connotative, and technical meanings; analyze the cumulative impact of specific word choices on meaning and tone (e.g., how the language of a court opinion differs from that of a newspaper).
5. Analyze in detail how an author's ideas or claims are developed and refined by particular sentences, paragraphs, or larger portions of a text (e.g., a section or chapter).

6. Determine an author's point of view or purpose in a text and analyze how an author uses rhetoric to advance that point of view or purpose.

The problem for education is created when the standards are framed by the TDI meme. First, note that the standards are framed as abstract sets of ideas and procedures. They are not framed in terms of how they impact student lives. While the Common Core materials themselves do not prescribe any type of pedagogy and do not call for the standards to be implemented in a linear way (see "Introduction"), in practice many educators simply deal with them sequentially and through the TDI meme so that they bear little or no relationship to the lives that students live nor to what they understand and care about. When pieces of text are used that are disconnected from life and student interests, the material is abstract, lacks any emotional bond, is usually perceived as meaninglessness and irrelevant, and tends to trigger the low road.

It should be mentioned that the need to bridge standards to reality is acknowledged in the Common Core materials. Unfortunately, many attempts to incorporate standards into student lives miss the point. It is all well and good to create a word problem that links standards to the real world. But that is radically different from living the standards through a project that actually engages the real world. It is the difference between a teacher giving the class the task of analyzing an article from a newspaper about immigration, for instance, and mentoring students who have chosen to examine immigration in their town and coming across that article in their search for information.

Second, note that when coverage of standards is uppermost in the minds of teachers, there tends to be little room for anything else. Student interests, sudden enthusiasm in a classroom about a real-world event, and alternative ways of thinking about the entire subject are simply preempted. This sucks the life out for both teachers and students. And so the gateway to the low road is opened.

Of course, the art of teaching should be to make these ideas meaningful by engaging them through P/AL. But for the most part, that calls for a sort of teaching that respects learning as the expansion of networks and aims for dynamic learning (Pessoa, 2008; South Australia, 2010).

Third, note that when content is fragmented, students memorize but do not understand. For instance, we have seen third and fourth graders ask questions that seemed unbelievably absurd because they reveal such an absence of coherent, integrated knowledge or broader knowledge network. A recent example is a third-grade classroom where students had seen a film on Plymouth Rock that focused on the landing of the Pilgrims. This "lesson" was to help students understand the origins of Thanksgiving. The teacher was inviting students to ask their personal, real questions. At first students did not seem to understand what was meant by "their own questions," because they were usually answering questions put by others rather than framing their own questions. But after repeated prompting by the teacher, they took the plunge. Two questions that stood out were:

> "Were the Pilgrims our enemies?"
> "Did this happen before or after the dinosaurs were on earth?"

In the example taken above from the Common Core Standards, memorization reveals itself in students who may "learn" a set of procedures for analyzing text and the craft of writing. They may, for instance, be able to define and explain "figurative, connotative, and technical meanings." And yet they may have almost no capacity to use these ideas and processes spontaneously and appropriately when seeking to read for information in the real world. These are students who can pass tests by recalling surface information and facts, but have no clue about the connections linking facts that are being "taught." What is in fact happening is that these students have information that is inadequately networked. Moreover, a vast wealth of information and experience to which many students do relate has to be ignored. These are precisely the sorts of practices that induce the low road.

When standards are interpreted in terms of traditional teaching practice, the high road is difficult to access and inclusion of technology becomes nonsensical.

Obsession with Standardized Tests

Ten years ago we did not take the pressure of testing that seriously. Every school we have ever worked with for a significant period of time had increased their test scores (Caine & Caine, 1997a; Caine, 2008). We did not anticipate the number of district-mandated procedures gathered to "help" schools succeed by requiring "teacher proof"; standardized material; single, adopted textbooks; and consultants. And all this was to ensure success spelled out almost exclusively in terms of the traditional meme tied to test scores.

The conceptual blind spot we have as a culture is to assume that test scores, genuine understanding, and real-world outcomes are directly linked. They are not. The link is indirect. That means that an obsession with test scores actually interferes with the sorts of processes that lead to the kind of learning students need to master most, such as higher order thinking and the development of rich, interconnected knowledge networks. And educators are not encouraged to look for more complex indicators that students have actually grasped what is being taught. They are, however, held accountable for success based almost exclusively on tests. This is even more pronounced because salaries, tenure and promotion, and even allowance of a school to keep its doors open are now in danger of being evaluated in terms of student test scores. All of this increases the distance between teachers and students and induces the helplessness that is at the heart of the low road.

Factory Models of Time Management Are Created

As illustrated in Chapter 3, most schools are managed like production lines. This supports learning at the bottom of the "V." Targets are set. Timelines are created. Modules of "learning" are prescribed to occur in prespecified chunks of time. The process is checked and rechecked. And so a context is created for standardized instruction and assessment. We appreciate that many schools are not like this, but they are very much in the minority. The key here is that administrator- and teacher-mandated strict time limits tend to be unrelated to the needs of the learner or tasks in question. Although deadlines are a fact of life, unrealistic timelines and relatively meaningless targets set by others contribute to the loss of control and sense of helplessness that trigger the low road.

Education Based Generally on Control and Coercion

Much of what is done to change teaching is done by coercion through the wielding of rewards and punishments, and much of the way that teachers manage students involves coercion, as we have shown in earlier chapters.

The disastrous consequence is that, in the name of raising standards, the system creates the conditions that inadvertently contribute to lowering standards. Compliance does not result in student-centered and purpose-driven learning. And fear of failure does not result in doing one's personal best.

How Students Respond

Students, like the rest of us, show what they value by how they spend their time. And as Chapter 1 points out, students spend over 50 hours a week on videotech. They are literally executing their own life choices. And largely as a consequence of how the system functions, most do not choose to spend time on "schoolwork." Today's students have access to an infinite number of options, and they can choose to embark on activities and have experiences that make them feel good about themselves or in which they are otherwise interested. Why should they prefer an environment that is largely unsupportive and where control is top-down? Why should they invest energy and enthusiasm in a system that insists they need to master what to them is not challenging, is little understood, and lacks personal meaning, creativity, and variety? "Nationwide, 7,000 students drop out every day and only about 70 percent of students graduate from high school with a regular high school diploma" (Miller, 2009; Vallerand, Fortier, & Guay, 1997).

Students can escape to worlds where they have choice and fun, where they can connect with others, involve themselves in possibilities, and have at least a minimal sense of having some personal control. And paradoxically, while schools have minimized the role of the arts or eliminated them entirely (despite all the research on the critical role of the arts to brain development), students everywhere are drawn to music, filming, experimenting with videos, designing Web sites, or exploring photography. And they flock to those who can teach them how to become participants in this explosion of the arts. Even more paradoxically, many spend much of their time learning more about perspective and other design principles.

The result is that many aspects of natural learning are occurring in student lives in the context of doing what they want and pursuing their own goals. For many, technology in all its forms becomes incredibly enticing and inviting. Others, less fortunate and usually with less access, drop out of school and seek other worlds that allow them to take action and experience a sense of self-worth or freedom, even if they end up being deprived in the longer term.

Students who end up feeling worthless, without a clear focus or sense of pride, are easy prey to the escapism that haunts our society from engaging in media overload to drug abuse.

A parent recently explained his frustration with a system that only acknowledges college entrance as the gold standard. "So many kids," he insisted, "want to do other things besides go to college." We agree. The goal should be achieving expertise, be it truck driving, construction, inventing Web sites, or any of the millions of jobs and professions that do not involve 4 years of college. Perhaps most important, he mentioned how many young people feel left out and useless in the current system.

DOES EVERYTHING ABOUT TRADITIONAL EDUCATION INDUCE THE LOW ROAD?

We have been emphasizing the most basic form of teaching, largely because so much current reform seems to be heading in that direction. In practice, as we mentioned earlier in this book, our research and experience suggest that approaches to schooling and teaching occur along a continuum. (We examine this topic in depth in our book *Seeing Education in a New Light*, in press).

Even the basic form of TDI can be enhanced and enlivened. For instance, when students are asked to memorize facts or procedures, there are many tools available to teachers to make the process enjoyable and successful. A teacher can create an environment of Relaxed Alertness for a while where the challenge to memorize material becomes fun. This is the thrust of much that is done in the name of accelerated learning, for instance (Rose, 1998). Provided this is done in an atmosphere of mutual respect, students can master basic dates and places, formulas, or other facts that help them do well on a test, and get good grades in the traditional approach. And the process itself, when it leads to success, can also help students (and teachers) feel a sense of empowerment and challenge, competence and confidence, so that they can successfully navigate assignments and other exams.

There are much more sophisticated approaches to direct instruction, approaches that have students interacting with each other, doing research, solving problems, working on projects, and so on. A very good set of ideas on how this is done can be found on the Annenberg Web site, with regular commentaries by Linda Darling-Hammond (http://www.learner.org/courses/learningclassroom). Another approach is Lauren Resnick's (2010) work on the "Thinking Curriculum." Both of these guide students to think in more complex ways and function at higher levels within the framework of the traditional model—provided system constraints make it possible. And when that happens, there is a move out of the reflexive and into the reflective state. Many more student capacities tend to come "online," intrinsic motivation climbs, and the extremes of the low road tend to be left behind.

Even with these high-level instructional approaches, however, there is a critical difference between students following a teacher's agenda and teachers embedding the standards as they nurture and support student choices and interests. Recall that we are after dynamic knowledge that can be applied spontaneously in situations that call for it. Memorizing a catalog of facts and procedures (even when it is fun to do so) or developing intellectual understanding that does not translate into real-world competence are still limited outcomes. The challenge still is to guide students into the use of higher order thinking, creativity, planning, and negotiating with others in the context of rigorous treatment of the standards. This type of higher order thinking requires a fundamentally different environment and philosophy of learning and teaching.

Does Technology Provide the Solution?

From our perspective this is not even a productive question. It is not either/or. Technology is relevant because of its immense power and the ways in which the larger environment has changed. Technology must be incorporated effectively and meaningfully into education. The goal is to ensure that full functioning of Perception/Action Learning, from the initial enthusiasm caught by a compelling idea to a final product produced for expert feedback in real-world settings. Technology alone does not ensure that. On the contrary, many professors at great institutions are observing a deplorable lack of focus in students who are literally wired around the clock (Dretzin, 2010). These students pride themselves on their ability to multitask and do five or six things at once. They are observed eating, talking on their phones, looking at multiple Web sites on their laptops, all while meeting with a group of "friends" for lunch.

Short-term manipulation of all sorts of information does not ensure excellence or mastery. Only moving through the phases essential for P/AL will do that. And learning that goes into depth, requires complex and meaningful decision making for a specific purpose of significance to the learner, cannot be done without focus, reflection, persistence, and feedback. These are built into P/AL.

Recall that the low road induces and is induced by fragmented thinking. What is needed for the knowledge age is an ability to recognize and deal with interconnectedness, thinking in terms of concepts and broader patterns of relationships, and higher order application and functioning. Unfortunately, there is significant evidence of student failure to function in those higher order ways induced to some extent by an oversaturation of technology, and a speed of human functioning that is actually most compatible with acquiring surface knowledge.

Next Steps Along the Way

As we have shown, a new approach to teaching is needed, one in which a high level of academic content and the real human being are both treated appropriately. And there are still some crucial elements of the behavior of human beings in their learning environments that need to be addressed. That is where we now turn.

CHAPTER 13

Working with Biological Predispositions

By higher level of psychic development we mean a behavior, which is more complex, more conscious and having greater freedom of choice, hence greater opportunity for self-determination.

— Kazimierz Dabrowski (in Cory & Gardner, 2002, p. 328)

THE LOW ROAD affects more than cognition. It affects human behavior and functioning in almost all aspects of life where it is expressed in invisible, automatic, and reflexive ways. Again we look to biology in order to seek a deeper insight into the influences that shape individual behavior and the larger culture. We do this in an effort to understand more about what impacts human behavior at its most basic level, and how the quality of behavior can be elevated when it comes under conscious control in education.

So far we have defined the perception/action dynamic in terms of reflexive actions that occur largely below the level of awareness and function largely in terms of automatic behaviors and responses in everyday life. We now look at another factor that impacts natural learning. We call them *biological predispositions* and there are many. We will focus our exploration on one perspective that we have found extremely valuable for educators.

Even with the best intentions, it is important to recognize that Perception/Action Learning doesn't just play itself out the way educators would like. Students and adults both are constantly diverted and influenced by forces that they do not understand or recognize. These patterns play themselves out in the everyday world as expressions of wants and needs, and they are activated by events and individuals in one's environment. This can be very frustrating to parents, educators, and the students themselves.

For each of us, the environment acts on an array of inbuilt perceptual *predispositions*—patterns that drive how we interpret, organize, and structure experience. The wafting smell of warm bread, the sound of a baby

146

laughing or crying, someone approaching on a dark street, encountering someone from another culture or value system—all of these instantly trigger the largely reflexive and unconscious perception/action dynamic in more or less automatic ways. More specifically, there is a set of deep, almost instinctual modes of perceiving and acting that we all share. We touch on some of them in this chapter.

Advertisers, publishers, media executives, and many video game designers know how to take advantage of these aspects of human nature. They understand how to activate, frame, and drive the predispositions at their most basic levels. Otherwise why would so much media focus on basic issues such as sex and violence? Why would a television station that calls itself the Weather Channel or the History Channel or one focused on nature focus so heavily on disasters in nature or sex and aggression in animals? These topics fascinate and tickle our most basic biological predispositions, but immersion in these issues rarely requires actual reflection, mathematical or scientific understanding, historical knowledge, further research, or literary depth.

A MAP FOR EDUCATORS

One of the most useful ways to get a handle on these deep, reflexive patterns of perception can be found in the triune brain theory of neuroscientist Paul MacLean (1978). MacLean's view of the development and structure of the brain did not include all the complex information neuroscience has added with the help of new technology including the most recent imaging techniques. In that sense his model is more general and simpler (LeDoux, 1996; Patton, 2008), but his theory of social and biological predispositions continues to intrigue biologists and neuroscientists (Panksepp, 1998).

As pointed out in Chapter 11, MacLean argues that the brain has three layers: The reptilian brain houses very basic instincts and was the first layer to evolve; the limbic system largely houses the emotions, and was the second layer to evolve; and the neocortex, the third layer to evolve, houses higher order functions. They all interact in complex networks, but the core point is that many of our basic, reptilian, perceptual predispositions still play themselves out in life in the way of the largely unconscious and reflexive perception/action dynamic. They cannot be eliminated or avoided. That means that they have to be acknowledged and managed.

MacLean's approach is extraordinarily useful for educators for two basic reasons.

1. His way of cataloging these characteristics and behaviors is a guide and way of seeing what is driving students as they act out in schools and classrooms.
2. It helps make sense of the fact that primitive, automatic, or reflexive modes of functioning are exacerbated when the survival response kicks in.

With these ideas we again cross the artificial threshold created between psychology, identity issues, and school-situated academics. The fundamental truths behind these predispositions reveal themselves in our society through media titles and stories as well as story line themes, myths, parables, fables, and magazine articles facing us on shelves lining the exit as we leave the grocery store.

The challenge is to recognize them and then to guide student behavior more intelligently. We begin by describing them and inviting the reader to explore their presence in their own experience.

Reality Check

In order to see how far we have to go in respect to this issue, imagine that we are visiting a typical traditional American high school. We find natural social hierarchies acting themselves out both within the larger community and the classroom. For instance, simply by observing the students in classes and the halls we can readily hear them as they identify the "jocks" and "nerds." We know that on any given day, most students have spent more time on selecting their clothes for that day than studying for the algebra test.

Walking into a classroom, we find students filing into "their" seats, while girls are combing their hair or checking their makeup. And there is the labeling and pigeonholing: So certain individuals are labeled as "smart" or "dumb," "funny" or "weird," based on their appearance or behavior, while other students continually scrutinize what is happening in order to determine their place and actions.

This is the same generation that also spends hours playing video games, watching DVDs or TV, e-mailing and talking with friends, "tweeting," and visiting Web sites like Facebook or MySpace. And here too we find student groups and social status expressed everywhere. They talk of their relationships, sports, YouTube shorts, and a host of topics emerging out of their lives.

Meanwhile, during their time at school, the school or district has restricted the use of personal computers, Web searches (by district-generated firewalls), and cell phones. Teachers come armed with standards and lesson plans for the purpose of having students "learn" using direct instruction (teacher-directed lessons) in order to achieve high test scores. We observe the teacher reminding students of the test on Friday, and with that barely camouflaged motivation-by-threat instilling a fear of failure, we finally see students settle down and listen to the teacher or do their "work."

Depending in part on the value parents have placed on education and the support they provide their adolescents on a consistent basis (limiting TV and entertainment time, having honest discussions, and most of all being present and involved in adolescent decisions) students vary widely in their interest in participating and caring about academics, the teacher's needs, and the social life of the school.

The teachers, of course, have their own legitimate worries. Student failure is *their* failure. Test scores are a matter of public record. And yet much of student attention and focus is out of their control. Others have designed the curriculum *for* students, not *with* students and an eye to student input or engagement. The administration also has been told that test scores must improve or else. As already mentioned, there are ongoing federal and state efforts to tie student test scores to teacher evaluations (see e.g., McNeil, 2009). And as a result the system focuses more and more of its energy on controlling or discouraging student "disruptive" or "inappropriate" behaviors.

Let us now look in a little more depth at some of the predispositions identified by MacLean and foreshadowed in the reality check above. In examining all of them, it is worthwhile asking how higher order thinking can help learners work their way out of being trapped in these basic instinctual patterns.

Flocking and Group Behavior

Flocking is an expression of the fact that the brain/mind is social. Almost everyone needs to belong to or connect with a group of some kind and address the natural need for contact with others. Groups range from families to clans to tribes to nations and include many different sorts of peer groups. MacLean's theory can act as a useful lens through which to view groups and group membership. Gangs and the mafia, as well as "good old boy" (or girl) networks in businesses, politics, and corporations, typically stake out and defend their territory, often through commitment to common beliefs and actions. Membership often requires ritualistic initiation or commitment to common values and beliefs. In schools, gangs come to mind with their signals of clothing and "tagging," as do fraternities, sororities, and the many social groups that make up our society. One can recognize them because participants tend to act and appear together (hence the word *flocking*).

Question: Where, in your experience, do you see flocking and group membership expressing itself in a classroom, in a school, in the community, in politics? In yourself? How could these be channeled in positive ways? Within schools, one suggestion might be to find ways to help more students become more proficient in the sorts of skills and actions that are grounded in student choice in school. The emphasis would be on becoming an expert in hiking, emergent computer technology, video design, or filming, to name a few. Having students organize around these subjects for the purpose of developing expertise, and not simply for the sake of social bonding or satisfying emotional needs, would go a long way to having them teach and support each other. Some schools manage this process by supporting minicourses taught by students to other students. A second suggestion is to find ways to help students notice, reflect on, and take more conscious charge of the ways in which flocking occurs and groups form in the course of their lives in school.

Territoriality

Animals tend to be very clear about their territory and mark or defend it in some way. Many years ago Robert Ardrey (1996) called this "the territorial imperative." In humans this concept tends to be more abstract, and is expressed, for instance, in the notion of ownership. Most people use the terms "*my* house," "*my* family," "*my* country," "*my* room," and "*my* team" to show that these things belong to them and in some way define them (even though land ownership itself is not valued by every culture). Wanting to own or be closely identified with something is part of this natural predisposition. It is not by chance that defense and conquest of territory defined as "mine" or "ours" is a big factor in starting wars. Ownership and territory also serve as themes for video games and is fundamental to many issues played out in sports and on the playground. The average parent and teacher observe these issues and resultant conflicts about "mine" or "my" every day. "My desk," "my friends," "my chair," "my room," "my things" are items to protect and defend. Certainly marking one's territory is a well-known part of what gangs do, rarely realizing that they are using a marking technique used by most animals.

Question: Where, in your experience, do you see territoriality expressing itself in a classroom, in a school, in the community? How might these needs be channeled instead of repressed? One suggestion would be to find authentic ways to have everyone honor the space of others, be it a desk, locker, cubbyhole, or chair. Seen from this perspective, adults simply invading a student's sacred space on the basis of a rumor or suspicion of wrongdoing should give everyone pause. Moving into the space of others should be done with extreme respect. As much as possible, adults should invite student understanding and permission because the level of trust and control that is lost for students can have serious consequences and create a sense of threat and helplessness. A second suggestion is for educators to intentionally raise the issue of territoriality and examine and process the ways in which it occurs in schools and in life. Of course, the challenge here is that adult territoriality becomes fair game in these discussions!

Preening and Ritualistic Display

We do what makes us stand out and attract attention, much like the peacock and other animals that wish to compete with powerful competitors or attract desirable mates. Such adornment may well go back an astonishing 100,000 years (Vanhaeren et al., 2006). This behavior is characterized by the sense of "look at me, I am unique, powerful, and desirable." Preening is revealed by magazine articles titled "Ten Ways to Dress Your Body Better." The television program *American Idol* might serve as a great example of how this behavior gets played out by human beings. Virtual worlds such as *Second Life* (http://secondlife.com/) also call for players to assume new identities and roles that make them more attractive, unique, and stand out from the crowd. In schools across the country students dress in whatever is new or will make them stand out. This includes tattoos, rings in their nose and other body parts, and provocative dress of all sorts. (Note that, paradoxically, they seek to belong and conform at the same time as they seek to stand out). Standing out as being daring or unique may also call for the use of invented or highly descriptive language. Not all students want to be publicly recognized but being recognized as special or unique in some way works for almost anyone.

Question: Where, in your experience, do you see preening and ritualistic display expressing itself in a classroom, in a school, in the community, in society at large? In yourself? Where do you see them in movies, TV programs, and video games? How might these patterns become a positive force and be channeled appropriately? Suggestions include recognizing exceptional achievement and excellence of all kinds including unique qualities, products, or performance. As much as possible recognition should be accompanied by nonjudgmental feedback that focuses on product, not person. And it is always possible to examine the topic deliberately. This can be done very effectively, for example, in courses on media literacy (e.g., see the New Mexico Media Literacy Project at http://www.nmmlp.org). But the issue can be raised in the course of dealing with many of the standards, ranging from literature and history to social studies and literacy (Cambourne, 1993).

Nesting Behaviors

Nesting behaviors have to do with securing and protecting a place of privacy and safety. It refers to establishing and protecting a place for mating and one's young. In contrast to territoriality, this refers to an intimate space. Birds provide, perhaps, the most obvious example, though nesting is an aspect of the use of animal dens of all kinds. In human beings nesting behaviors lead to the creation of a place where one is "at home." The phrase "a house is not a home" conveys the sense of what is meant by nesting.

Schools also need to provide places that are created for the purpose of intimate conversations that are free from interference or control by others. Students and teachers alike need places where genuine safety and relaxation can be experienced. "Time out" in such places should be available to everyone when the need arises.

The concept of "safe space" has been abstracted in many ways. This may be why almost all video games include a "home" base and why almost every Web site has a front page called "home." "Homeroom" is also a familiar term to most Americans. Notice how the word *home* has become metaphorical because how the word is now used may have little if anything to do with the original, concrete meaning. Note that territoriality and nesting overlap. The emphasis here is on the degree of safety, comfort, and warmth of home.

Question: Where, in your experience, do you see nesting behavior and a sense of home expressing itself in a classroom, in a school, in the community? How might this become more effective? Excellent examples come from schools that have taken Relaxed Alertness (creating the optimum state for learning) seriously such as Armeda Middle School in Michigan where the principal has used comfortable furniture and decorative plants to create places in public areas in the school where students and adults can gather. Classical music is also played in the halls and has contributed to the reduction of unwanted behaviors. We have also been struck by the success that some schools have had when students begin to voluntarily participate in cleaning, monitoring, and protecting the school so that it becomes "theirs."

Mating Rituals

Flirting is a mating ritual in any language. It is tied to one of the most primitive survival responses as a species—procreation. Much of what motivates human beings to lose weight or have plastic surgery or wear "the latest" in fashion is motivated by the need to attract sexual partners, even if this is only at an unconscious or reflexive level. Here, too, we recognize the themes that permeate television, movies, video games, and other aspects of the world of entertainment. Mating rituals can sometimes be seen to be encouraged in the early grades and even in small children (such as infant beauty contests) where such behavior is supported by parents. Just look at titles from the magazine stand with headlines that include multiple references to articles on mating, such as "10 Ways to Please Your Man"or "Four Things All Guys Keep Private."

Question: Where, in your experience, do you see mating rituals expressing themselves in a classroom, in a school, in the community? Other than by way of rules enforced by adults, how could the use of seductive clothing be reduced? On television? Commercials? How might this seductive behavior be dealt with more effectively? Although we support variety and diversity of all sorts, we have become advocates of school uniforms. Preening and seductive clothing with the latest in clothing fad or fads of almost any kind really distract from other aspects of education. However, because of the need to have input and control over one's identity, it seems to us that uniforms should be designed with a great deal of input from students, along with periodic rethinking as tastes and design issues emerge.

Deceptive Behaviors

There are many reasons for being deceptive, and David Livingstone Smith (2007) confirms that "the roots of deceit lie deep in our biological past" (p. 10). The general purpose is to help a person (or an animal) get its way. Sometimes animals, such as the chameleon, deceive in order to forestall or confuse their enemy or prey. In human beings, deceptive behaviors can take the form of subverted direct aggression. And it shows up in lying. According to Smith, "Lying can be conscious or unconscious, verbal or nonverbal, stated or unstated" (p. 14). Politics and corporate life provide many examples. In many video games, one of the primary tools is the creation of an image that fools others. An example in schools is cheating on an assignment or a test. Note, also, that deception includes all manner of pretending, from phony smiles to the ways we dress, and the selection of people with whom we associate.

Question: Where, in your experience, do you see camouflage and deceptive behavior expressing itself in a classroom, in a school, in the community and society, and in yourself? How might this be dealt with more effectively? How can raising these issues and applying higher order reasoning help? Examining this issue honestly in groups can be very powerful. Much of the problem, it appears to us, is that deception becomes a key to survival and success within the context of the TDI meme. So an essential key is to adopt an approach to teaching that actually benefits from more openness and honesty. That is one of the virtues of the Guided Experience Approach to instruction that we have begun in these pages.

Establishing and Maintaining Social Hierarchies

Most groups are hierarchical in some way, and so there are patterns of dominance and submission, of leaders and followers. Despite ostensible commitment to democratic processes, most organizations and much of our culture is based on what have been called "dominance hierarchies" (Eisler, 1994). Dominance can be perceived and expressed in a wide range of ways including biological, intellectual, social, and physical superiority. It plays itself out on the playground, in video games, in the teachers lounge. and throughout the community in spheres ranging from sports to business to politics to who counts as a celebrity.

Donald Trump's show, *The Apprentice*, is a perfect example of how a dominance hierarchy plays itself out on television. Dominance hierarchies are reflected, among other things, in the selection and power of leaders and in the relative obedience of followers (MacLean, 1978, p. 322). In video games this is often an overriding theme as well as is the success of players often held in high esteem in their everyday worlds by friends and others.

Question: Where, in your experience, do you see dominance and the maintenance of social hierarchies expressing themselves in a classroom, in a school, in the community? In yourself? One suggestion for reducing the impact of dominance hierarchies is to allow almost everyone to have an opportunity to be recognized for expertise or responsibility of some kind. Our approach to the creation of professional learning communities uses a circle as a vehicle for developing a sense of equality and a field of listening so that educators can become freer and more equal in status (Caine & Caine, 2010). Similar processes can work very well with students in classrooms (Caine et. al., 2009).

THE LOW ROAD REVISITED

As shown in the previous two chapters, people can either operate from the high road or the low road or somewhere along the continuum. However, when students are in low road mode and higher order functioning is suppressed or hijacked, the predispositions assume a much higher profile. The survival response comes to the fore, as LeDoux described. Emotional and reptilian responses then prevail. Les Hart (1978) coined the word *downshifting* to describe this phenomenon.

In practice, this means that the various predispositions are triggered more quickly and reflexively, and operate more intensely and in very stark, black-and-white ways. For example, if some violation of territoriality is deeply felt, then someone who might otherwise just be a person with whom one has a disagreement may end up being perceived as an enemy. Similarly, an opponent in a highly contested competition to get a promotion at an office (or school) may become quite vicious. And the behaviors associated with strong territoriality can play themselves out very dramatically in the classroom, on the playground, and in the adult world.

The problem is that all the predispositions interact, and when in survival mode, a host of tension-generating responses and behaviors can express themselves, both directly and indirectly, in educators and students. In Chapter 12, for instance, we introduced the notion of threat rigidity. That phenomenon can now be reframed in terms of the set of predispositions discussed in this chapter. To begin with, threat rigidity experienced when forced changes are imposed on a school illustrates dominance hierarchies in action. Territoriality, deception, and preening also loom large. Cliques are formed, such that some people are on the "inside" and others are not. And effective functioning is largely undermined.

Power plays by teachers and administrators tend to have a similar impact on students. The sorts of behaviors that we describe when the lower portion of the "V" is activated are all expressions of the predispositions spelled out in this chapter.

The essential point, then, is that biology does not go away. The alternative to ignoring it, then, is to understand and work with it.

Educators and Society at Large Need to Ask Some Hard Questions

Educators are quite right to be concerned about predispositions and related behaviors getting out of hand. Recall how mind states are often influenced by the outside world and how important it is to apply higher order thinking.

And we must stress that we are *not* advocating an end to all disciplinary endeavors. Schools are social organizations where people need to be safe. The point is that the rule of law—the power of imposed discipline—should not be primary. Good teaching in a good atmosphere, where the various predispositions are recognized, can enhance the learning experience for everyone and capitalize on all the predispositions. Media literacy, for instance, can become a vehicle for helping students grasp how the media and technology of all kinds are constructed and what influences their message. By addressing and mastering the basic predispositions in our lives we can gain power over them and learn.

Most of the time, unfortunately, the approaches adopted by schools are to manage, control, and constrain basic tendencies and patterns of functioning, without awareness of what is actually happening and without helping students recognize what is going on. So, as already pointed out, many "discipline" programs have been established for schools based on rewards and punishments, the goal of which is to suppress or eliminate the more automatic types of behavior in students.

One major problem of course is that most of the tools of traditional classroom management tend to trigger the survival response, so that the basic predispositions take over, usually with the teacher being seen as a dominant and hostile member of a different tribe or group.

The sad fact is that the system tends to ignore or suppress the basic, innate, behavioral tendencies of students, and by doing so it activates them to its own disadvantage. Then when extra suppressive measures are introduced, the survival response is simply accentuated. And the predispositions that educators are seeking to control are actually energized. Students become rebellious, angry, violent, withdrawn, disinterested, and more. One reason for adopting a radically different approach to teaching, and to move beyond the TDI meme, is to create the conditions that capitalize effectively and appropriately on the basic biological predispositions of students and staff. If schools or learning environments are to be positive and coherent with everyone adhering to common codes, then everyone must be appropriately involved in designing and maintaining those. Understanding one's own behavior is a big part of that.

When students are not seen as valued and respected participants in school life, when they rarely have a designated place or territory of their own (even lockers have been eliminated in many schools), they are at the bottom of the hierarchy, leaving them to act out the need to be superior in some fashion (bullying may be one example). They dress to please each other or to rebel against adult society; they engage in deception by trying to outwit teachers; and so on. In effect, some of the most powerful driving forces that guide the ways in which students perceive their world—and the curriculum—are used to protect themselves, often by treating curriculum as irrelevant. The old approach of controlling behavior using coercion plays havoc with these natural needs, distorts them, and must be reexamined.

Perhaps most important, relationships need to be nurtured, and communities need to be built on common understandings and goals that foster collaboration. What educators need to do, in effect, is to translate the power of these basic aspects of the perception/action dynamic into a more intelligent type of healthy social environment. How can students learn to relate to issues of ownership, sexual attraction, and one-upmanship? Where are the opportunities for students to be heard, have significant input, and get recognized? How can all students experience leadership? And how can we integrate this more sophisticated way of functioning as human beings into the ways in which students experience literature, history, science, and mathematics?

This is certainly where some sophisticated video gaming is ahead of most schooling. Shaffer (2006) refers to some of these games as epistemic games. Here students not only learn about science but venture into science as scientists. They make discoveries by applying rules of conduct as well as using scientific procedures that mirror the world of a scientist. By dealing with academic fields as historians, inventors, writers, and artists, students not only learn how to practice their craft but how to act and interact in a world filled with real-world consequences. As they compete with others or work together on projects, they are exposed to ways of behaving and negotiating, solving personal and interpersonal dilemmas, and dealing with moral and ethical issues as they apply to their goals and work. These are beautiful examples of how to integrate the social world and academics—which are not separated or isolated in real-world experiences or in the brain.

What Might It Look Like?

Applying these practices to a learning environment in schools will require a totally new way of looking at instruction. This is what is essential to Perception/Action Learning and what the Guided Experience Approach models (Chapters 15–18). All of it will require a different kind of social community.

By way of example, Geoffrey visited an elementary school in Colorado some time ago. As he walked into a math class he initially thought that he was in a traditional classroom. Students were in chairs and one was at the blackboard writing. As he stayed longer he realized that the students were largely in charge, writing their solutions on the board and being systematically questioned and challenged by their peers. The entire process was orderly and students were fully engaged with what was happening. Here was a superb example of students being heard, having significant input, and getting recognized for their work and ideas. The point is that all the basic drives and instincts—for belonging, for recognition, for safety, for a place in the group and more were being satisfied while at the time the focus was on mathematics.

WHERE TO BEGIN?

The conclusion is as simple as it is daunting. Students bring the totality of their humanity to school with them. And *all* of it is engaged in the perception/ action dynamic, cycle, and P/AL. The fundamental predispositions described above operate throughout a student's life in school. When they are suppressed, they still operate in stealth mode. So they either detract from learning, or they can be recognized and worked with in order to support learning. The latter is much more difficult, but that is the path of natural learning. And it is one of the secrets to accessing many of the unused capacities available to every student that can help them enjoy education, access creativity and innovation, and function at much higher levels.

Thus the place to begin is with a view of learning and teaching that naturally works with the innate predispositions of students and guides them into more appropriate modes of expression. We take the first step along that path with the Guided Experience Approach introduced in Part IV.

CHAPTER 14

How a Village, School, and Society Teach

Our mirror neurons fire as we watch someone else, for example, scratch their head or wipe away a tear, so that a portion of the pattern of neuronal firing in our brain mimics theirs. This maps the identical information from what we are seeing onto our own motor neurons, letting us participate in the other person's actions as if we were executing that action.

—Daniel Goleman (2006, p. 42)

IN THE EARLY 1950s when television began to play a regular role in many households, a remarkable thing happened. Little boys started to wear "invisible" gun belts and pull out "invisible" guns much like their cowboy heroes. Eventually, they urged for the production of more solid belts and plastic guns and practiced their ability to be the "fastest gun in the West." No one taught these children directly about cowboys, belts, and guns. They learned from watching their heroes act on television and automatically began to emulate them.

Even more amazing is the fact that adults thought the actions of the children were "cute," never questioning what was going on here, nor what else children automatically might be learning from television and what they saw adult actors do. In fact, much of the adult response amounted to encouraging the playing out these TV stimulated roles.

In this case, all of the factors that we have discussed so far were involved:

- Children were being motivated by needs and desires over which they had relatively little conscious control. One clear motivating force evidenced in the above example is the desire to be like people who matter to us.
- Innate predispositions were being activated. While the specifics are unclear (depending on individual episodes and plots) and given the

previous chapter, it could also look as though issues of territoriality (protecting individuals from those who might bring harm to their home or land), social groups, and dominance and submission (the "sheriff" and "bad guys") were touched on.

- Every need, predisposition, and action was folded into the perception/action cycle as children (1) experienced the program as something important to them, (2) interpreted what they saw, (3) made decisions, (4) created something (got "holsters" and "guns" and practiced their "draw"), and (5) received feedback on their actions (admiration, approval, or disapproval) and learned.

We are talking here of the social nature of learning, which has actually been investigated in depth for years. One of the fathers of this way of thinking is Vygotsky (1993) who suggested that children only acquire an inner voice after they experience outer communication with others. Sociologists, anthropologists, and social psychologists have also explored the notion in depth. Hence the emergence in cognitive psychology of the notion of *situated cognition* (Lave & Wenger, 1991), a notion that suggests that the way that people perceive, understand, and participate in their worlds is deeply influenced by the social context.

THE BIOLOGICAL FOUNDATIONS OF SOCIAL LEARNING

New research is now showing that students of all ages are born ready to identify and act out the best of what others have to offer—and the worst. In effect, it is now known that much, perhaps most, of the development of beliefs, attitudes, and behaviors may have a biological foundation. And that foundation lies in the ability to "mirror" another's behaviors and feelings and anticipate their actions:

> The brain's capacity to echo the perception of the faces and gestures of others and code them immediately in visceromotor terms supplies the neural substrate for an empathic sharing that, albeit in different ways and at diverse levels, substantiates and directs our conduct and our individual relationships. (Rizzolatti & Sinigaglia, 2006, p. 192)

Research on mirror neurons lends strong support to the old adage, "It is not what you say, but what you do, that will shape a child."

Mirror Neurons

As briefly introduced in Chapter 1 and the opening quote by Goleman, *mirror neurons* are neurons in the brain of an observer that respond in the same or a similar way to the neurons in the brain of the actor. Mirror neurons respond both to actions and the expression of emotions in others, and the result is that observers unconsciously imitate, experience, and frequently adopt the behavior and emotions of others without being consciously aware of doing so.

Mirror neurons probably play an important role when anyone "picks up" the culture of a profession, and even in mastering the nuances in a specific field of expertise. According to Daniel Goleman (2006), "They explain a huge swath of life, from emotional contagion and social synchrony to how infants learn" (p. 42).

Here is an example. At a high school in-service, teachers were seated in rows in auditorium style with seats rising as one moved up the rows. The person doing the in-service took a few moments to allow everyone to settle down and stop talking. He began by making a joke or two and then looked at all the teachers and asked, "How many of you came here ready to do some grading during my talk?" After a little coaxing to be honest, several people raised their hands looking a bit embarrassed. He then asked how many had brought that morning's newspaper so they could read in case the speaker got boring. Again, hands went up very slowly as people began to believe that they could be honest. Then he asked how many of them would rather have gone out for a long breakfast that morning or even have stayed in their rooms working on something they cared about. More hands went up as it became clear that almost no one wanted to be in this auditorium listening to someone talk about something they had little or no interest in. He then waited a few seconds and looked at those teachers and asked, "What makes you think that your students feel any different when they are in your classrooms?" We have often observed how high school teachers act like their students, be it the way they joke, try to get approval, or want to be popular or "cool." Is it possible that a continuous and close relationship with students begins to influence some of a teacher's values and behaviors, both positively and negatively over time?

Although most researchers agree that relationship and social context exert great influence in both development and social learning, not all agree on the specifics of mirror neurons (Lingnau, Gesierich, & Caramazza, 2009). It is also important to mention that mirror neurons are tied to greater networks sparked by the context and associated to past personal experience.

The original research reported by Giacomo Rizzolatti and his Italian team is rapidly being expanded. Today, mirror neurons are also seen as involved in more complex learning. They are at work in every aspect of the life of children in their homes and in their interactions with their parents and peers. They appear to be essential to mastering ways of communicating, social interactions, appropriate emotional expressions, and use of language. In fact, mirror neurons appear to be necessary in order to understand the beliefs of others and to translate those beliefs into one's own. They may influence responses to conflict and moral dilemmas. They may play a substantial role in helping children build what some scientists call a "theory of mind" (Cozolino, 2006; Meltzoff & Gopnik, 1993). A theory of mind is the foundation for a sense of what others are likely to do or want or know and may be the basis for how children and adults alike "read" their environment. Multiple opportunities for mirroring also help learners develop alternative solutions and anticipate the results of possible actions.

The message of mirror neurons is that what we experience from significant others as we move through the Perception/Action Learning phases is coded at low levels of awareness into our neural networks and influences our own reactions and future actions. And the closer to us those others are, the more likely we are to adopt what they do (Rizzolatti & Sinigaglia, 2008; Rowe, 2009). Proximity matters, but so do excitement, heightened emotions, trust in the other, and status and closeness of relationship (Iacoboni et al., 1999). It does not take a great deal of imagination to see that attitudes to violence, drug use, and sex, as well as kindness, compassion, and even a love for reading, are "picked up" by what important people do in a child's life. Alfred Bandura (2000) pointed this out years ago.

Although much still needs to be understood about how mirror neurons organize themselves, researchers have found that mirror neurons may play an essential role in several important areas:

- Understanding someone's intentions—internally predicting what they're about to do (Fogassi et al., 2005; Meltzoff & Gopnik, 1993; Iacoboni et al., 2005)
- Learning by imitation and modeling—this probably includes language and all the learning that involves cultural transmission (Arbib, 2006; Iacoboni et al., 1999; Rizzolatti & Arbib, 1998; Tettamanti, Buccino, Succuman, Gallese, Danna, Scifo et al., 2005)
- Bonding between mother and child and the finding that babies imitate from the first hour of life (Cozolino, 2006; Falck-Ytter, Gredeback, & Hofsten, 2006)

- The evolution of human culture and the transmission of culture across generations (Cantrell, 2006)

Mirror neurons provide a fitting explanation for many largely unconscious reactions that mesh emotions and action. Watching a football game and the almost instantaneous and visceral reactions that occur "in chorus" as the crowd responds to actions on the field may be one example. Feeling one's body respond automatically to watching dancers on stage, or "feeling felt" (Siegel, 1999) by another whose understanding reflects one's own sentiments and emotions are other examples.

Mirror Neurons and Emotions—A Closer Look

Research demonstrates that mirror neuron systems are deeply involved in emotional connections. Here are some different ways of describing the process that together illustrate how deep the connection is.

- People can identify with the feelings of others more or less automatically without being aware or analyzing their own response (Iacoboni et al., 1999; Siegel, 1999). So mirror neurons are involved in developing empathy—understanding others' feelings; experiencing the social emotions that allow people to coexist; understanding social meanings (Decety & Jackson, 2004; Preston & de Waal, 2002).
- One of the primary researchers on mirror neurons, Giacomo Rizzolatti, suggests that mirror neurons "allow us to grasp the minds of others not through conceptual reasoning but through direct simulation; by feeling, not by thinking" (quoted in Blakelee, 2006). This means that mirror neuron system activity appears to trigger responses that emulate another's actual emotional state such as feeling sad or angry when sadness or anger is observed in another (Iacoboni et al., 1999).
- Daniel Goleman (2006) further tells us that what we are experiencing are literally emotions that are contagious. Like Daniel Siegel (1999) he emphasizes that this is how we stay "in synch" with someone and follow what they are doing or telling us. "We 'feel' the other in the broadest sense of the word: sensing their sentiments, their movements, their sensations, their emotions as they act inside us" (Goleman, 2006, p. 42).
- Mirror neurons are also involved in understanding the mental states that motivate the actions of others (Iacoboni et al., 1999).

- Mirror neurons may someday explain why children who are bullied often turn around and bully the next person down the pecking order, or why children of alcoholics or abusers find themselves attracted to similar individuals as adults despite cognitively expressing dislike of such individuals and their behavior.
- Because mirror neurons are involved in responding emotionally, they contribute to the bypassing of conscious control of such things as violence in media (Hurley, 2006b).

As human beings watch significant others around them, their own brains and minds are picking up how to behave, how to express feelings, and generally how to anticipate and respond to the events and experiences around them.

The Impact of Violence

When we take the research on mirror neurons seriously we have to come to the conclusion that immersing children in violence (remember our little cowboys) or being exposed to pornography or drug use (prescription or recreational use) is not OK, even when it is masked as entertainment. "The results of the controlled experiments with children in laboratory settings could not be more clear and unequivocal: exposure to media violence has a strong effect on imitative violence" (Iacoboni, 2008, p. 206).

Having said this, we must repeat that when children and adolescents are emotionally connected to, and in conversation with, healthy adults and peers, many issues can be put into perspective and the negative impact of some exposure can be prevented.

For a clearer understanding about what happens, it is important to use research appropriately. For instance, it is a mistake to assume that simple, short-term cause-effect studies can accurately capture the impact of exposure to violence. Longitudinal studies, however, which document changes over time, are far more reliable and they do exist. Marco Iacoboni (2008) describes how a study, begun in the 1960s with close to 1,000 young people, demonstrated that early exposure to watching media violence was highly correlated with aggressive and antisocial behavior when these kids were followed into adulthood. They were first followed up on 10 years later at high school graduation and then again after another 10 years (a 23-year span in total). The results were definitive in that early media viewing of violence and early aggressive behavior correlated with criminal behavior at age 30. This study controlled for early aggressive and other major variables including education and social class.

FIGURE 14.1. Perception/Action Cycle and Social Impact

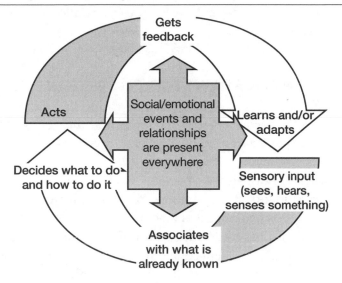

> The effect of media violence on imitative violence is observed in children from preschool to adolescence, in both boys and girls, in both naturally aggressive and nonaggressive children and in different races. The results are quite convincing. (Iacoboni, 2008, p. 206)

Those in the business of creating and promoting media and video games that focus on violence as a form of entertainment will often say that correlational studies do not prove cause and effect. As Iacoboni points out, few of us have a problem in associating smoking and lung cancer, or asbestos exposure and cancer, or bone mass and calcium intake. Yet, he assures us, the correlation between violence and media is greater than any of the above.

What is beginning to be understood is that although human beings can make rational decisions and anticipate the results of their actions, it is foolish to assume that they are not affected by events deeply tied to their biology and that these events have a largely unconscious effect on us all. Ariely (2008, p. iii) writes of "the hidden forces that shape our decisions." The idea that we are totally rational and have complete freedom of choice has been challenged by many disciplines and is continuing to be challenged and clarified by neuroscience. So, as the conclusion of Chapters 5 and 6 of this book suggest, we literally "become" our experiences. In Figure 14.1 we have expanded our original diagram of the P/A cycle (Chapter 6). We include a visual reference to the social contest, because it really impacts so powerfully.

Given the research on mirror neurons, can anyone still doubt that being with adults or peers who openly engage in dangerous behaviors has an effect on young people, especially on the most vulnerable who have little or no connections with parents, the culture, or other emotionally healthy significant and caring adults?

IMPLICATIONS FOR EDUCATION

The impact of the social/emotional context and the power of mirror neurons impact learners in two significant ways that interact with each other.

- One has to do with the personal qualities that educators (and others) have. Students model the sorts of people that others are. We could say that this can impact character development.
- The second has to do with how the curriculum and standards and expertise are experienced and modeled. It refers to the nature of the actual exposure of students to academic material. This has to do with how academic competence is modeled, not just presented. For instance, enthusiasm and conviction, as well as authoritative knowledge, appear to be a powerful combination in a teacher.

In brief, if we want students to become healthy human beings, achieve high excellence in any field, and develop higher order capacities to think, plan, anticipate, decide, and monitor themselves, then all of these must be experienced in the learning environment and modeled by significant peers and adults (Sternberg, & Grigorenko, 2001).

This is illustrated by Renate's research almost 30 years ago and mirror neurons may provide much of the explanation for her results. Her work focused on the effect that the teacher's use of "I-messages" and active listening (Gordon, 1975) had on student self-concept and attitude toward school and teachers. Using I-messages, a teacher might say, "I become frustrated whenever this happens" instead of "whenever you do this . . . ." *Active listening* for the study was defined primarily as restating a student's comment or explanation before entering into a discussion.

Two very closely matched groups of teachers were included in the study. One group was trained in the use of I-messages and active listening, which they would practice for 6 months with their students. The others acted as the control group and changed nothing in the way they had been communicating.

> Six months later the students in classes where teachers used "I" mes-
> sages and active listening had a significant positive change in self-esteem
> and attitude towards school and teachers. The latter is important be-
> cause attitude has been positively correlated with achievement. (Martin
> & Dowson, 2009)

This research convinced her of something that permeates our approach to professional development to this day. We suspect that teacher behavior and interactions are immensely potent and that it matters how the teacher models respect, knowledge of subject matter, and expertise, and listens to students. Can this effect be the same for teachers who model enthusiasm and love of learning for students?

The research looking at teacher influence on student learning has been mixed, but it suggests that teacher influence can be different for different students, depending on how closely students identify with, like, and respect the teacher. The research on resilience (Gillham, 2000) is also helpful in dem-onstrating that having only one powerful, loving, and supportive individual in one's life can make a significant difference. So personal connection and respect or admiration count. The same may apply to how students are or are not affected by peer pressure.

Character Development

The personal qualities and characteristics of teachers, parents, and admin-istrators and the extent to which they are knowledgeable, caring, and emo-tionally healthy human beings matter more than is generally understood, in part because mirroring requires a sense of relationship with another. Sarcasm, a noncaring attitude, and severe criticism of student learning, as well as poor commitment to scholarship, can impact the extent to which students master academic knowledge. Educators must model behaviors that lead to the devel-opment of healthy, connected, compassionate, and whole human beings.

Who and what connects with our students becomes very important. Ado-lescents, in particular, are influenced by what's "cool" as issues of identity emerge. Moving into an adult identity can be fraught with insecurity and un-certainty, two powerful forces for stress and engaging the low road. If students become aware of what is happening to them, they can learn to take charge of their own decisions using reflection and higher order thinking processes. This new understanding is at the heart of the Guided Experience Approach, which provides direction for what educators have to do differently.

Memes may one day be understood as mirror neurons at work. Their unconscious scripting steers much of what we do, particularly when we are on "automatic." But the subtle power of memes to make us act often eludes detection." (Goleman, 2006, p. 46)

When it comes to mirror neurons, we cannot specifically predict who will be affected or how it will happen. We can only know that the people who surround our children must be emotionally and socially healthy and, if possible, possess the kinds of skills we would want our children to emulate. Is this possible in a complex world? We would answer that we must strive for this because the price of exposing younger generations to destructive influences is far too high.

All of the influences that continually bombard students need to become visible. Open discussions and debates on sensitive issues with a responsible and able adult who challenges student thinking become critical. Students benefit from the opportunity to comment on issues like drug use, racial conflict, violence, and sex, either at home or in special forums with responsible adults or peers they respect. However, addicted students are another matter entirely. Once the physiology has been hijacked, much stronger issues are in place.

Immersion in Standards with a Teacher Who Models Excellence

Imagine a teacher who doesn't just teach math as a subject but loves teaching and students, and can demonstrate how math is alive in the real world. With such a teacher students can experience firsthand the kind of mathematical thinking rarely encountered in textbooks or math classes taught by teachers who have little enthusiasm for the subject. Students are not only learning math, their mirror neurons are picking up on the love of math.

Educators have to learn how to embed the curriculum intelligently while engaging students in the many natural ways that the human brain learns. There is good evidence for the importance of immersion and socialization in the development of expertise. It is clear that, in addition to motivation and deliberate practice over a long period of time, one of the key ingredients in the development of expertise is immersion in a world in which the ideas, concepts, procedures, and practices are explored, modeled, discussed, and lived as a matter of course (Lave & Wenger, 1991; Mieg, 2006). This notion has been best expressed in terms of the idea of communities of practice (Wenger, 1998, 2008) and is now in vogue as a leading-edge process in the world of professional development in large organizations. It is also one of the reasons we advocate Process Learning Circles for educators who want to take charge of their profession by engaging in ongoing learning (Caine & Caine, 2010).

Actually, the same idea has been evident in the world of reading for a long time. It is clear, for instance, that the children who come to school best equipped to learn to read come from environments where there has been a lot of reading. And one of the best ways to develop reading skills is to have a practice that requires reading across the curriculum. It is not simply that children learn to read using "scientifically proven" isolated skills. Rather, they are immersed in a social environment where reading is experienced as an integral part of any learning environment. Children see, perceive, experience— mirror—the process of reading. Whole language learning (Goodman, 2005) was and remains incredibly intelligent in this respect. Some years ago Jerome Harste (1989) demonstrated the benefits of embedding specific skills while paying full attention to reading as part of the child's experience as a reader.

What works best for the learning of reading and for becoming expert in any field or profession applies to every subject in the curriculum. One of the best practices that educators can use is for their students to be exposed to the authentic practice of a subject in the course of their everyday lives. That is why it is so much better for teachers to know how to apply math rather than limit it to abstract formulas. The more naturally knowledge and skills are embedded in any situation, the easier the learning for students. This is also why the actual rules of engagement and agreed-upon procedures that are employed in a school have such a large impact on whether or not students actually grasp the essence, say, of democracy in action.

Part IV

THE GUIDED EXPERIENCE APPROACH

CHAPTER 15

Implementing the Guided Experience Approach: The Three Critical Elements

T HROUGHOUT THIS BOOK we have explored the fact that the brain is a parallel processor where multiple operations take place simultaneously. As we have seen in previous chapters, Perception/Action Learning engages the brain, body, and mind at the same time. The way for educators to optimize the process is by means of what we call the Guided Experience Approach to teaching. The Guided Experience Approach requires educators to blend academic content, skills, thinking, and action, while students are in a continuously monitored healthy environment and motivated to create something of personal meaning and significance.

In Part III, as well as examining many of the unused or underused capacities of students, we looked at the hidden forces that keep students from pursuing P/AL. These include incompatible mind states for deep learning; a curriculum that does not relate to what is exciting, challenging, and meaningful for the learner; and a practice of relying on assessments that are externally controlled and largely summative. We also gave an example of teaching about digestion that contrasted the traditional approach to instruction and the Guided Experience Approach. The problem with spelling out the research as we have done, is that there is much too much for educators to deal with, one ingredient at a time. The challenge, therefore, is to connect and integrate the research so that it provides an in-depth foundation to support the Guided Experience Approach.

In our opinion, first presented in 1991, the key is to integrate three overlapping and general elements that together allow educators to effectively engage Perception/Action Learning.

THREE FOUNDATIONAL ELEMENTS THAT UNDERGIRD THE GUIDED EXPERIENCE APPROACH

The three foundational elements of the Guided Experience Approach (GEA) to teaching are discussed separately below, but act in concert in the classroom to activate the Perception/Action Learning phases.

Relaxed Alertness as an Optimal State of Mind

All learning is impacted by the state of mind of the learner and the atmosphere and culture that permeate a learning environment. Our research across disciplines, and the conclusions that we derive from Chapters 10 and 11 in particular (on motivation and state of mind), suggests that the optimal state of mind and atmosphere are what we call Relaxed Alertness.

Relaxed Alertness is a combination of high challenge (high intrinsic motivation) and high expectations with low threat and a relative absence of helplessness in individuals and the learning community as a whole (the high road). Another way to frame this state of mind is as a combination of competence, confidence, and intrinsic motivation and challenge. When in this state of mind, students are ready and able to respond to new subject matter or curriculum by asking questions that personally interest them.

The core foundation for developing Relaxed Alertness is an orderly (but not rigid) and caring community in which healthy relationships based on respectful and coherent procedures are infused throughout. There is an ongoing attention to maintaining and creating positive relationships, and these are grounded in mutual respect throughout the community. Both adults and students honor boundaries that have been established with input from everyone (Caine & Caine, 1997a, 2010).

Orchestrated Immersion in Complex Experience

The only way to simultaneously engage the many processes and capacities reflected in P/AL is through complex experience. Perception/Action Learning activates body, brain, and mind in a physical and social context. Every component of the learner as a living system is involved interactively. That is what is meant by "experience."

The way to translate this into education is to orchestrate the immersion of learners in experiences in which content is embedded. This is, in fact, precisely how the worlds of management, business, and the many professions operate. There, individuals are immersed in a world that requires competence with specific skills and a range of knowledge for specific purposes.

We wish to emphasize again that *none* of this discounts the importance of transmission of information, direct instruction, practice and rehearsal, and so on. It simply calls for all of these to be integrated in meaningful ways that contribute to the learner's larger experience. The consequence is that students have opportunities to begin to *think* mathematically or historically instead of just acquiring some math knowledge or historical facts.

Active Processing of Experience

Although students learn much from experience, they do not automatically master new concepts, academic practices, skills, or procedures without the right sort of practice and application. Research confirms this.

- One thrust of the perception/action cycle is that it invites the discernment of new patterns, and much of the time that calls for detailed observation of phenomena.
- Part of becoming a good learner is being able to take charge of one's own learning and engage the executive functions, one aspect of which is metacognition (Perfect & Schwartz, 2002).
- Although some memories are formed instantly, it has been known for many years that the keys to forming long-term memories are multiple iterations and deep processing (Craik & Lockart, 1975).

The key is for the teacher to ensure that students have many opportunities to receive feedback, digest, think about, question, examine, see from differing perspectives and with the benefit of additional information, and process what they are experiencing—guided by teachers and the questions asked by teachers, peers, and others.

This continuous and personal reflective participation by students is what we mean by Active Processing. Active Processing, therefore, constantly enriches and deepens different aspects of P/AL and ensures that cycles are continually completed and reinvigorated. A perfect (though often low-level) example can be found in some of the discussions that take place between friends and online as gamers penetrate deeper and deeper into their games. In the course of this ongoing type of exchange they experience layer after layer of similar skills as they occur in different contexts.

The Three GEA Elements Dance Interactively

These three elements are naturally active in any learning situation, and they happen in parallel: (1) States of mind and the *social/emotional* context interact with and are a significant part of (2) the *intellectual/instructional* context that, in turn, affects and interacts with (3) the ongoing and dynamic process that maximizes *feedback and consolidation* of new learning.

All three elements must be present because each impacts and shapes the others. The existence of community and healthy relationships is an essential aspect of Orchestrated Immersion in Complex Experience. And Active Processing relies on complex experience and healthy relationships in order to ensure that there is healthy and rigorous feedback that empowers learners.

TWO RUNNING EXAMPLES

There are many schools across the world and brave individual teachers and schools that have explored natural learning in different ways (though using different terms and modes of organization). One is the MET (the Metropolitan Regional Career and Technical Center) which is a state-funded public school district that serves six small schools in Rhode Island and which has inspired a national network of about 50 other such schools (http://www.themetschool.org/Metcenter/home.html). Another example, one of our favorites, is the Bidwell Training Center, founded in the heart of Pittsburgh (http://www.bidwell-training.org/).

In the next three chapters we illustrate what we have been writing about using two examples with which we have some personal contact. One is Bridgewater Primary School, a small, public middle school in South Australia. The other is Gary and Jerri-Ann Jakobs High Tech High, a larger, but still small, charter high school in San Diego. We have visited Gary and Jerri-Ann Jakobs High Tech High (http://www.realizethedream.org/programs/high-tech-high.html) and met with some of its leaders and spoke with students. It is also superbly described by Tony Wagner in his book *The Global Achievement Gap* (2008), and we will draw extensively from his descriptions, our visit, and their own Web site.

High Tech High

As their Web site says: "High Tech High began in 2000 as a single charter high school launched by a coalition of San Diego business leaders and educators. It has evolved into an integrated network of schools spanning grades

K–12, housing a comprehensive teacher certification program and a new, innovative Graduate School of Education." (http://www.hightechhigh.org) "The network" is dedicated to a small school model: No more than 500 students, and no more than 25 students per class. (A fascinating insight into this type of learning and teaching can be found in a publication provided by the HTH Graduate School of Education entitled "Unboxed—A Journal of Adult Learning in Schools." Issues can be found on their Web site at www. hightechhigh.org/unboxed.)

The network now consists of five high schools, three middle schools, and one elementary school, with a total population of 3,500 students. Students are chosen by lottery to represent the demographics of the area. So there is extensive representation of minority populations, special ed students, and those who qualify for a free lunch. Their cost per student matches the California cost per student in public schools.

While the philosophy and approach are the same in each school, the focus of the curriculum varies. For example, one school focuses on international studies, another on the media arts. And as for results? Tony Wagner notes that since graduating its first class in 2003, *all* High Tech High students have been accepted to college, including MIT, University of California–Berkeley, University of Southern California, and Johns Hopkins University. And while their test scores are among the highest in the state, teachers resolutely refuse to teach to the test.

Both High Tech High and Bridgewater rely heavily on the application of knowledge through projects and in the process gain what we have called *dynamic knowledge*. The products are of the highest standards. High Tech High, for example, has student-authored books that are truly impressive and leave no one in doubt as to student mastery of the English language, science, math, and technology, as testified in Jane Goodall's foreword to a student-authored book, *San Diego Bay: A Call for Conservation*: "Most people are amazed that such important results can be achieved by high school students. I am not one of those! I know this group of students—the 'High Tech High Roots & Shoots' team—and have become familiar with their high standards of excellence. Each year they design innovative ways of working within their communities to improve the lives not only of wildlife but also the human population of San Diego." (A similar book entitled *Perspectives of San Diego Bay—A Field Guide* is authored by the school and was published in 2005.)

Bridgewater Primary School

We selected our other example, Bridgewater, in part because it is a participant in a leading edge, systemwide project in South Australia with which we were involved for over 10 years. That project was originally called *Learning to Learn*. Schools initially volunteered to participate and were given immense freedom to create their own school communities. The project supported each school and provided access to leading thinkers, visionaries, and practitioners on a more or less ongoing basis. *Learning to Learn* officially ended as a separate program in 2009, but has since been absorbed into the South Australia Department of Education and Children's Services as *Teaching for Effective Learning*. *Teaching for Effective Learning* represents the official pedagogy for South Australia and is captured in the *South Australia Teaching for Effective Learning Framework Guide* (or SATfEL guide) published by the S.A. Department of Education and Children's Services (2010). It is also a superb summary of the theory and practices we advocate in this book.

We were fortunate enough to launch the project in Adelaide with a 2-day in-service for the first cohort of schools. We introduced our 12 Brain/Mind Learning Principles and based the in-service on our *Process Learning Circles* (described in depth in Caine & Caine, 2010). Participants were initially confused because we were clearly questioning some of their basic assumptions and practices. Yet over time, and with all the input they had from various thinkers (systems thinking), practitioners (predominately constructivist), and support that was provided, some wonderful shifts began to occur. We are delighted to have maintained our relationship with these remarkable educators.

Learning to Learn did not present everyone with some formula or road map they could follow, only an understanding of how people learn and skills that support an environment of Relaxed Alertness, Orchestrated Immersion in Complex Experience, and Active Processing. So every school was different. What they shared was access to some of the best thinking about learning and teaching, and the SACSA Frameworks (S.A. Department of of Education and Children's Services, 2010; see also Chapter 4), which are the equivalent of the U.S. state standards. Learning to Learn also demonstrated that it takes a substantial investment over time if genuine change is to take place.

Several years ago we asked Margot Foster, the incredibly talented visionary and manager of the original project, to suggest a school she felt exemplified our work the most. She recommended that we visit Bridgewater Primary School near Adelaide. The school is a small combination upper primary and middle school with approximately 157 students and includes parent and community involvement. Although a small school, it represents an exceptional model and study of what we advocate in this book. What was most amazing to us was the fact that the school had anticipated many of the ideas we had developed but not yet published or shared with them directly. It further confirmed that natural learning can be harnessed by schools once the conditions and human capacities have been allowed to take hold.

While the school makes significant use of technology, what we wish to demonstrate is how a school is formed and emerges as an organic whole when some core conditions are established, the three elements operate, and everyone participates in continuous learning and personal development, and ongoing processing. The school is described in the Working with Outcomes Web site (which can be accessed through http://www.sacsa.sa.edu.au/). The material is provided with permission of Bridgewater Primary School. An interview on ABC radio can be found online (http://mpegmedia.abc.net.au/rn/podcast/2009/04/lms_20090420_0930.mp3).

Even from this modest description, the three elements—Relaxed Alertness, Orchestrated Immersion in Complex Experience, and Active Processing—can be identified as they occur in a natural and integrative fashion.

Bridgewater: In Their Own Words

Bridgewater Primary is 10 years into an exciting learning journey (www.bridgeps.sa.edu.au). Our focus is on supporting and challenging students to engage in rigorous, engaging, and meaningful learning. Key to our approach is the partnership among members of the school community. The student is at the center supported by teachers, parents, and appropriate support staff. Supported by much of the recent research into the brain and learning, we have recognized that choice and ownership of learning is a key motivating force for student engagement.

Imagine coming into our school any time after 8:50 in the morning. As you wander into the Yellow Learning Area you would see clusters of students ranging in age from 9 to 13 engaged in their learning.

- Scattered around the room working individually are about 10 students. Each is working on something different. One might be working on a cardboard model of a building, while several others are writing around their research. Some are working on computers, others at a desk using pen and paper.
- Four girls on the floor clustered around an Apple iBook, webcam, and small stage filled with clay figures are discussing where to go next on their claymation of an aboriginal creation myth.
- Three boys clustered around a desktop computer are speaking and gesturing quietly as they view a Flash animation that one of them has created, offering advice on possible changes.
- Just across from them a group of four students are working with an adult who is running a focus session on planning and setting deadlines for their current unit of work.

- Just across the passage in a small room two students are sitting around another computer. One has a keyboard plugged into an Emac and is playing a sequence, while the other is checking the input which is coming into GarageBand.
- In the main hall is a group of eight students working with a parent, designing and developing a dance based around their research into Indonesian culture. (Bridgewater Primary, 2010)

Students are working on their Personal Learning. At the end of the term there is to be an Open Night and Exhibition. Guided by clear and negotiated criteria for success students know what they are doing, are clear about expectations, and have made clear choices around the learning that they are engaged in.

Comment

All three elements that we have described are clearly embedded throughout the two schools we use as examples. In each we find a superb climate and attitude of students, their immersion in a variety of projects that deal with content and standards, and a variety of ways to process experience for content and for higher order functioning. Now let us unpack the three elements and see in more detail how they play themselves out. We will also see how the Guided Experience Approach is woven throughout.

CHAPTER 16

Relaxed Alertness

GOOD COMMUNITY and healthy relationships are essential, and these need to be matched with a deep commitment by participants to continuous and authentic learning. This means that Relaxed Alertness is an atmosphere, a spirit, an environment that pervades a school. It begins with shared values and beliefs. And it requires individuals to be prepared to constantly learn from all that is happening and includes the impact they have and contributions they make to the community. This is challenging. It calls for good communication skills, a sense of process, an ability to be truthful with oneself and others, and for all of this to take place in difficult times as well as easy ones. So educators and staff are committed to expanding their own skills and knowledge and contributing these to the community through their work. Creativity and problem solving become the hallmark of the community and wisdom is respected.

In our work, we have found that adults and staff benefit from a core set of basic skills:

- Ways of listening to each other, including active listening
- Ways of communicating, including the use of I-messages
- Effective classroom meetings
- Conflict resolution

We do not have the space to describe these in any detail, but have provided our own approach in two books (Caine & Caine, in press; Caine et. al., 2009). Practical applications are also beautifully spelled out in the *South Australian Teaching for Effective Learning Framework Guide* (South Australia, 2010) discussed in the last chapter. For a comprehensive coverage of many of these and other skills, see also Larrivee (2009).

The core point is that Relaxed Alertness in a school as a whole and in individual students and educators emerges as a result of the interaction of a host of different elements that work together. In the language of systems theory, we would argue that Relaxed Alertness cannot be imposed or manufactured.

Rather, it is an emergent phenomenon that occurs because so many other things are done right.

In the rest of this chapter we discuss some of the ways in which relaxed alertness is generated at Bridgewater and High Tech High.

ORGANIZATION AND STRUCTURE AT BRIDGEWATER

The processes and structures at Bridgewater form a network that sustains Relaxed Alertness. We discuss several of these features below and tell how they bring about Relaxed Alertness.

A Vision Reinforced by Honest Inquiry

The vision for the school is as follows: "Bridgewater Primary School staff and students are committed to lifelong learning that is relevant, enriched, and passionate, and which uses the best of learning energies for everybody" (Bridgewater Primary, 2010).

A vision can, of course, just be a convenient set of words. Bridgewater goes further, because opportunities are provided for students to explicitly question pedagogy. So there are times when students are asked, and discuss responses to, such questions as "What is the purpose of school?" and "What do we, as a community, need to learn?"

Respect Made Real

Like other schools, Bridgewater has a code—a set of rules and procedures that govern how people interact and that contribute to a respectful attitude. The difference? The staffs apply to themselves the same rules that apply to students! It is important to understand that there cannot be one set of rules for all schools. Rules are negotiated and based on actual needs regarding community, adherence to negotiated time schedules, allocation of space, maintenance, allocation of work areas, and agreements on what constitutes excellence.

> We don't believe there should be two sets of rules—one for teachers and one for kids. None of this could work if you didn't have two-way respect. It's up to us as teachers to demonstrate that—we are the ones that need to break down the barriers. (Bridgewater Primary, 2010)

Honoring Individual Choice and Stage of development

Students and teachers understand that learning is an individual as well as a shared experience. A whole class is not put into the same learning situation where, in their words, "you have a third who already know, a third who may be receptive to it, and a third who are not ready for it" (Bridgewater, 2010). Rather, individual learning allows students to see their learning as relevant because they have many choices and schedules that are adapted to their stage of development. This taps into student motivation and provides them with an added sense of control, both of which are important for maintaining the high road. At least two processes work toward these ends.

Personal Learning Plans—The Ultimate Differentiated Instruction

The primary and middle years program at Bridgewater Primary School, spanning what would be Grades 5 to 8 in the United States, gives ownership of learning to students. This ownership contributes enormously to a sense of safety and to motivation, both of which strengthen the high road. In addition to, as well as incorporating, the three core elements listed above, students undertake their own personal learning. They can choose any topic they want, with no topic being considered inappropriate, although there are times when teachers may have to guide the learning around a topic.

Within a specific application of the GEA, individual interests are triggered and personal questions are asked. However, the overall topic itself tends to be set by the teacher. In addition, at Bridgewater, students have extensive opportunities to select areas of personal interest and pursue them. A joint responsibility of teachers and students is to then connect those larger personal interests with the SACSA Frameworks or standards.

It is important to remind the reader that this is a culture of collaboration. Almost all students *want* to be here because the entire school is about them. And a great deal of learning is collaborative, tied to group projects, so peer support is available. Most parents and the community stand ready to help. All students are not interested in all academics even if they do have choice. When a teacher finds a student not cooperating or ignoring math, they notice. There are small "catch up" sessions students can sign up for and they do. They are encouraged to recognize their own skill level (metacognition) and empowered to see that they can take action.

Students complete a "planning a new learning unit" booklet. There are two versions of the booklet—one for novice learners and another for advanced learners. Both can be viewed on the Web site. The booklet is a guide to the process, which must be undertaken to ensure success (notice the steps of PA/L). These include:

- Choosing the topic
- Determining what they already know
- Developing some questions or issues
- Demonstrating new learning will occur
- Considering methodology and resources
- Planning the final presentation
- Setting criteria for success

All of these areas are unpacked and nurtured by means of Active Processing (see Chapter 18). Teachers and students together assess the situation, ask different types of questions, and generally clarify what is going to be done.

Balancing Personal Learning and Teacher Instruction

At Bridgewater, each student completes a personal timetable on a daily basis during circle meetings, which occur first thing each morning. This group time also presents an opportunity for any issues to be raised and for teachers to give notice to students of other discussions groups, such as global issues discussions.

On 4 days of the week, a set time is allocated to acquiring skills in math and language, although within this time students have choices about where their focus will lie. Sports and fitness are also at set times, with students signing up for their chosen sport. Wednesday is set aside almost exclusively for personal learning. There are also set times allocated to silent time, often used for sustained writing.

A Focus on Self-Management

Development of executive functions of planning and decision-making and more is a crucial aspect of preparation for the future. Bridgewater addresses this in two ways. First, a great deal of self-assessment and self-management is built into the learning generally. In addition, Bridgewater provides for students to be placed in groups, according to their ability to learn and to plan and organize. Thus students are given ownership of their own learning by celebrating what they know and establishing what they don't know. There are three layers of organization competence:

- Novice—all students new to middle and upper primary, either from junior primary or new to the school.
- Learner—students who have acquired some skills as an organizer and/or learner.
- Advanced learner—students who require little adult intervention in organizing and learning; many advanced learners may embed their learning by teaching novices.

It is not a matter of total student self-selection because a regular review process occurs. As students demonstrate increasing ability to organize and take responsibility for their learning, they are moved into a more advanced group. Similarly, students requiring further help with organizational skills may be moved into a group where added assistance is provided.

Each organizational group has circle meetings in which agenda items, which are contributed by teachers as well as students, are discussed. Students take on a variety of roles, such as manager, lunch monitor, and chairperson for the group.

The process is initiated for every student at the beginning of each year. Each one answers the following questions:

- What do you feel competent/confident about?
- What would you like to learn?

Skills and understandings are therefore tracked. For example, ICT (Information and Communication Technology) students identify their ICT skill level and learning goals. Students identify themselves as novice, learner, or advanced learner and provide examples of how they have demonstrated their skills. (A PowerPoint presentation, which demonstrates how the tracking booklet works, is available on the Web site.)

Note that the Essential Learning of "Identity" (from the *Essential Learnings* that constitute the second aspect of the curriculum in South Australia and which are dealt with in more detail in the next chapter) plays a significant role in this model of learning. Teachers state that it is much easier to keep track of each learner's progress because of the individuality of the program, making it easier to remember what each learner is doing. As one teacher said: "I can give you a detailed description of each student's personal learning. But best of all is that we've got rid of 'OK-ness' and mediocrity from the classroom."

Teacher Buy-in

Relaxed Alertness needs to be manifested in the entire community, in staff as well as students. One key is for the staff to be interested in and committed to the process—for their intrinsic motivation to be activated. As one of the teachers remarked: "Teachers have to buy into it when they are ready—choice is essential. You can't tell people to think in this way—you have to actually believe in it."

Teachers Supporting Each Other in Supporting Students

In order to schedule programs at Bridgewater, communication between teachers is paramount. While each student will complete their timetable in their circle group, teachers need to also be aware of each other's movement and availability. For example, the success of focus groups depends on an adult being able to uninterruptedly teach a small group. Therefore, another adult must be available who can act as the "touch-base" person to facilitate learning for other students, as well as assign movement and resource notes.

The system is structured so that students are always with adults who know them, including the principal or other staff, who teach specialist subjects, such as drama or sport. Relieving teachers (substitute teachers) are familiar with the system at Bridgewater and know that they are coming in to act as a "touch-base" person for students who already have individual learning plans; they therefore do not have to spend time preparing lessons to enrich students' learning, which may interest some but not all students.

Student Responsibility for Operating the School

Giving students increased responsibility for and ownership of their school is further evidence of change in culture; students take an active role in the running of the school, such as answering phones, dealing with mail and greeting visitors, with students volunteering for "office duties," even during lunch breaks and recess. Student involvement is therefore not just tokenistic, but highly valued in the day-to-day running of the school. A student comments, "This is much more interesting than going out to play. We learn so much more about life and it's good responsibility. I think it's much more like university."

This of course hints at the sort of flexible scheduling that the school provides for students. This is challenging but doable as students have schedules for the week and confirm specifics every morning before the day begins.

Effective Behavior Management

Because all students are engaged, there are very few behavior issues to deal with. Rather than taking punitive measures, those students requiring help with behavior issues are encouraged to change their behavior and move on. The "Kids' Club" is available for reflection on personal issues and assists them in finding strategies such as anger management. Students also have the right to request a short "chill-out time" if they need time out from their learning in order to get back on task. Thus the culture has changed from one of denial to one of ownership, and responsibility has become prevalent.

THE PHILOSOPHY AND CULTURE OF HIGH TECH HIGH

High Tech High (HTH) shares the same deep underlying philosophy of learning, teaching, and being as Bridgewater. Its mission is equally profound, though with a different focus. High Tech High's mission is to develop and support innovative public schools where all students develop the academic, workplace, and citizenship skills for postsecondary success. This is unpacked in a set of goals that include the following:

- Serve a student body that mirrors the ethnic and socioeconomic diversity of the local community
- Integrate technical and academic education to prepare students for postsecondary education in both high tech and liberal arts fields
- Increase the number of educationally disadvantaged students in math and engineering who succeed in high school and postsecondary education
- Graduate students who will be thoughtful, engaged citizens

Some modes of organization are similar and others are different. But the net effect is a culture that generates and sustains Relaxed Alertness. Here are some aspects of the way that this state of mind and atmosphere are generated.

The Adult Community

A core belief of High Tech High is that "if you want to build a good learning environment for students, it must also be a good place of learning for adults" (http://www.hightechhigh.org/). This is precisely right. Everything that we have addressed in this book points to the need for a coherent culture of learning, so that students are immersed in a way of being that supports their learning. This approach extends into the support that staff is offered. For example, one of the great barriers to building an effective learning and teaching culture in most schools is the absence of time for staff to plan and work together. At HTH teacher teams have ample planning time to devise integrated projects, common rubrics for assessment, and common rituals by which all students demonstrate their learning and progress toward graduation. To this end school begins at 8:30 a.m. (a time supported by research into when adolescents function best) rather than at 7:00 a.m.

> "[Teachers] have an hour together in school every day before students get here, when we'll do things like look at samples of student work and talk about what's good and what could be better. Every teacher works in a team with one other teacher and, together, they are responsible for fifty students. They meet twice a week to plan and to talk about their kids and their work." (Principal Ben Daley, quoted in Wagner, 2008, p. 224)

Note here, as in Bridgewater, the emphasis is on teachers working together in order to help students. This is supplemented in a range of other ways.

Personalization

One of the key design principles for HTH is *personalization*. Each student has a staff adviser, who monitors the student's personal and academic development and serves as the point of contact for the family. Students with special needs receive individual attention in a full inclusion model. Facilities are tailored to individual and small-group learning, including networked wireless laptops, project rooms for hands-on activities, and exhibition spaces for individual work.

The Physical Space

The physical spaces are designed to support key program elements such as team teaching, integrated curriculum, and project-based learning. The emphasis is on adequate and useful space with attention paid to color, the use of comfortable furniture, both formal and informal meeting areas, and the use of many windows to emphasize their design notion of transparency. One of the powerful aspects of their approach is the use of what they call essential spaces. These include a Commons Room, which is a centrally located area for student gatherings and community meetings; Teaching Clusters, which are small "neighborhoods" of seminar rooms, studio spaces, and teachers' offices; Multipurpose Seminar Rooms with flexible use that can also be adapted to accommodate direct instruction; Studio Areas; Specialty Labs; and Outdoor Learning Spaces. Note also that while HTH has been supported by some moderate grants, it manages on the same amount of money per student that every charter school in California receives.

Student Motivation

At the heart of Relaxed Alertness is the combination of low-threat and high-challenge or intrinsic motivation. That means, as we point out in the body of this book, that the key to driving Perception/Action Learning is student interest, nurtured and guided by teachers who introduce the need for rigor in a psychologically safe way. HTH thrives on projects that engage and stimulate students, framed to suit their interests while dealing with the complexities of the various subjects that are being explored (for examples see Web site at http://www.hightechhigh.org/projects/). It seems to us that Bridgewater actually insists on a greater degree of student autonomy and choice, including the selection of their projects, and are more involved in the design of rubrics. However, our conversations with students and the founder indicate that the notion of student autonomy is very important to High Tech High.

A Comment

It is impossible to catalog all the features that collectively give rise to a climate of Relaxed Alertness. We have identified some of them in order to provide a general sense of what is involved. Remember that all three elements of the GEA are interwoven like a triple helix. So the treatment of Orchestrated Immersion and Active Processing, in the pages to follow, also contribute to Relaxed Alertness.

The key is for educators to "get it." In particular, they need to get the interconnectedness of it all, and the enormous power and potential that is unleashed when this approach is given full reign. With the best will in the world, some people just don't grasp the interconnectedness of it all. This is a practical philosophy, and not a recipe.

CHAPTER 17

Orchestrated Immersion

ACTIVELY LEARNING, even when one's own ideas and interests are included, may still be difficult for many students raised in an environment and culture driven by the transmission/direct instruction meme. In our experience, without first developing a culture of Relaxed Alertness, Orchestrated Immersion in Complex Experience is simply not possible. To repeat, the Guided Experience Approach depends upon mutual respect, collective understanding, and appropriate communication techniques, ranging from I-messages to conflict resolution. Students or teachers who feel isolated or inadequate will simply not participate in the same way that empowered individuals will. The Guided Experience Approach cannot be forced. It emerges out of hard work and collaboration by committed individuals.

STANDARDS

We begin with the fact that learners are immersed in experience *in which the standards are embedded*. Students are being prepared for participation in their worlds, and much of that preparation can and should, we believe, be determined by the larger community that is served by education.

Bridgewater

Bridgewater implements the SACSA Framework (*South Australian Curriculum Standards and Accountability Framework*). They are organized in a relatively sophisticated way. As we briefly touch on in Chapter 4, on the one hand are the more traditional "learning areas," which embrace English, math, science, and more. On the other hand are what they call "essential learnings," which embrace systems theory, a sense of the future, the notions of identity and interdependence, and a general sense of how people think and communicate in an interconnected world (South Australia, 2001).

All teachers are required to know the standards and to be proficient in core subject areas. In addition, *the students* are encouraged to be aware of the

SACSA Framework and the various strands. Bridgewater then goes further: "We have a look at what the Key Ideas and Outcomes say and make them work for our situation"(http://www.hightechhigh.org/).

High Tech High

High Tech High adopts a similar two-pronged approach. While they do not teach for results on standardized tests, and much of what they do is interdisciplinary, their curriculum largely reflects recognizable big subject areas such as humanities, math/physics, biology, English, and chemistry. However, their entire philosophy is to interweave what we would call a second curriculum throughout the life of the school. This is expressed in several different ways. One example is intellectual rigor. And so one of their staff positions is humorously—but seriously—called Emperor of Rigor. The post is held by an extraordinarily highly qualified person who helps to ensure that learning and teaching are rigorous. Another example is expressed in some of their design principles, which include personalization and adult world connection. The thrust is to integrate academics with the development of healthy, competent citizens.

THE PHASES

Although they use different language, both High Tech High and Bridgewater essentially implement the Guided Experience Approach. In the list given here, we simply mention the core elements of Orchestrated Immersion for the Guided Experience Approach. (The steps are expanded in the next section.) The key is to grasp the essence and underlying concept behind each element, and then to blend them as appropriate.

The Multisensory Immersive Experience. This is a direct, real-world experience that introduces or exposes students to a new subject or material to be dealt with.

Sensory Processing. This expands awareness of the details and previous experience and triggers greater interest.

Actor- (Student-)Centered Adaptive Questions. These are based on authentic student interests and may call for dealing with their own lives in some way.

Planning, Organizing, and Doing Research and Skill Development. Here begins the real inquiry into the topic. It combines student research, collective and individual inquiry, teacher-led sessions, explanations, and direct instruction on occasion. Skill development is incorporated as students read, write, research, or pursue deeper understanding and do more processing.

Creating a Product That Requires Use of New Learning. This is where new skills and new understanding are applied. At the core is practical application that both enhances accuracy and demonstrates what has been understood and mastered.

Formative and Summative Assessments Handled with Ongoing Active Processing. Active Processing is essential and nonnegotiable. Throughout the entire process of student-driven learning, the teacher continually challenges student thinking, expressed assumptions, mastery of concepts, and accuracy.

Formal Feedback. Final products are essential to this process. Public demonstrations, presentations, models, or documentations of all kinds take place. Attention is paid to issues ranging from the appropriate use of vocabulary to the ability to answer spontaneous questions from experts or novices.

Technology Can Be Infused Throughout. Technology can be used at every stage, ranging from communication tools and resources for research to the creation and presentation of final projects.

The Natural Inclusion of Executive Functions of the Human Brain. In the course of this approach, there is constant decision making, planning, negotiating, and reflection, both individual and collective.

THE GUIDED EXPERIENCE APPROACH EXPANDED

The last sections listed the core elements of Orchestrated Immersion for the Guided Experience Approach. Each phase has a considerable amount of depth, as we explain below. We illustrate them by liberally referencing both High Tech High and Bridgewater.

Multisensory Immersive Experiences: Setting the Stage

Much of what is done in schools is abstract and doesn't engage one's senses the way the real-world does. Bridgewater calls the Multisensory Immersive Experience "Front Loading," and Kovalic and Olsen (1994) call it a "Being There" experience. Regardless of what it is called, it refers to a complex event that engages multiple senses and frames material in a meaningful way. Students often don't know how things happen in real time or the real world and the Multisensory Immersive Experience begins here.

In general, therefore, new topics should be prefaced by the Multisensory Immersive Experiences (MIE) we described in Chapters 7 and 9. It is important to recall that the purpose of the Multisensory Immersive Experience (MIE) is to trigger student questions—questions that get at their motivation to learn more. So it is a good idea to think of the Multisensory Immersive Experience as the engine that generates student interests and questions. We should repeat, however, that the process is nonlinear. That means that the MIE need not be the first exposure that a student has to a subject. For example, one of the key ingredients of the High Tech High curriculum is a 10-week internship with a nonprofit organization or local company in a student's junior year. Another is the extensive use of complex projects. Here is an excerpt from an entry on their Web site by teacher Angela Guerrero (http://www.hightechhigh.org/unboxed/issue3/where_do_projects_come_from/):

> So, where do projects come from? My answer is this: they are born in the places we love to visit, the things we love to see, the tasks we love to lose ourselves in. They are the things we find exciting. They are the things we deem worthy of writing essays and graphing charts about. They come from teachers who fall in love with something and decide to share that something with their students.

But student interests still provide the spark. And so here is another way in which projects and research begin: "We listen to them {students} when planning a project. If a student says, 'I'm interested in learning about surfing,' we try to find a way to accommodate that in the project" (Wagner, 2008, p. 221).

One of the major ways in which technology is changing what education can be is that it provides a huge range of opportunities for constructing Multisensory Immersive Experiences.

Brief Multisensory Immersive Experience. Multisensory Immersive Experiences come in all shapes and sizes. They can be very artistic, and the best ones spark the imagination or engage a sense of wonder and possibility. Technology also assists educators in providing complex experiences for students. Recall video games: Sophisticated video games can act as wonderful MIEs. Multisensory Immersive Experiences can also be specific and structured, provided that real life is introduced in some way. We frequently use YouTube videos to highlight certain abstractions and make them more lifelike or real. We have also used parts of movies that illustrate abstract notions such as "expertise" or the "value of a human life."

Comprehensive Multisensory Immersive Experience. The Comprehensive Multisensory Immersive Experience is quite long. For example, Bridgewater and some U.S. schools take students on overnight camping trips. The High Tech High internships would feature here. This kind of experience can lead to investigations into scientific studies of water quality, weather variations, and the environmental impact of weather on plants and animals. We have developed a rather in-depth Multisensory Immersive Experience on the Civil War. As long as the emotional impact is handled with sensitivity (this frequently requires some training), issues related to war and separation generally can be introduced. (Following a Multisensory Immersive Experience in science, one Bridgewater student became passionate about researching breast cancer because her mother had cancer.)

Sensory Processing

The Multisensory Immersive Experience is just a first step. Processing sensory detail enhances attention and focus. So students are guided in ways that make the experience more vivid. A teacher may ask questions such as "What did you recognize?" "What colors did you observe?" "What did you notice about size, distances, proximity?" "What was familiar?" "New?" Through more detailed sensory observation students also make initial connections to what they already know.

Actor- (Student-)Centered Adaptive Questions

Following sensory processing, the teacher works with students to ascertain what interests them, individually and collectively. This phase is handled much like a brainstorming session. A teacher may ask: "What are you curious about?" "What struck you as you watched?" "What do you want to know more about?" The questions are placed on the interactive whiteboard, and students can decide which aspect they want to investigate. They can decide to pursue the question in pairs, small groups, or as individuals. The result is that students can connect to topics of personal interest to them. As long as they lead to the essential skills and knowledge to be mastered, individual choice is essential for motivation and pursuing P/AL.

In Chapter 9, for instance, in the lesson on digestion students were free to select any of the issues that emerged during the process. They could choose to:

- Focus on personal issues such as individuals they knew who had dietary problems or diabetic or obesity issues

- Care about the food available to the poor and the effect of cheap food on digestion and health
- Investigate different ethnic diets and how changing from one culture to another can affect digestion
- Find out what to know about digestion when traveling to a third world country

Note that if questions do not arise immediately, other options are available to teachers. They can themselves introduce topics and raise realistic questions that matter to them personally and see if there are any that strike a chord in the students collectively. The art of the teacher, in part, is to find a way to connect those personally relevant questions to the topic and standards under discussion.

Planning, Organizing, and Doing Research and Skill Development

Once initial questions have been formulated, students are given relatively free rein to conduct their research—either alone, in pairs, or in research groups (their choice). Once again technology becomes essential as students use the Internet, reference sites, or contact expert sources and actual experts in the community on the Web or by e-mail. Web research (including Wikipedia), in particular, needs to be cross-checked since information is often superficial or incorrect. Students and teachers may want to create a set of responsible Web sites. If schools house their own server, students can create their own in-house Wikis where responsible information is housed and monitored by students and staff alike. Books are scanned and read, and a variety of other sources can become relevant.

As students gather essential facts, view more real-life examples, or use technology, and begin to unpack concepts and issues, the data and ideas are processed and discussed by students and the teacher in a respectful exchange. In the course of all of this, the teacher assists students to develop critical thinking skills and summarize essential ideas relating to their topic. One student at High Tech High worked on a biology project and helped to write a book (now for sale at the natural history museum) on animal species in San Diego Bay.

> [He]researched the snowy plover—its habitat, the biology of the bird, its population growth and decline, and the ways in which it is endangered. [He continued,] "I'd never contributed to a book before. It's hard to make the writing sound interesting, instead of like a usual research paper. I also got an understanding of how important the environment is. I didn't understand before how important just one creature

could be. The plover eat the larvae of bar flies—if they become extinct,
our beach will be infested with flies." (Wagner, 2008, p. 227)

Both directly and indirectly, the teacher will guide students in using new
vocabulary. As students talk about their findings, a lively exchange of information and conjecture takes place. Essential facts and issues are recorded as they
emerge (written on blackboards or recorded electronically on an interactive
whiteboard) from student research. Students discuss what they are finding
and explain and discuss possible implications and contradictions and conclusions. We need to note a reminder here that all learning is developmental.
Sometimes the developmental issues take care of themselves, as students do
what they can manage; sometimes more guidance is required from teachers.
This is just one reason why teaching is such an art.

Creating or Designing Something

Students need to decide how to document their new understanding. They
may choose to graph patterns, build or grow things, write papers, create a
model, generate a multimedia presentation, and so forth. The use of projects,
both simple and complex, is at the heart of the High Tech High philosophy.
Regardless of the method they choose, there should be rigorous attention to
quality and proficiency. That is why teachers and peers process and work with
each other in an ongoing way to constantly improve: This ranges from editing
and reediting papers and presentations to rethinking and rebuilding products.
The beauty of this process is that a great deal of additional understanding and
competence develops in the course of generating or compiling the product or
procedure or presentation.

Public Presentations

Finally the project becomes public for fellow students, teachers, parents,
and discipline experts to comment on. A central aspect of the High Tech High
process, for instance, is to make student work public.

> We have many different ways of getting kids to put their work out
> there, such as inviting people from the outside to look at it with us—
> parents who view the students' digital portfolios and presentations, of
> course, but also engineers for an engineering project, architects for an
> architecture project, and not just at the end, but also along the way, so
> the feedback is much more meaningful. (Principal Ben Daley, quoted in
> Wagner, 2008, p. 223)

Students listen to, and show that they understand and can respond to critique, make essential changes, and demonstrate their learning.

Feedback from others can be simple or complex. It can occur in the form of small "stickies" next to a particular product. And it can consist of intensive, long discussions. All feedback must be specific and worded respectfully. Thus the provision of feedback also becomes a teaching tool that adds an additional layer to the whole process. As students observe and process feedback, they acquire additional abilities to discriminate between poor and high quality and how to critique each other constructively and respectfully.

General Comment

All the above take place within a larger context. Sometimes it may become clear that a set of skills or concepts (say, additional math or the skills needed to prepare a better report) need to be addressed before students can continue. Sometimes interests and other projects are interwoven. There will always be multiple strands of activity because different competencies will be developing in parallel (e.g., math and science or reading and history). Sometimes larger schoolwide activities need to be dealt with. And so on. This constant activity and multiple agendas need to be managed or facilitated without losing the spirit and the dynamic of the GEA. For instance, there may be a clear need for some direct instruction every now and then. That is fine. The key, always, is to nurture and respect and expand students' interests and their own sense of control, so that the essence of the high road is sustained. Bridgewater does this. But it is a complex process, as can be seen below.

HOW BRIDGEWATER STRENGTHENS THE GUIDED EXPERIENCE APPROACH

Bridgewater sustains the overall GEA by means of many processes and procedures that are described and embraced by its organizational philosophy.

Ensuring Learning Areas Are Covered

As we noted, Bridgewater requires teachers to be familiar with the SACSA Framework and how it is structured. Math and English are clearly integral to students' personal learning, as are society and environment. Their philosophy is that much of this can be easily incorporated into most projects. They feel that almost everything can be taught across the curriculum to some extent.

However, they know that more is often needed:

- They happily do some explicit teaching of core skills in math, language, and ICT (information and communication technology) in order to ensure that students have a set of basic skills for further learning.
- Where other Learning Areas are missing in personal learning, they are made up for through electives in the Widening Horizons program (to be described later).
- Specific holes are also filled. For instance, Bridgewater recognized that one learning area that was underrepresented was science. This was remedied by a whole school, 2-week, intensive science focus in which everyone participated. This included deconstructing science and the strands, how to develop experiments, how to develop procedural writing, and how to test theories.
- They look for areas of collective student interest. Deconstruction of Key Ideas and Outcomes has been a theme when working with students to increase their familiarity with the SACSA Framework. And the following questions, for example, gained a highly enthusiastic student response and influenced a number of future personal learning plans:

    "What can you measure?"
    "What attributes can you measure?"
    "What tools would you use to measure?"
    "What language would you use to share your findings?"

Personalized Timetables and Schedules

Teaching and running a school in the way we describe calls for a dance between structure and freedom, overall organization and self-organization. Each school must decide what works for it and for the students when they have multiple choices of where they will learn best.

At Bridgewater each student completes a personal timetable on a daily basis during circle meetings (which occur first thing each morning). This group time also presents an opportunity for any issues to be raised and for teachers to give notice to students of other opportunities or group meetings.

Recall that on 4 days of the week, a set time is allocated to acquiring skills in math and language, although within this time students have choices about where their focus will lie. Sports and fitness are also at set times, with students signing up for their chosen sport. We also mentioned that Wednesday is set aside almost exclusively for personal learning. There are also set times allocated to silent time, often used for sustained writing.

In addition to maintaining their personal timetables, students also need to book computer and teacher time, as well as write into their timetables any Widening Horizons, focus groups, or Creative Ideas groups they are participating in.

At the end of each term, students in the "novice" group (see the section on organizational competence in Chapter 16) create a large erasable class timetable for the following term. The timetable is maintained by each circle group during the course of the term and is finalized for the day during circle meetings. The timetable includes items which will occur over the day or the week as they become known, so that students can add these to their personal timetables and know when and where they can access things getting offered. The class timetable also allows teachers to know when students are accessing additional activities, such as choir.

Movement Notes

Because students are undertaking so much individual study, they may be utilizing many areas of the school as their resource. This is managed by using movement notes to gain permission to utilize areas such as the tech room, which may only be utilized in the presence of a teacher, or for working outside.

Obviously this many choices and variations need to be well organized. So the staff also looks for ways that everyone can keep track of students by use of electronic boards where students can record where they are or where they are going for a specific activity.

Additional Practices

The GEA is always part of a more comprehensive way of doing things. This can be illustrated by several Bridgewater practices, which include:

- The use of personal learning plans (see also Chapter 16)
- Student groupings according to capacity to plan and organize
- Planning meetings with mentors
- Attending focus groups

A Word About Focus Groups. We want to emphasize the use of focus groups here to indicate that some explicit, direct instruction can be incorporated into the larger GEA when appropriate. Students may sign themselves into focus groups or they may be identified by teachers. Focus groups offer explicit learning opportunities, such as gaining a better understanding of fractions or writing more colorful fiction characters. Focus meetings are very short—often only 10 minutes duration—as they are intended to meet immediate and specific needs and involve small groups of only about 6–10 students. Focusing on a specific area, there are usually 2–3 sessions on the selected topic, with one teacher explicitly teaching in an uninterrupted way. Sign up sheets identify the subject of the focus group, e.g., how to write a newspaper article; and the identified group of learners, e.g., novice. Once numbers have been established, the group is given a timetable slot and students are informed of the time and location.

Enrichment and Expansion

The SACSA Frameworks are important but they're not everything. Bridgewater takes to heart the notion that understanding and skills need to be expanded and deepened. In effect, the goal is to continuously expand the rich knowledge networks that we describe in Chapter 7. They do this in at least two additional ways.

Widening Horizons. Further enrichment is added to the program through *Widening Horizons*, where adults, be they teachers, parents, or outside specialists, offer programs and units for which they may have a passion and which are frequently mapped to the SACSA Framework. Students indicate their interest via a sign-on sheet, which indicates the topic, the adult or topic leader, the time, place, and length of commitment. Recent *Widening Horizons* have included art, square dancing, using the video camera, and creative cookery.

Creative Ideas. Creative Ideas work in a similar fashion to *Widening Horizons* but are offered by students to other students. Students need to apply to run a Creative Ideas session by completing:

- A description of the activity
- How many people they are running the activity for
- The resources they will require
- Whether adult help is needed
- Where they will run the group

Students can choose any topic on which to base their Creative Ideas, as long as they complete an application which meets the above criteria and have their application approved by a teacher. Recent topics have included computer games, Monopoly, propagating plants, and still life drawing.

Assessment

A running log should be kept by student and teachers, which demonstrates progress, improvement, and gained expertise. These are discussed and documented with evidence from writing samples, projects, and other exhibits. Since the emphasis with the Guided Experience Approach focuses on competence, confidence, and motivation to demonstrate or do more, and include dynamic knowledge and higher order thinking, we suggest that much can be learned from student competitions of all kinds. These can be in-house, local, national, and international contests or competitions and include video, Web site, and multimedia demonstrations. Success in such competitions can serve as documentation of achievement.

Reporting to Parents

Parents are kept informed through each student's timetable booklet, which includes feedback on their Personal Learning Projects and their learning in math, literacy, and ICTs, together with a reflection page, written by teachers and students. Timetable booklets go home each week and keep parents in touch.

And Then There's Additional Technology

By and large, our experience suggests that the restrictions on the use of technology are much more severe in the United States than in many other first world nations. Here is a range of examples of what can be done (when students are a part of a caring, coherent learning community).

- Students can create their own Web pages, as can cohorts of students.
- Students can engage in extensive research and collaboration with others around the world.
- Students could be equipped with their own laptops. And, of course, access to cell phones and their communication and networking capacities could be made use of in schools for all sorts of nonfrivolous purposes.

- Other types of technology and complex relationships can be formed. One example is the teaming of McComb Academy in Michigan and Motorola, where the students have the opportunity to genuinely test equipment and provide results to the manufacturer.

CHAPTER 18

Active Processing

ACTIVE PROCESSING gives life, dynamism, and substance to everything else that is done, and it is just as important as Relaxed Alertness and Orchestrated Immersion in Complex Experience. It is through the use of questions that engage "in-the-moment" thought and actions that both formative and summative assessments operate. Active Processing is ongoing and dynamic, and is key to ensuring depth, breadth, and learning rigor. It is through Active Processing that teachers emphasize important issues and invoke higher order thinking and students share their ongoing conclusions and understanding.

Active Processing enhances attention and focus, integrates various learning strands and subject matter, and becomes the window through which executive functions are highlighted and expanded. In general, the way for educators to act is to use questions instead of lectures, challenges instead of predetermined answers, and help the learner see what isn't obvious and remains to be discovered.

THE SPIRIT OF PROCESS

Active Processing is more than a set of strategies. There is a larger spirit or philosophy that it serves. The key, in essence, is that learning is ongoing. There are bumps in the road, high points, and plateaus. Students and staff need to grasp the constant ongoing nature of learning and persist with it even while they take time out to celebrate completed goals and achievements.

For this spirit to be fully appreciated, staffs need to apply it to themselves as well as their students. Learning theory and the research on mirror neurons tells us that students pick up a great deal both indirectly and from modeling. When the staff is seen to be learning and to be engaged themselves in processing, students treat Active Processing as normal—as the way things are. And so resistance to questions is replaced by the acceptance, and often the joy, of penetrating stuff in depth and becoming more proficient along the way.

Much, but not all, of this happens in the world of videotech. Many game players like to learn more and get better and test themselves and exchange ideas and generally observe their own performance. So we are not introducing something alien into education. Rather, we are calling for what is now known to be implemented where it is most needed—in education.

And note, finally, how much Active Processing both invokes and strengthens executive functions. One of the fundamental goals of education is for students who graduate to be ready for a career and ready to live in the knowledge age. This does not occur by accident. Rather, the skills and processes that students experience throughout their young lives largely determine the skills and processes that they carry with them into the world beyond school and a life of continuous learning. They will always be immersed in experience. The ability to process that experience and adequately benefit from what it has to offer is, perhaps, the greatest gift with which they can leave the nurturing environment called school.

As Bridgewater and High Tech High are seen in context, Active Processing is ongoing and everywhere. Here, for instance, is one aspect of how HTH approaches this general goal, as related by founder Larry Rosenstock:

> What we're trying to do is create future leaders—civic, nonprofit, and profit—who have a sense of who they are, have a passion with purpose, and have a set of skills. We want them to be able to think, to work in groups, and to work independently. We want them to have a set of intellectual behaviors—Deborah Meier . . . calls them "habits of mind": to think about significance—why is it important; perspective—what is the point of view; evidence—how do you know; connection—how does it apply; supposition—what if it were different. These habits of mind are really habits of question asking. There's something about being perplexed that is at the core of inquiry: problem posing is more important than problem solving. (quoted in Wagner, 2008, p. 214)

ACTIVE PROCESSING FLESHES OUT AND ENLIVENS THE GUIDED EXPERIENCE APPROACH

In this section we move through the phases of the Guided Experience Approach and include Active Processing in each. Imagine, now, that students in a class have been immersed in a Multisensory Immersive Experience and are beginning to explore it for the first time and to deal with what interests them. The task of the teacher is to work with the students to process the experience and to go into it in more depth.

Processing Sensory Elements

Processing sensory detail engages attention and focus, both of which need to be present if neurons are to connect and networks are to be created or expanded. Using Active Processing language, sensory processing can become very sophisticated as students explore how their sensory experiences can be enhanced and sharpened.

In a "being there" experience such as a visit to an engineering site, a trip down a river, or a visit to a zoo, there would also be many actual events and details to recall. Depending on the established relationships and other aspects of Relaxed Alertness, the teacher may have to lead the initial discussion, but eventually students can take over. They can make notes as a group, put things in sequence, organize items they observed, or brainstorm what they would do if they had a chance to repeat the experience.

Questions might begin with the basics: "How high or wide is it?" "What color differentiations do you see?" "What are the dimensions?" Questions become more complex by asking, for instance: "What are the similarities to and differences from . . . ?"

The students also benefit from what others recognize and have observed. This can be documented more formally. Through it all, the teacher asks deeper questions, sometimes summarizes, and generally nurtures student enthusiasm for what they already know.

To some extent, associations to what has been learned previously will be made automatically because that is how the brain works, but it is essential to bring surface connections and articulate and expand them. Again, the primary way to do this is by means of a series of questions, and the elaboration that follows. Examples are "Where have you seen or experienced this before?" "What does it remind you of?" "How similar is it to . . . ?"

Planning, Organizing, and Doing Research and Developing Skills Using Multiple Modes of Questioning

As students pursue their research and investigation, teachers guide and support them in numerous ways. Many different modes of questions can be used for this purpose by the teacher (and sometimes by fellow students). These questions serve different purposes:

Add rigor and depth to research and incorporate expert knowledge: "Where else might you look or who else might you ask?" "When you were reading up on this issue, did you deal with the issue of . . . ?" "What would (expert) suggest?" "Are there examples available that can help you?" and "Who might model this for you?"

Challenge chosen resources: "What evidence do you see that tells you that the information on this Web site is accurate?" "Have you found additional supporting evidence?" "What counterarguments or information have you found?"

Focus on right and wrong answers: "What is the distance?" "Can you Google the answer?" "What is the formula?"

Elicit learner-centered adaptive questions: "What do you see as most urgent?" "How much time might it take?" "What are some possible solutions?"

Analyze data and sources: "What is the evidence for this?" "What would be revealed if you graphed these?" "Are there any other types of data that we might have overlooked?"

Much of what is dealt with in school is skill based. Skills may be part of the content as in reading and writing. Or skills may be supportive, as in the development of presentations for the public. In each case, teachers support and guide students in their practice. It may be through general questions such as "How will you practice your piece of music? "How will you make your presentation to parents?" "How will you demonstrate what you know or have done?" It may be through direct coaching, as teacher and student work together to assess what is or is not working and then design steps to improve. And it may be through self-assessment. For instance, in Bridgewater, students are largely responsible for deciding for themselves how well organized they are.

Processing for Creating a Product That Reflects New Learning

Recall that P/AL requires actual application. Students are thus urged to create a product that includes newly mastered knowledge and skills. To help a student decide on a product, a teacher may ask questions such as these: "How might you best demonstrate what you have learned so far?" "On the basis of your research, how would you document your new knowledge of skills?" "Can you capture what you now know in a Multisensory Immersive Experience?" "What talent or skill (that you have) could you use to demonstrate what you have learned?"

To process the product as it is created, the teacher may ask questions such as: "How accurate is your representation?" "What formula(s) did you use?" "What questions can you anticipate on the basis of your work?" "What does it still need?" "Have you been able to check for details?"

Active Processing in the Context of Assessment and Feedback

Active Processing is doubly useful because it simultaneously provides feedback for both teachers and students while it can be used to expand and deepen student thinking. As Fullan and his colleagues point out (2006), the timing of feedback and the timing of responses to feedback is critical. In this way formative and summative assessment are largely integrated.

Assessment at Bridgewater. Assessment is undertaken by holding initial evaluation meetings, where students may be assessed by teachers and their peers. They also self-assess their work. In some instances, students will present their work to the whole group of students. Final assessment determines the ability grouping of the student for different aspects of the learning unit, with novice being celebrated as much as advanced learner. Assessment will be for demonstration of:

- Planning/mind mapping
- Challenging and relevant questions
- Literacy skills
- Numeracy skills
- ICTs (information and communication technology)
- Presentation of the learning unit

All students participate, as required, in the tests administered by the state of South Australia, and their performance is well above state averages. However, neither staff nor students view these state tests as the most important modes of assessment to be used.

Assessment at High Tech High. HTH is equally adamant about not teaching to the test and about not being dominated by test results. All students take the California high school exit exam. They also take the STAR tests (the California Standardized and Reporting Program) by which schools are assessed. But assessment is performance based: All students develop projects, solve problems, and present findings to community panels. They write long papers. And there are many individual staff/student conversations along the way.

Active Processing as a Tool for Guiding Students Generally

It is crucial to help students take charge of their own learning and expand their capacities for self-discipline and self-regulation. As we have seen, each student at both Bridgewater and HTH has a staff adviser. In addition, there is planning for projects in several different ways. They engage in narrative writing. And there are many opportunities to reflect on experience. Both schools use planning meetings.

We think it would be helpful here to take an extended look at the use of planning meetings at Bridgewater. We use some of the materials supplied to us directly by Bridgewater (Sheperd & Love, 2009). The material is provided with permission of Bridgewater Primary School.

In the course of developing their individual learning plans, Bridgewater students must arrange a planning meeting with an adult. The adult acts as a mentor, ensuring the learning has rigor and challenge while also determining, in discussion with students, how outcomes can be matched to their learning. Here are some questions that they ask:

- Why is this topic of real significance and/or importance to you?
- What is/are the new learning(s) that you hope to acquire through this unit?
- Where does this Personal Learning fit within the contexts of the curriculum and previous personal learnings?
- Can you access the expertise/information/help that you will require to successfully complete this Personal Learning?

Similarly, students are aware of three stages: gathering, processing, and applying. Thus using an adaptation of Bloom's Taxonomy, students indicate which "story" they are in and how their journey to the next story might look and be achieved.

At planning meetings it is the adult's responsibility to ensure depth and breadth of learning, and to provide students with every opportunity to explore their chosen area of learning. Nevertheless, it is the students who must demonstrate that their topic does involve new levels of mastery and is not just revisiting old learning. Teachers who discover students are maintaining too narrow a choice will encourage students to explore more widely.

Note the issue of safety and avoidance of the low road:

Because you're in a smaller group, and everybody is there for the same reason as you, you don't get embarrassed. In a large group

you could get embarrassed also that you were holding back the
whole class.
—Year 6 student

Planning meetings also avoid insularity; they might include other students and discussions may include relevant challenging issues, such as multi-
culturalism or gender balance. This way debate is kept alive and students have
opportunities to examine issues and processes, which might impact on their
learning, creating still greater learning opportunities.

Students are responsible for setting timelines and deadlines for the com-
pletion of the planning unit. Any fixed dates, such as excursions or visiting
speakers, students write in their term planners and timetables.

CHAPTER 19

Window Into Tomorrow

AS VALUABLE AS all the examples from Bridgewater and High Tech High are, they are only the tip of the iceberg of what is possible. We chose Bridgewater and HTH because they exemplify the naturalness of the approach to learning we have outlined in this book. Bridgewater and HTH consist of students from different cultures and of a variety of abilities and talents. They are examples of what can happen when real people come together to create something unique and extraordinary. Those involved with Bridgewater and HTH have created schools that exemplify natural learning and the Guided Experience Approach.

Once again we want to emphasize that this book is not offering a formula. There are parameters, but each school will ultimately look different. Nature has infinite variety and is continually changing and evolving. The implementation of natural learning is just like that.

What is important, however, is that all the phases of Perception/Action Learning are engaged and that teaching must include all of them. There must be an initial experience that activates student interest and focus; actor-centered questions must be formulated by students; immersion in research, modeling, and expert knowledge must follow; something has to be created that demonstrates what has been learned; and all this must be made public in some way for feedback.

But even when the Perception/Action Learning phases are incorporated, success is not assured. Ongoing attention must be paid to Relaxed Alertness. Active Processing must include higher order thinking and must be ongoing as well. Unless the entire process is dynamic and emergent, control and reliance on old methods will take hold once again. This is why we developed the Guided Experience Approach. It relies on all three elements as they play out in a dynamic learning environment. This is also what Bridgewater and HTH demonstrate.

And just as important, teachers and educators need to apply the same process to their own continuous learning and development. Lectures, top-down instructions, and two-dimensional learning have a limited role, but they are totally inadequate for good professional development. Becoming familiar with ongoing research and mastering new technology requires collaboration, discussion, exploration, and implementation. Group work and research within schools is essential.

In effect, schools need to acquire their own in-house capacity for ongoing development and not just rely on outside experts, nor simply respond to edicts from individuals and state or government agencies. Educators *must* take charge of their own learning. That is the thrust of our approach to the development of professional learning communities in schools and districts, the goal of which is to generate in-house capacity for professional development, using the principles and processes dealt with in this book (Caine & Caine, 2010).

Where do we go from here? Technology will take on a life of its own. The challenge for educators and those interested in education is to help bring forth something that nurtures the human spirit while expanding knowledge and intelligence into places that have not yet been imagined. But the perception/action foundation of natural learning remains, regardless of how complex technology becomes. Here is an excerpt from a newsletter from Singapore in June 2008 that gives these comments meaning:

Singapore Schools Look to the Future

> Immersive 3D and 4D environments, avatars powered by artificial intelligence, virtual field trips, real-time classes over the Internet and computer-based games will soon be a reality for Singapore's pioneer batch of FutureSchools: Beacon Primary School, Canberra Primary School, Crescent Girls' School, Jurong Secondary School and Hwa Chong Institution.
>
> For Crescent Girls' School, it is all about changing the way the children learn. "To excel in an increasingly complex and globalised economy, students need to be active self-driven learners with a passion for lifelong learning. They also need to acquire ease in working collaboratively, leading virtual teams, and harnessing technology to achieve effective outcomes," said its principal, Ms. Eugenia Lim.
>
> Not only is technology being used to make learning more engaging and experiential at Crescent Girls' School, it will also personalize each student's journey. It will be used in the assessment of key concepts and skills, and to track the student's learning progression. The role of the teacher thus becomes more of a designer, facilitator and manager of learning. ("Singapore schools," 2008)

The words, of course, are easy to speak and to write. The key is to grasp and live the spirit and philosophy that gives meaning to the words and flesh to the experience. The future calls for a reimagining of what teaching looks

like and how education works in the age of knowledge and technology. Fortunately, we can get there. The task, if we are to significantly elevate the quality
of education for all children, is to work with the capacities with which every
one of them is naturally endowed—all races, all ethnic groups, all ages, all
genders, all nationalities. Everywhere.

Glossary

Active Processing of Experience—The continuous and personal engagement of the learner in the process of making sense of experience. It includes many opportunities to digest, think about, question, examine, see from differing perspectives, and receive feedback guided by teachers, experts, peers, and others.

Actor-centered adaptive questions—Questions and decisions that have meaning to actors (students) and arise out of their need to know and therefore sustain the perception/action cycle.

Biological predispositions—Instinctual modes of perceiving and acting that play themselves out in the everyday world as expressions of wants and needs related to survival such as procreation, social group behaviors, and the search for food and shelter.

Bridgewater Primary School—Bridgewater is a small school with 14 teachers and approximately 157 students. It combines upper primary and middle school, and is located near Adelaide in South Australia. Although a small school it is an exceptional example of what we advocate in this book.

Cortex—The outer layer of the brain that houses thought, language, and consciousness.

Dynamic knowledge—Knowledge that can be applied in the real world, in both planned and spontaneous and ambiguous situations; also called performance knowledge.

Executive functions—Higher order thinking skills and capacities housed in the prefrontal cortex of the brain. They include planning, analysis, logical thought, and emotional control.

Extrinsic motivation—Externally imposed factors that "make" or "compel" or "drive" a person to act in some way largely independent of personal choice or meaning.

High road—According to LeDoux, one of the two major pathways in the brain, the one that taps into and engages higher order capacities. (See also *low road*.)

High Tech High (HTH)—Began in 2000 as a single charter high school launched by a coalition of San Diego business leaders and educators. It has evolved into an integrated network of schools spanning grades K–12, housing a comprehensive teacher certification program and a new, innovative Graduate School of Education.

Higher order functioning—The term used by psychologists for the thinking skills and capacities that are part of the executive functions of the prefrontal cortex. It includes logical and moral or ethical thought processes.

Intrinsic motivation—Intrinsic refers to the urges, persuasions, and forces, including personal wants and needs, that come from inside a person and that lead to actor-centered adaptive questions and the resultant personal decisions and actions. Intrinsic motivation is internal, personal, and meaningful.

Knowledge networks—All knowledge and skills are networked in the brain. No unit of knowledge or concept in the brain occurs in isolation.

Learning to Learn—A 10-year, leading-edge, educational reform project in South Australia with which the Caines worked as international colleagues. Learning to Learn officially ended as a separate program in 2009 and has since been absorbed into the S.A. Department of Education and Children's Services as the foundation for their approach to Teaching for Effective Learning.

Low Road—According to LeDoux, one of the two major pathways in the brain, the reflexive and automatic survival response that bypasses much of higher order functionings. (See also *high road*.)

Meme—A unit of cultural information that is taken for granted and results in the repeated generation of the same sorts of ideas and actions. It is sometimes described as an idea that has a life of its own.

Metacognition—The ability to reflect on one's own actions, knowledge, thinking, and behavior. It may be described as "knowing that you know."

Mind state—A person's inner state, or state of mind, is the total pattern of activation of the brain, involving body, cognition, and emotion, at any point in time (Siegel, 1999) and is influenced by the totality of the conditions in which people find themselves.

Mind state continuum—There is a path between the low road and the high road. There are degrees of fear and helplessness associated with survival, and there are degrees of higher order functioning.

Mirror neurons—Mirror neurons are neurons in an observer that respond both to actions and the expression of emotions in others, with the result that observers unconsciously imitate, experience, and frequently adopt the behavior and emotions of others without being consciously aware of doing so.

Multisensory Immersive Experience (MIE)—This is a direct, real-world experience that introduces or exposes students to a new subject or topic, or new material to be examined.

Natural learning—The way that all humans are biologically and psychologically designed to learn from life. It is organized in terms of the perception/action dynamic, perception/action cycle, and Perception/Action Learning.

Neuroplasticity—The capacity of the brain to reorganize itself on the basis of experience.

Orchestrated Immersion in Complex Experience—One of the three essential elements of teaching with natural learning in mind. It is the process of teaching by involving students in selected or designed lifelike situations, activities, events, and procedures in which content is embedded naturally.

Perception/action cycle—The process that all people use naturally for recognizing and solving everyday problems.

Perception/action dynamic—All human beings are constantly engaged in the dance of perception and action. At its most elemental, it occurs below the threshold of consciousness and is as simple as an eye blink that occurs spontaneously in response to dust in the air or a bright light. The response is automatic and executed by the body itself.

Perception/Action Learning (P/AL)—Purposeful learning that is grounded in, makes use of, and goes beyond the perception/action cycle.

Perception/Action Learning phases—P/AL consists of a number of critical phases: a lifelike, real-world event as an initial experience; searching for and making initial associations; actor-centered adaptive questions; opportunities to gather information and develop a product or performance based on new knowledge or skills. These are presented for feedback.

Positive Affect—A mind state accompanied by a mild increase in positive feelings brought about by common everyday events. These feelings include moments of contentment and joy, interspersed with hard work that is intrinsically motivating (Ashby et. al., 1999).

Relaxed Alertness—The optimal state of mind for powerful learning. It consists of a combination of high challenge (high intrinsic motivation) and high expectations with low threat and a relative absence of helplessness in individuals and the learning community as a whole.

SATfEL guide—*South Australia Teaching for Effective Learning Framework Guide* (South Australia, 2010).

Self-efficacy—A concept attributed to Alfred Bandura (1997), refers to the belief that people have about their own effectiveness. The more personally effective people believe themselves to be, the more they are motivated to act—and to learn.

Sensory processing—An aspect of Active Processing that expands awareness of details of current experience and links to previous experience.

Surface knowledge—Knowledge largely limited to memorized facts and procedures and shallow understanding that require very little activation of the different aspects of P/AL.

TDI meme—Transmission/direct instruction meme that represents the traditional view of education.

Technical/scholastic knowledge—Knowledge that involves a grasp of key concepts and competence that incorporate relatively structured skills and procedures. It has more depth than surface knowledge because it includes deeper understanding.

Spirit of Process—Learning is seen as ongoing. Although there are bumps in the road, with high points, plateaus, and valleys, students and staff need to grasp the constant ongoing nature of learning, and to persist with it even while they take time out to celebrate completed goals and achievements.

Videotech—The world of media including television, technology, and video gaming.

References

Alexander, C. N., & Langer, E. J. (1990). *Higher stages of human development: Perspectives on adult growth*. New York: Oxford University Press.

Anderson, C. A. (2003). An update on the effects of playing violent video games. *Journal of Adolescence, 27,* 113–122. Retrieved from www.sciencedirect.com

Anderson, C. A., Gentile, D. A., & Buckley, K. E. (2006). *Violent video game effects on children and adolescents*. Oxford: Oxford University Press.

Annenberg Media. (2003). *The learning classroom: Theory into practice*. Retrieved from http://www.learner.org/resources/series172.html

Arbib, M. A., Bonaiuto, J., & Rosta, E. (2006). The Mirror System Hypothesis: Linking Language to Theory of Mind. Retrieved from arbib06mirrorSystemH#30ª864.pdf

Ardrey, R. (1996). *The territorial imperative: A personal inquiry into the animal origins of property and nations*. New York: Atheneum.

Ariely, D. (2008). *Predictably irrational: The hidden forces that shape our decisions*. New York: Harper Collins.

Ashby, F. G., Isen, A. M., & Turken, U. (1999). A neuropsychological theory of positive affect and its influence on cognition. *Psychological Review, 106*(3), 529–550.

Bandura, A. (1997). *Self-efficacy: The exercise of control*. New York: Freeman.

Bandura, A. (2000). Self-efficacy: The foundation of agency. In W. J. Perrig (Ed.), *Control of human behavior, mental processes, and consciousness* (pp. 17–33). Mahwah, NJ: Erlbaum.

Bateson, G. (2002). *Mind and nature: A necessary unity (advances in systems theory, complexity, and the human sciences)*. New York: Hampton Press.

Begley, S. (2007). *Train your mind change your brain: How a new science reveals our extraordinary potential to transform ourselves*. New York: Ballantine Books.

Bell, P., Lewenstein, B., Shous, A. W., & Feder, M. A. (Eds.). (2009). *Learning science in informal environments: People, places, and pursuits*. Washington, DC: The National Academies Press.

Blackmore, S. (2000). *The meme machine*. Oxford: Oxford University Press.

Blakelee, S. (2006, January 10). Cells that read minds. *New York Times*. p. C3.

Bloom, B. S. (1984). *Taxonomy of educational objectives*. New York: Longman. (Original work published 1956)

Boleyn-Fitzgerald, M. (2010). *Pictures of the mind: What the new neuroscience tells us about who we are*. Upper Saddle River, NJ: Pearson.

Boone, K. (1999). Neuropsychological assessment of executive functions. In B. Miller & J. Cummings (Eds.), *The human frontal lobes: Functions and disorders*. New York: Guilford Press.

Brady, M. (2007). *An any-century curriculum*. Retrieved from www.marionbrady.com/documents/AnAny-CenturyCurriculu.pdf

Bridgewater Primary. (2010). Retrieved from http://www.sacsa.sa.edu.au/ ATT/%7BAE62BB45-DD21-498D-ACA4-55114418E11C%7D/outcomes/sites/ bridgewater2.html

Brodie, R. (1996). *Virus of the mind: The new science of the meme*. Carlsbad, CA: Hay House.

Bronson, P., & Merryman, A. (2010, July 10). The creativity crisis. *Newsweek*. Retrieved from http://www.newsweek.com/2010/07/10/the -creativity-crisis.html

Brothers, L. (1997). *Friday's footprint: How society shapes the human mind*. New York: Oxford University Press.

Buccino, G., Riggio, L., Melli, G., Binkofski, F., Gallese, V., & Rizzolatti, G. (2005). Listening to action-related sentences modulates the activity of the motor system: A combined TMS and behavioral study. *Cognitive Brain Research*, 24, 355–363. Retrieved from http://www.sciencedirect.com

Caine, G., & Caine, R. N. (2001). *The brain, education and the competitive edge*. Lanham, MD: Scarecrow Press.

Caine G., & Caine, R. N. (2010). *Strengthening and enriching your professional learning community: The art of learning together*. Alexandria, VA: Association for Supervision and Curriculum Development.

Caine, G., & Caine, R. N. (in press). *Seeing education in a new light*. New York: Teachers College Press.

Caine, R. N. (2008). How neuroscience informs our teaching of elementary students. In C. Block, S. Parris, & P. Afflerbach (Eds.), *Comprehension instruction* (2nd ed.). New York: Guilford Press.

Caine, R. N., & Caine, G. (1994). *Making connections: Teaching and the human brain*. Menlo Park, CA: Addison-Wesley.

Caine, R. N., & Caine, G. (1997a). *Education on the edge of possibility*. Alexandria, VA: Association for Supervision and Curriculum Development.

Caine, R. N., Caine, G., McClintic, C., & Klimek, K. (2009). *12 brain/mind learning principles in action: Developing executive functions of the human brain* (2nd ed.). Thousand Oaks, CA: Corwin Press.

California State University–San Bernardino. (2009). *Welcome to the holistic and integrative program*. Retrieved from http://www.csusb.edu/coe/programs/holistic_integ_ed/ index.htm

Cambourne, B. (1993). *The whole story: Natural learning and the acquisition of literacy in the classroom*. New York: Scholastic.

Cameron, J., Banko, K. M., & Pierce, W. D. (2001, Spring). Pervasive negative effects of rewards on intrinsic motivation: The myth continues. *The Behavior Analyst, 24*(1), 1–44.

Cantell, D. (2006). Mirror neurons—A primer. *Intelligence River—RiverTown News*. Posted 2006/03/26. Retrieved from http://intelligenceriver.net/news/2006/03/26/121

Carnagey, N. L., Anderson, C. A., & Bushman, B. J. (2007). The effect of video game violence on physiological desensitization to real-life violence. *Journal of Experimental Social Psychology, 43*, 489–496. Retrieved from www.sciencedirect.com

Christakis, D. A., Zimmerman, F. J., DiGiuseppe, D. L., & McCarty, C. A. (2004). Early television exposure and subsequent attention problems in children. *Pediatrics: Official Journal of the American Academy of Pediatrics, 113*(4), 708–713.

Christensen, C., Horn, M., & Johnson, C. (2008). *Disrupting class: how disruptive innovation will change the way the world learns*. New York: McGraw-Hill.

Clark, A. S. (2006). *Detox for video game addiction?* Retrieved from http://www.cbsnews. com/stories/2006)07/03/health/webmd/main1773956.shtml

Clark, B. (2004). Leaving children behind: Exam privatization threatens public schools. *CorpWatch*. Retrieved from http://www.corpwatch.org/article.php?id=11543

Claxton, G. (1997). *Hare brain tortoise mind: Why intelligence increases when you think less.* London: Fourth Estate.

Cloud, J. (2009, March 25). Kids with ADHD may learn better by fidgeting. *Time* [Online edition]. Retrieved from http://www.time.com/time/health/ article/o,8599,1887486,00.html

Cole, K. C. (1999, October 13). Nobel prizes go to Caltech chemist, Dutch physicists. *Los Angeles Times,* pp. 1, 15.

Collins, A., & Halverson, R. (2009). *Rethinking education in the age of technology: The digital revolution and schooling in America.* New York: Teachers College Press.

Combs, A., & Snygg, D. (1959). *Individual behavior.* New York: Harper & Row.

Combs, A. W. (1999). *Being and becoming: A field approach to psychology.* New York: Springer.

Common Core States Standards Initiatve (CCSSI). (2010, March 10). *Draft K–12 Common Core state standards available for comment..* Retrieved from http://www.corestandards.org

Conlan, R. (Ed.). (1999). *States of mind: New discoveries about how our brains make us who we are.* New York: Wiley.

Cory, G. A., Jr., & Gardner, R., Jr. (Eds.). (2002). *The evolutionary neurothology of Paul MacLean.* Westport, CT: Praeger.

Costa, A. L., & Kallick, B. (Eds.). (2008). *Learning and leading with habits of mind: 16 essential characteristics for success.* Alexandria, VA: Association for Supervision and Curriculum Development.

Covey, S. R. (1990). *The 7 habits of highly effective people: Powerful lessons in personal change.* New York: Fireside.

Cozolino, L. (2006). *The neuroscience of human relationships: Attachment and the developing social brain.* New York: W. W. Norton.

Craik, F. J. M., & Lockhart, R. S. (1972). Levels of processing: A framework for memory research. *Journal of Verbal Learning and Verbal Behavior,* 11, 671–684.

Csikszentmihalyi, M. (2008). *Flow: The psychology of optimal experience.* New York: Harper Perennial. (Original work published 1990)

Damasio, A. R. (1994). *Descartes' error: Emotion, reason and the human brain.* New York: Avon Books.

Damasio, A. R. (1999). *The feeling of what happens: Body and emotion in the making of consciousness.* New York: Harcourt Brace.

Damasio, A. R. (2003). *Looking for Spinoza: Joy, sorrow, and the feeling brain.* New York: Harcourt.

Dawkins, R. (1976). *The selfish gene.* Oxford: Oxford University Press.

Decety, J., & Jackson, P. L. (2004). The functional architecture of human empathy. *Behavioral and Cognitive Neurscience Reviews,* 3, 71–100.

Deci, E. L., Koestner, R., & Ryan, R. M. (1999). A meta-analytic review of experiments examining the effects of extrinsic rewards on intrinsic motivation. *Psychological Bulletin: American Psychological Association,* 125(6), 627–668.

Denkla, M. B. (1999). A theory and model of executive function: A neuropsychological perspective. In G. Lyon & N. Krasnegor (Eds.), *Attention, memory, and executive function* (pp. 263–278). Baltimore, MD: Brookes.

Dewey, J. (1980). *The need for social psychology.* In J. A. Boydston (Ed.), *John Dewey: The middle works, 1899–1924,* (Vol. 10, pp. 53–63). Carbondale, IL: Southern Illinois University. (Original work published 1916)

Dewey, J. (1997). *Experience and education.* New York: Macmillan. (Original work published 1938)

Dewey, J. (2010). *Democracy and education: An introduction to the philosophy of education.* Retrieved from http://www.forgottenbooks.org/read.php?a=144004497X (Original work published 1916)

Diamond, M. C., & Hobson, J. (1998). *Magic trees of the mind.* New York: Penguin Putnam.

Doidge, N. (2007). *The brain that changes itself.* New York: Penguin Group.

Dretzin, R. (Producer). (2010, February). Digital nation [Television series episode]. In *Frontline.* Washington, DC: Public Broadcasting Service. Retrieved from http://www.pbs.org/wgbh/pages/frontline/digitalnation/view/

Dugandzic, R., Dodds, L., Stieb, D., & Smith-Doiron, M. (2006). The association between low level exposures to ambient air pollution and term low birth weight: a retrospective cohort study. *Environ Health, (5)*3.

Dunlosky, J., & Metcalfe, J. (2009). *Metacognition.* Thousand Oaks, CA: Sage Publications.

Dweck, C. S. (2000). *Self-theories: Their role in motivation, personality, and development.* Essays in Social Psychology. Philadelphia: Psychology Press.

Dweck, C. S. (2006). *Mindset: The new psychology of success.* New York: Ballantine Books.

Eisler, R. (1994). *The chalice and the blade: our history, our future.* Gloucester, MA: P. Smith.

Engel, A. (2009). *Seeds of tomorrow.* Boulder, CO: Paradigm.

Entertainment Software Association. (2010). *Sales & genre data.* Retrieved from http://www.theesa.com/facts/salesandgenre.asp

Ericsson, K. A. (2006). The influence of expertise and deliberate practice on the development of superior expert performance. In K. A. Ericsson, N. Charness, P. J. Feltovich, & R. R. Hoffman (Eds.), *Cambridge handbook of expertise and expert performance* (pp. 683–703). Cambridge: Cambridge University Press.

Falck-Ytter, T., Gredeback, G., & Hofsten, C. von. (2006). Infants predict other people's action goals. *Nature Neuroscience, 9,* 878–879.

Farrace-Di Zinno, A. M., Douglas, G., Houghton, S., Lawrence, V., West J., & Whiting, K., (2001). Body movements of boys with attention deficit hyperactivity disorder (ADHD) during computer video game play. *British Journal of Educational Technology, 32*(5), 607–618.

Federation of American Scientists. (2006). *Study recommends fix to digital disconnect in us education and workforce training: Features of video and computer games teach skills in demand by present-day employers.* Retrieved December 8, 2010, from http://www.fas.org/press/news/2006/2006oct_digitaldisconnect.html

Fogassi L., Ferrari, P. F., Gesierich, B., Rozzi, S., Chersi, F., & Rizzolatti, G. (2005). Parietal lobe: From action organization to intention understanding. *Science,* Vol. 302, 662–667.

Fredrickson, B. L. (2009). *Positivity: Groundbreaking research reveals how to embrace the hidden strength of positive emotions, overcome negativity, and thrive.* New York: Crown.

Freire, P. (2000). *Pedagogy of the oppressed* (30th anniversary ed.; M. B. Ramos, Trans.). New York: Continuum. (Original work published in English 1970)

Fullan, M., Hill, P., & Coevola, C. (2006). *Breakthrough*. Thousand Oaks, CA: Corwin Press.

Fuster, J. M. (2003). *Cortex and mind: Unifying cognition*. New York: Oxford University Press.

Garan, E. M. (2004). *In defense of our children: When politics, profit, and education collide*. Portsmouth, NH: Heinemann.

Gardner, H. (2006). *Multiple intelligences: New horizons* (Rev. ed.). New York: Basic Books.

Gazzaniga, M. (1988). *Mind matters: How mind and brain interact to create our conscious lives*. Boston, MA: Houghton Mifflin.

Gee, J. P. (2007). *What video games have to teach us about learning and literacy*. New York: Palgrave Macmillan.

Gibbs, R. W. (2007). *Embodiment and cognitive science*. New York: Cambridge University Press.

Gillham, J. E. (2000). *The science of optimism and hope: Research essays in honor of Martin E .P. Seligman*. Radnor, PA: Templeton Foundation Press.

Goldberg, E. (2001). *The executive brain: Frontal lobes and the civilized mind*. New York: Oxford University Press.

Goleman, D. (2006). *Social intelligence: The new science of human relationships*. New York: Bantam Books.

Goodman, K. (2005). *What's whole in whole language* (20th anniversary ed.). Muskegon, MI: RDR Books.

Gopnik, A., & Meltzoff, A. N. (1997). *Words, thoughts and theories*. Cambridge: MIT Press.

Gopnik, A., Meltsoff, A. N., & Kuhl, P. (1999). *The scientist in the crib: Minds, brains, and how children learn*. New York: William Morrow.

Gordon, T. (1975). *P.E.T. parent effectiveness training*. New York: New American Library.

Greene, A. J. (2010, July/August). Making connections: The essence of memory is linking one thought to another. *Scientific American Mind, 21*, 22–29.

Greenfield, S. (2008). Society hard-wired for a fall. *The Australian*. Retrieved from http://www.theaustralian.news.com.au/story/O,25197,23858718-28737,00.html

Haines, L. (2005). Violent video games do not cause aggression. *The Register*. Retrieved from http://www.theregister.co.uk/2005/08/15/video_games_and_aggression/

Harste, J. C. (1989). *New policy guidelines for reading: Connecting research and practice*. Urbana, IL: National Council of Teachers of English and the ERIC Clearinghouse on Reading and Communication Skills.

Hart, L. A. (1983). *Human brain and human learning*. White Plains, NY: Longman.

Hayward, M. (1998). *Embodied cognition and the percept/concept distinction*. Retrieved from http://hci.uscd.edu/lab/publications/1995-1999.htm

Healy, J. M. (1990). *Endangered minds: Why our children don't think*. New York: Simon & Schuster.

Healy, J. M. (1998). *Failure to connect: How computers affect our children's minds—for better and worse*. New York: Simon & Schuster.

Herr, N. (2007). *Television & health*. Retrieved from http://www.csun.edu/science/health/does/tv&health.html

High Tech High. (2005). *Perspectives of San Diego Bay—A field guide*. Providence, RI: The Next Generation Press.

High Tech High. (2010). *San Diego Bay: A call for conservation*. San Diego, CA: The California Sea Grant College Program of the University of California.

Hillman, J. (1996). *The soul's code: In search of character and calling.* New York: Warner Books.

Hirshberg, C. (1999, September). How good are our schools? *LIFE Magazine,* 40, 43.

Hirst, P. H., & Peters, R. S. (1970). *The logic of education.* New York: Routledge.

Houghton, S., Milner, N., West, J., Douglas, G., Lawrence, V., Whiting, K., et al. (2004). Motor control and sequencing of boys with attention-deficit/hyperactivity disorder (ADHD) during computer game play. *British Journal of Educational Technology, 35*(1), 21–34.

Hunt, J. B. (1998). Organizing for learning: The view from the governor's office. *American Association of Higher Education.* Retrieved from http://www.highereducation.org/reports/learning/learning3.shtml

Hurley, S. L. (2006). Bypassing conscious control: Media violence, unconscious imitation, and freedom of speech. In S. Pockett, W. Banks, S. Gallagher (Eds.), *Does consciousness cause behavior? An investigation of the nature of volition.* Cambridge, MA: MIT Press.

Hurley, S. L. (2006). Active perception and perceiving action: The shared circuits model. In T. S. Gendler & J. Hawthorne (Eds.), *Perceptual experience.* Oxford: Oxford University Press.

Huttenlocher, P. R. (2002). *Neural plasticity; The effects of environment on the development of the cerebral cortex.* Perspectives in Cognitive Neuroscience. Cambridge, MA: Harvard University Press.

Iacoboni, M. (2008). *Mirroring people: The new science of how we connect with others.* New York: Farrar, Straus & Gitroux.

Iacoboni, M., Molnar-Szakacs, I., Gallese, V., Buccino, G., Mazziotta, J. C., & Rizzolatti, G. (2005, March). Grasping the intentions of others with one's own mirror neuron system. *PLoS Biology, 3*(3), Retrieved from www.plosbiology.org/article/info:doi/10.1371/journal.pbio.0030079

Iacoboni, M., Woods, R. P., Brass, M., Bekkering, H., Mazziotta, J. C., & Rizzolatti, G. (1999). Cortical mechanisms of human imitation. *Science, 286,* 2526–2528.

Iiyoshi, T., & Kumar, M. S. V. (Eds.). (2008). *Opening up education: The collective advancement of education through open technology, open content, and openknowledge.* Cambridge, MA: MIT Press. Retrieved from mitpress.mit.edu/books/chapters/0262033712chapt25.pdf

Jenkins, D. (2006). NPD data claims younger gamers still dominant. *Gamasutra: Industry News.* Retrieved from http://www.gamasutra.com/php-bin/news_index.php/news_index.php?story=10923

Jukes, I., & Walker Tilesto, D. (2009). *Understanding digital kids: Teaching and learning in the new digital landscape.* Thousand Oaks, CA: Corwin Press.

Kelly, F. S., McCain, T., & Jukes, I. (2009). *Teaching the digital generation: No more cookie-cutter high schools.* Thousand Oaks, CA: Corwin Press.

Kihlstrom, J. F. (2007). *The rediscovery of the unconscious.* Retrieved from http://socrates.berkeley.edu/~kihlstrm/rediscovery.htm

King, B. (2003). Educators turn to games for help. *Wired.com.* Retrieved from http://www.wired.com/gaming/gamingreviews?news/2003/08/59855

King, M. L., Jr. (1947). The purpose of education. *Morehouse College Student Paper, The Maroon Tiger.* Retrieved from http://www.drmartinlutherkingjr.com/thepurposeofeducation.htm

Kohlberg, L. (1984). *The psychology of moral development: The nature and validity of moral stages.* San Francisco: Harper & Row.

Kohn, A. (2000a). *The case against standardized testing.* Portsmouth, NH: Heinemann.

Kohn, A. (2002). The 500-pound gorilla: The corporate role in the high-stakes testing obsession and other methods of turning education into business. *Reclaim Democracy.* Retrieved from http://reclaimdemocracy.org/weekly_article/corporate_influence_education_kohn.html

Kovalik, S. J., & Olsen, K. D. (1994). *ITI model: Integrated Thematic Instruction* (3rd ed.). Kent, WA: Books for Educators.

Krasnegor, N. A., Lyon, G. R., & Goldman-Rakic, P. S. (Eds.). (1997). *Development of the prefrontal cortex: Evolution, neurobiology, and behavior.* Baltimore: Paul H. Brookes.

Lakoff, G. (1987). *Women, fire, and dangerous things: What categories reveal about the mind.* Chicago: University of Chicago Press.

Lakoff, G., & Johnson, M. (1999). *Philosophy in the flesh: The embodied mind and its challenge to Western thought.* New York: Basic Books.

Lakoff, G., & Johnson, M. (2003). *Metaphors we live by.* Chicago: University of Chicago Press.

Langer, E. J. (1997). *The power of mindful learning.* New York: Pereus Book Group.

Langford, N. J. & Ferner, R. E. (1999). Toxicity of mercury. *Journal of Human Hypertension.* Retrieved from: http://www.nature.com/jhh/journal/v13/n10/abs/1000896a.html

Larrivee, B. (2009). *Authentic classroom management: Creating a learning community and building reflective practic* (3rd ed.). Columbus, OH: Pearson.

Lave, J., & Wenger, E. (1991). *Situated learning: Legitimate peripheral participation.* New York: Cambridge University Press.

Lawrence, V., Houghton, S., Tannock, R., Douglas, G., Durkin, K., & Whiting, K. (2004). *ADHD outside the laboratory: Boys' executive function performance on tasks in videogame play and on a visit to the zoo.* Retrieved from http://www.eric.ed.gov/ERICWebPortal/Home.portal;jsessionid;HhzSwDc1sPMS

Lazarus, R. S. (1999). *Stress and emotion: A new synthesis.* New York: Springer.

LeDoux, J. E. (1994, June). Emotion, memory and the brain. *Scientific American, 270*(6), 50–57.

LeDoux, J. E. (1996). *The emotional brain.* New York: Simon & Schuster.

LeDoux, J. E. (2002). *The synaptic self: How our brains become who we are.* New York: Penguin Group.

Leonard, D., & Swap, W. (2005). *Deep smarts: How to cultivate and transfer enduring business wisdom.* Boston: Harvard Business School Press.

Lingnau, A., Gesierich, B., & Caramazza, A. (2009). A symmetric fMRI adaptation reveals no evidence for mirror neurons in humans. *PNAS, 106*(24), 9925–9930.

Lozanov, G. (1978). *Suggestology and outlines of suggestopedy.* New York: Gordon & Breach.

Lyon, G. R., & Krasnegor, N. A. (Eds.). (1996). *Attention, memory, and executive function.* Baltimore: Brookes.

MacLean, P. D. (1978). A mind of three minds: Educating the triune brain. In J. Chall & A. Mirsky (Eds.), *Education and the brain* (pp. 308–342). Chicago: University of Chicago Press.

Martin, A. J., & Dowson, M. (2009). Interpersonal relationships, motivation, engagement, and achievement: Yields for theory, current issues, and educational practice. *Review of*

Educational Research, 79(1), 327–365.

Maslow, A. H. (1954). *Motivation and personality.* New York: Harper.

Maslow, A. H. (1968). *Towards a psychology of being* (3rd ed.). New York: Wiley.

Masullo, M., & Ruiz, A. (2000). People are the only thing that matter. *New Horizons.* Retrieved from http://www.newhorizons.org/strategies/technology/masullo.htm

Maturana, H. R., Varela, F. J., & Paolucci, R. (1998). *The tree of knowledge: The biological roots of human understanding.* Boston: Shambhala Publications.

McCain, T., & Jukes, I. (2001). *Windows on the Future: Education in the Age of Technology.* Thousand Oaks, CA: Corwin Press.

McCombs, B. L., & Miller, L. (2008). *The school leader's guide to learner-centered education: From complexity to simplicity.* Thousand Oaks, CA: Corwin Press.

McNeil, M. (2009, June 8). Duncan to states: Test scores and teacher evaluations do mix. *Edweek.* Retrieved from http://blogs.edweek.org/edweek/campaign-k-12/2009/06/duncan_to_states_dont_bar.html

Meier, D. (2000). *Will standards save public education?* Boston, MA: Beacon Press.

Meltzoff, A. N., & Gopnik, A. (1993). The role of imitation in understanding persons and developing theories of mind. In S. Baron-Cohent & H. Tager-Flusberg (Eds.), *Understanding other mind: Perspectives from autism.* Oxford: Oxford Univesity Press.

Meltzoff, A. N., Kuhl, P. K., Movellan, J., & Sejnowski, T. J. (2009, July 17). Foundations for a new science of learning, *Science, 325*(5938), 284–288. Retrieved from http://www.sciencemag.org/cgi/content/full/325/5938/284?ijkey=/.hRjgiY2QsOs&keytype=ref&siteid=sci

Mieg, H. (2006). Social and sociological factors in the development of expertise. In K. A. Ericsson, N. Charness, P. J. Feltovich, & R. R. Hoffman (Eds.), *The Cambridge handbook of expertise and expert performance.* Cambridge: Cambridge University Press.

Miller, B. L., & Cummings, J. L. (1999). *The human frontal lobes.* New York: Guilford Press.

Miller, E. K., & Cohen, J. D. (2001). An integrative theory of prefrontal cortex function. *Annual Review of Neuroscience, 24,* 167–202.

Miller, Hon. George Chairman (2009). *High school dropout crisis threatens U.S. economic growth and competiveness, witnesses tell house panel.* Committee on Education and Labor. Retrieved from http://edlabor.house.gov/newsroom/2009/05/high-school-dropout-crisis-thr.shtrnl

National Center on Education and the Economy. (2007). *Tough choices or tough times: The report of the new commission on the skills of the American workforce.* San Francisco: Wiley.

National Commission on Excellence in Education. (1983). *A nation at risk: An imperative for education reform.* Retrieved from http://www2.ed.gov/pubs/NatAtRisk/index.html

No Child Left Behind Act of 2001 (NCLB), Pub. L. No. 107-110 (2002). Retrieved from http://www.ed.gov/policy/elsec/leg/esea02/index.html

Noe, A. (2004). *Action in perception.* Cambridge, MA: MIT Press.

Olsen, B., & Sexton, D. (2008, July 29). Threat rigidity, school reform, and how teachers view their work inside current education policy contexts. *American Educational Research Journal.* Retrieved from http://aer.sagepub.com/content/46/1/9.full

Ormrod, J. E. (2007). *Human learning* (5th ed.). Upper Saddle River, NJ: Prentice Hall.

Ormrod, J. E. (2010). *Educational psychology: Developing learners* (7th ed.). Upper Saddle River, NJ: Prentice Hall.

Panksepp, J. (1998). *Affective neuroscience*. New York: Oxford University Press.

Patton, P. (2008, December). One world, many minds: Intelligence in the animal kingdom. *Scientific American*. Retrieved from http://www.sciam.com/article.cfm?id=one-world-many-minds

Pearce, J. C. (2002). *The biology of transcendence: A blueprint of the human spirit*. South Paris, ME: Park Street Press.

Pennington, B., Vennetto, L., McAleer, O., & Roberts, R., Jr. (1999). Executive functions and working memory: Theoretical and measurement issues. In G. Lyon & N. Krasnegor (Eds.), *Attention, memory, and executive function* (pp. 327–348). Baltimore: Brookes.

Perfect, T. J., & Schwartz, B. L. (Eds.). (2002). *Applied metacognition*. New York: Cambridge University Press.

Perry, B. D. (2000). The neuropsychological impact of childhood trauma. In I. Schultz & D. Brady (Eds.), *Handbook of psychological injuries: Evaluation, treatment, and compensable damages*. Chicago: American Bar Association.

Perry, B. D. (2003, October 8). Workshop at the Second Annual Southwest Family Violence Conference presented by the Alternatives to Domestic Violence and Prevent Child Abuse Council of Southwest Riverside County, CA.

Perry, B. D., Pollard, R. A., Blakley, T. L., Baker, W. L., & Vigilante, D. (1995). Childhood trauma, the neurobiology of adaptation and the use-dependent development of the brain: How states become traits. *Infant Mental Health Journal, 16*(4), 271–291.

Pert, C. B. (1997). *Molecules of emotion*. New York: Scribner.

Pessoa, L. (2008, February). Opinion: On the Relationship between emotion and cognition. *Nature Reviews Neuroscience, 9*, 148–158.

Petri, H. L., & Govern, J. M. (2003). *Motivation: Theory, research, and applications* (5th ed.). Florence, KY: Wadsworth Publishing.

Phillips, H. (2007, April 19). Mind-altering media. *New Scientist*, No. 2600. Retrieved from http://www.newscientist.com/article/mg19426001.900-mindaltering-media.html

Piaget, J. (1976). *To understand is to invent: The future of education*. New York: Penguin.

Piaget, J. (1977). *The development of thought: Equilibrium of cognitive structures*. New York: Viking Press.

Porter, T. (2005, February 12). Reading the vanishing newspaper, 6. Readability. *First Draft by Tim Porter: Newspapering, Readership & Relevance in a Digital Age* [Blog]. Retrieved from http://timporter.com/firstdraft/archives/000418.html

Prensky, M. (2001a, October). Digital natives, digital immigrants. *On the Horizon, 9*(5), 1–6. Retrieved from http://www.marcprensky.com/writing/Prensky%20-%20Digital%20 Natives,%20Digital%20Immigrants%20-%20Part2.pdf

Prensky, M. (2001b, December). Digital natives, digital immigrants, part 2: Do they really think differently? *On the Horizon, 9*(6), 1–6. Retrieved from http://www.marcprensky. com/writing/Prensky%20-%20Digital%20Natives,%20Digital%20Immigrants%20-%20 Part2.pdf

Prensky, M. (2006). *Don't bother me, mom—I'm learning*. St. Paul, MN: Paragon House.

Prensky, M. (2009). *Marc Prensky's essential 21st century skills*. Retrieved from http:// portfolio.jblearning.com/learning-technology/2009/7/8/marc-prenskys-essential-skills-for-the-21st-century.html

Preston, S. D., & de Waal, F. B. M. (2002). Empathy: Its ultimate and proximate bases. *Behavioral and Brain Sciences, 25*, 1–72.

Ravitch, D. (2010). *The death and life of the great American school system: How testing and choice are undermining education.* New York: Basic Books.

Ready, T., Edley, C., Jr., & Snow, C. (Eds.). (2002). *Achieving high educational standards for all.* Washington, DC: National Academies Press.

Resnick, L. B. (2010, April). Nested learning systems for the thinking curriculum. *Educational Researcher, 39*(3), 183–197.

Restak, R. M. (2001). *The secret life of the brain.* Washington, DC: Joseph Henry Press.

Richards, A. (Ed.). (In press). *Matters of consequence: Selected writings of Arthur W. Combs, PhD.* Carrollton, GA: The Field Psych Trust.

Rideout, V., Foehr, U. G., & Roberts, D. F. (2010). Generation M2: Media in the lives of 8–18 year-olds. *Kaiser Family FoundationvStudy.* Retrieved from http://www.kff.org/entmedia/7251.cfm

Rizzolatti, G., & Arbib, M. A. (1998). Language within our grasp. *Trends in Neuroscience, 21*(5), 188–194.

Rizzolatti, G., & Sinigaglia, C. (2006). *Mirrors in the brain: How our minds share actions and emotions.* Oxford: Oxford University Press.

Roald, T. (2007). *Cognition in emotion: An investigation through experiences with art.* New York: Rodopi.

Rogers, C. R. (1969). *Freedom to learn: A view of what education might become.* Columbus, OH: Charles Merill.

Rose, C. (1998). *Accelerated learning for the 21st century: The six-step plan to unlock your master-mind.* New York: Dell Press.

Rowe, A. (2009). Mirror neurons fire better at close range. *Wired.* Retrieved from http://www.wired.com/wiredscience/2009/04/mirrormirror/

Sapolsky, R. (1998). *Why zebras don't get ulcers: An updated guide to stress, stress-related diseases, and coping.* New York: W. H. Freeman.

Saxon, J. N. (2004). *Saxon math.* Boston: Houghton Mifflin Harcourt. Retrieved from http://www.hmhco.com/about-us.html

Schank, R. (1992, December). *Goal-based scenarios* (Tech. Rep. No. 36). Evanston, lL: Institute for the Learning Sciences, Northwest University. Retrieved from http://cogprints.org/624/1/V11ANSEK.html

Schlimme, M. (2002). *Video games: A source of benefits or addictions?* Retrieved from http://serendip.brynmawr.edu/bb/neuro/neuro02/web3/mschlimme.html

Seligman, M. E. P. (1990). *Learned optimism.* New York: Knopf.

Selye, H. (1956). *The stress of life.* New York: McGraw-Hill.

Selye, H. (1974). *Stress without distress.* New York: Lippincott.

Shaffer, D. W. (2006). *How computer games help children learn.* New York: Palgrave Macmillan.

Shaffer, D. W., Squire, K., & Gee, J. (2004). *Video games and the future of learning.* University of Wisconsin–Madison and Academic Advanced Distributed Learning Co-Laboratory Retrieved from http://www.discoverproject.net/italy/images/gappspaper.pdf

Shepard, R., & Love, I. (2009). Bridgewater Primary School Personal Learning Plans.

Siegel, D. J. (1999). *The developing mind: Toward a neurobiology of interpersonal experience.* New York: Guilford Press.

Siegel, D. J. (2001). *The developing mind: How relationships and the brain interact to shape who we are.* New York: Guilford Press.

Singapore schools look to the future. (2008, June 1). *iN-SG [Newsletter].* Retrieved from http://www.ida.gov.sg/insg/post/Singapore-schools-look-to-the-future.aspx

Skinner, B. F. (1976). *Walden Two.* New York: Macmillan. (Original work published 1948)

Skinner, B. F. (2002). *Beyond freedom and dignity.* Indianapolis: Hakett. (Original work published 1971)

Small, G., & Vorgan, G. (2009). *iBrain: Surviving the technological alteration of the modern mind.* New York: Harper Books.

Smith, D. L. (2007). *Why we lie: The evolutionary roots of deception and the unconscious mind.* New York: St. Martin's Griffin.

South Australia Department of Education and Children's Services. (2001). *South Australian curriculum, standards, and accountability (SACSA) framework.* Retrieved from www.sacsa.sa.edu.au/

South Australia. Department of Education and Children's Services. (2010). *South Australian teaching for effective learning framework guide.* Camden Park, South Australia: Lane Print & Post.

Stansbury, M. (2009). Survey shows barriers to Web 2.0 in schools. *eSchool News.* Retrieved from http://www.eschoolnews.com/2009/04/16/survey-shows-barriers-to-web-2-0-in-schools/

Sternberg, R., & Grigorenko, E. (2001). *Environmental effects on cognitive abilities.* Mahwah, NJ: Erlbaum.

Stoddard, L., & Dallman-Jones, A. (2010). *Educating for human greatness* (2nd ed.). Sarasota, FL: Peppertree Press.

Strommen, E. F., & Lincoln, B. (1992). Constructivism, technology, and the future of classroom learning. *Education and Urban Society, 24*(4), 466–76. Retrieved from www.playfulefforts.com/archives/papers/EUS-1992.pdf

Sylwester, R. (2002). *A biological brain in a cultural classroom* (2nd ed.). Thousand Oaks, CA: Corwin Press.

Sylwester, R. (2007). *The adolescent brain: Reaching for autonomy.* Thousand Oaks, CA: Corwin Press.

Temple, C. (1997). *Developmental cognitive neuropsychology.* East Sussex, UK: Psychology Press.

Tettamanti, M., Buccino, G., Succuman, M. C., Gallese, V., Danna, M., Scifo, P., et al. (2005). Listening to action-related sentences acivates fronto-parietal motor circuits. *Journal of Cognitive Neuroscience, 17*(2), 273–281.

Thompson, E. (2007). *Mind in life: biology, phenomenology, and the science of mind.* Boston: Belknap Press of Harvard University Press.

Vallerand, R. J., Fortier, M. S., & Guay, F. (1997). Self-determination and persistence in a real-life setting: Toward a motivational model of high school dropout. *Journal of Personality and Social Psychology, 72*(5), 1161–1176.

Vandewater, E., Shim, M., & Caplovitz, A. (2004). Linking obesity and activity level with children's television and video game use. *Journal of Adolescence, 27,* 71–85. Retrieved from http://www.arasite.org/kcobesity.html

Vanhaeren, M., d'Errico, F., Stringer, C., James, L. J., Todd, J. A., & Mienis, H. K. (2006, June). Middle Palaeolithic shell beads in Israel and Algeria. *Science, 312*(5781), 1785–1788.

Varela, F. J., Thompson, E., & Rosch, E. (1991). *The embodied mind: cognitive science and human experience.* Cambridge: MIT Press.

Velmans, M. & Schneider, S. (Eds.) (2007). *The Blackwell Companion to Consciousness.* Malden, MA: Blackwell.

Vygotsky, L. S. (1993). *The collected works of L. S. Vygotsky* (R. W. Rieber & A. S. Carton, Eds.). New York: Plenum Press.

Wagner, T. (2008). *The global achievement gap.* New York: Basic Books.

Walsh, D., Gentile, D., Walsh, E., & Bennett, N. (2006). *11th annual MediaWise video game report card.* Minneapolis, MN: National Institute on Media and the Family. Retrieved from http://www.mediafamily.org/research/report_vgrc_2006.shtml

Wenger, E. (1998). *Communities of practice: Learning, meaning, and identity.* New York: Cambridge University Press.

Wenger, E. (2008). *Communities of practice: A brief introduction.* Retrieved from http://www.ewenger.com/theory/index.htm

Wenger, E., McDermott, R. G., & Snyder, W. M. (2002). *Cultivating communities of practice: A guide to managing knowledge.* Boston: Harvard Business School Press.

What's with the newspapers? (2005). *Plain-language newsletter. Impact information plain-language services.* Retrieved from http://www.impact-information.com/impactinfo/newsletter/plwork15.htm

Wheatley, M. (1999). *Leadership and the new science: Discovering order in a chaotic world* (2nd ed.). San Francisco, CA: Berrett-Koehler.

Whitehead, A. N. (1929). *The aims of education and other essays.* New York: Free Press.

Wiedermann, J. (2004). Building a bridge between mirror neurons and theory of embodied cognition. In P. Boas, J. Pokorny, M. Bielikova, & J. Stuller (Eds.), *SOFSEM 2004: Theory and practice of computer science* (pp. 159–68). Lecture Notes in Computer Science (Vol. 2932). Berlin: Springer. Retrieved from http://www.springerlink.com/content/fe3h9uxa3vr7wwkp/

Wilber, K. (2001). *Sex, ecology, spirituality* (2nd ed.). Boston: Shambhala Publications.

Wilber, K., Engler, J., & Brown, D. P. (1986). *Transformations of consciousness: Conventional and contemplative perspectives on development.* Boston: Shambhala Publications.

Winerman, L. (2005). The mind's mirror. *Monitor of Psychology, 36*(9). Retrieved from http://www.apa.org/monitor/oct05/mirror.html

Wright, W. (2006, April). Dream machines. *Wired Magazine* (Issue 14.04). Retrieved from http://www.wired.com/wired/archive/14.04/wright.html

Youth crime in N.C. linked to media violence. (1992, Fall). *The New Citizen, 1*(2). Retrieved from http://www.main.nc.us/cml/new_citizen/v1n2/fall92b.html

Zelazo, P. D., Carter, A., Reznick, J. S., & Frye, D. (1997). Early development of executive function: A problem-solving framework. *Review of General Psychology, 1*(2), 198–226.

Zimmerman, B. J., Bandura, A., & Martinez-Pons, M. (1992). Self-motivation for academic attainment: The role of self-efficacy beliefs and personal goal setting. *American Educational Research Journal, 29*(3), 663–676.

Zsambok, C. E., & Klein, G. (1997). *Naturalistic decision making.* Mahwah, NJ: Erlbaum.

Zuckerman, M., Porac, J., Lathin, D., Smith, R., & Deci, E. L. (1978). On the importance of self-determination for intrinsically motivated behavior. *Personality and Social Psychology Bulletin, 41*(3), 443–446.

Links

Apple. *Challenge Based Learning*: http://ali.apple.com/cbl/

Bridgewater Primary School, Rosslyn Shepherd Principal: http://www.bridgeps.sa.edu.au

Common Core State Standards Initiative (CCSSI): http://www.corestandards.org/

Convergence Education Foundation: http://www.cef-tree.org/Home.html

Creative Learning Plaza: http://www.creativelearningsystems.com/prod/clp.asp

Educating for Human Greatness: http://definegreat.ning.com

George Lucas Foundation. Retrieved from Edutopia: http://www.globalschoolnet.org/gsnprojects/GLEF/indes.cfm

Institute for Habits of Mind: http://www.instituteforhabitsofmind.com/what-are-habits-mind

Linda Darling-Hammond: http://www.learner.org/courses/learningclassroom

Monticello Web site: http://www.monticellocatalog.org/200168.html

National Board for Professional Teaching Standards: http://www.nbpts.org

Personality Theories: http://webspace.ship.edu/cgboer/snygg&combs.html

Second Life: http://secondlife.com/

Wikipedia: http://www.wikipedia.org/

Index

About the Authors

Renate N. Caine, PhD, is an education consultant, researcher, and writer. She is a codirector of the Caine Learning Center, the Director of Research and Professional Development of the Natural Learning Research Institute, and Professor Emerita of Education at California State University in San Bernardino (CSUSB). She has taught or worked with teachers at every level from kindergarten to university, and her work with schools has been featured on *Teacher TV* and on the Discovery Channel, *Wizards of Wisdom* shown on PBS. She teaches workshops and courses on the Brain/Mind Learning Principles and on natural learning at the Caine Learning Center in Idyllwild, California. She consults throughout the world on the implementation of natural learning, and works with schools and districts interested in long-term restructuring. She has been an international colleague of one of the world's leading-edge educational reform projects, *Learning to Learn* in South Australia.

Geoffrey Caine, LLM, is a learning consultant, process coach, and writer. He is a codirector of the Caine Learning Center and is the Executive Director of the Natural Learning Research Institute. He has an extensive background in adult education, having been a tenured member of a faculty of law in Australia, Education Services Manager of National Software Company, and National Director of the Mind/Brain Network of the American Society of Training and Development. He consults throughout the world on the implementation of natural learning, and works with and gives talks to schools and educational organizations as well as nonprofits, foundations, and business. He was also an international colleague of one of the world's leading-edge educational reform projects, *Learning to Learn* in South Australia.

The Caines have co-authored eight books and many chapters and articles on learning and education. Their first book was *Making Connections: Teaching and the Human Brain* (ASCD, 1991; Addison-Wesley, 1994). John Dunworth, past president of the American Association of Colleges for Teacher Education, said, "*Making Connections* ranks among the most significant publications in the field of teaching and learning in this century."